DAYS IN THE CAUCASUS

BANINE

TRANSLATED FROM THE FRENCH
BY ANNE THOMPSON-AHMADOVA

PUSHKIN PRESS CLASSICS

Pushkin Press
Somerset House, Strand
London WC2R 1LA

Days in the Caucasus was first published as *Jours caucasiens* in Paris, 1945

First published by Pushkin Press in 2019
This edition published in 2025

ISBN 13: 978-1-80533-220-6

Map by Alex Swanston, The Map Archive

A CIP catalogue record for this title is available from the British Library

The authorised representative in the EEA is
eucomply OÜ, Pärnu mnt. 139b-14, 11317, Tallinn, Estonia,
hello@eucompliancepartner.com, +33757690241

Designed and typeset by Tetragon, London
Printed and bound in the United Kingdom by Clays Ltd, Elcograf S.p.A.

Pushkin Press is committed to a sustainable future for our business, our readers and our planet. This book is made from paper from forests that support responsible forestry.

MIX
Paper | Supporting responsible forestry
FSC® C018072

www.pushkinpress.com

3 5 7 9 8 6 4 2

PUSHKIN PRESS CLASSICS

DAYS IN THE CAUCASUS

'Introduces the reader to an exotic, antique world and to characters so vividly drawn that their raucous voices seem to echo long after they have vanished from sight'

WALL STREET JOURNAL

'A voice so vivid it seems impossible that it should ever have been forgotten'

EVENING STANDARD

'Banine tells her story with wit and warmth… Her company – and her memoir – is a delight'

TATLER

BANINE was born Umm El-Banu Assadullayeva in 1905, into a wealthy family in Baku, then part of the Russian Empire. Following the Russian Revolution and the subsequent fall of the Azerbaijan Democratic Republic, Banine was forced to flee her home country—first to Istanbul, and then to Paris. In Paris she formed a wide circle of literary acquaintances including Nikos Kazantzakis, André Malraux, Ivan Bunin and Teffi, and eventually began writing herself—all of which is brought to life in *Parisian Days*, also available from Pushkin Press.

ANNE THOMPSON-AHMADOVA is a writer and translator from Azerbaijani, French and Russian. She lived in Baku for twenty years, moving there in 1997 initially to set up a Caucasus bureau for the BBC Monitoring Service. She has also translated *Parisian Days* for Pushkin Press.

Contents

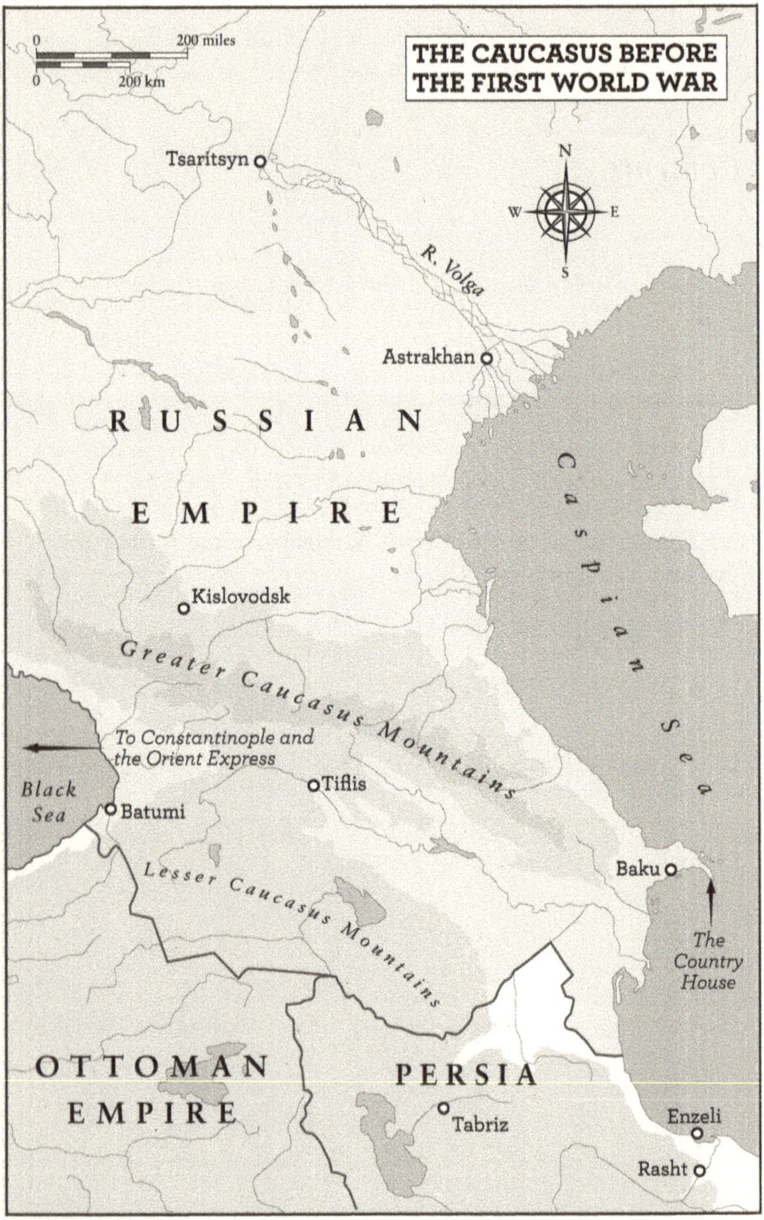

THE CAUCASUS BEFORE THE FIRST WORLD WAR
0
200 miles
0
200 km
N
W
E
S
Tsaritsyn
R. Volga
Astrakhan
RUSSIAN
EMPIRE
Caspian Sea
Kislovodsk
Greater Caucasus Mountains
To Constantinople and the Orient Express
Black Sea
Batumi
Tiflis
Lesser Caucasus Mountains
Baku
The Country House
OTTOMAN
EMPIRE
PERSIA
Tabriz
Enzeli
Rasht

Foreword by the Translator

The Caucasus—a range of majestic mountains and gentler foothills where Europe meets Asia. The Black Sea laps at the western edge, the Caspian at the east. This natural barrier separates Russia from Azerbaijan, Georgia and Armenia and, farther south, Iran and Turkey. It was in the Azerbaijani city of Baku that the author of *Days in the Caucasus*, Banine, was born in 1905.

Ummulbanu Asadullayeva, to give Banine her full name, was the granddaughter of peasants who had become fabulously wealthy through oil. Her maternal grandfather, Musa Naghiyev, struck oil on his patch of land and became one of the richest men in the Russian Empire, while her paternal grandfather, Shamsi Asadullayev, built a flourishing oil business through shrewd investment.

Oil had turned Banine's Baku from a sleepy port on the Caspian Sea into a bustling, booming city, bursting with ideas. This was an era of enlightenment, of social and political ferment, of growing self-awareness for the Muslim Azerbaijani population and for all workers, regardless of ethnicity. Education made huge strides—in 1901 the first secular school for Muslim girls opened in Baku, where Banine was so unhappy she 'cried every day for two months'. Newspapers were published in Azerbaijani Turkish. The first opera in the Muslim world, a fusion of traditional *mugham* and European operatic style, was performed in Baku in 1908.

This was an era too of unrest and upheaval. The tsar was deposed and the Russian Empire collapsed in 1917. A year later the Azerbaijan Democratic Republic was proclaimed, with universal suffrage, including for women, enshrined in its constitution. The Democratic Republic, in which Banine's father was a government minister, was to be short-lived, however. She describes the arrival of Russian Bolshevik troops in Baku in 1920: 'In a matter of moments, without a shot being fired, the Azerbaijani army had melted away. The Republic was dead and victorious Russia was reclaiming its subjects. With my own eyes I had seen the end of a world.'

Pogroms, revolutions and the end of empire are the backdrop to Banine's coming-of-age tale. She dreams of romantic love and burns with idealism, even sporting a badge of Lenin. Banine escapes into the realm of the imagination and these escapes are mirrored in real life when she flees to Persia, Tiflis, Constantinople, Paris.

In Paris Banine worked as a model for several years, before becoming a writer. Her first book, a novel titled *Nami*, was published in 1942. But it was her second book, *Jours caucasiens* or *Days in the Caucasus*, that received critical acclaim. Published in the French capital in 1945, the memoir established Banine in literary and émigré circles. 'I started to leaf through the book and was soon engrossed,' the Russian émigré author Teffi wrote in a review in the journal *Nouvelles russes*. 'So vividly and wittily does the author reveal to us an utterly unfamiliar world.'

Banine wrote a sequel to *Days in the Caucasus*, *Days in Paris*, published in 1947. The most successful of her later works was an account of her conversion to Christianity, *I Chose Opium*. She translated widely into French, including works by Dostoevsky, Tatyana Tolstaya and the German author Ernst Jünger, who became a good friend.

Banine died in Paris in 1992 at the age of eighty-six.

She came to public attention in her homeland only in the late 1980s, when the Soviet newspaper *Literaturnaya gazeta* published an article about her friendship and correspondence with the Nobel Prize-winning Russian author Ivan Bunin. I first heard of Banine in 2000 when I lived in Baku and wondered about the fate of the oil barons who had left behind such remarkable buildings. Hamlet Qoca's Azerbaijani translation of *Days in the Caucasus* was published in Baku in 2006, and was itself translated into Russian by Gulshan Tofiq Qizi. A translation from the original French into Russian by Ulviyya Akhundova came out in Baku in 2016.

Reading Banine's gripping memoir, I was struck by similarities between Baku in the early twentieth century and the city in the early twenty-first. The excitement of the first years of the independent Azerbaijan Republic after the collapse of the Soviet Union mirrored the heady days of the Democratic Republic created in 1918 after the collapse of the Russian Empire. Though the highest hopes have yet to be fulfilled, the Azerbaijan Republic marks its twenty-eighth birthday in 2019.

The cultural tensions so vividly illustrated by Banine continue in Baku to this day, contributing to the city's energy and verve. Russian language and culture still thrive in the capital, alongside the much more widespread Azerbaijani culture. Religion is regaining ground, though in the early twenty-first century it is more often the young who turn to Islam, their grandparents having grown up under the anti-religious Soviet system. Churches too are growing, and services are held in the Lutheran Church, whose Frauenverein (Women's Union) the young Banine frequented with enthusiasm.

Banine slightly revised the text of *Days in the Caucasus* and republished it in France in 1985. It is the 1985 version that has been translated here. Banine wrote in French, though she spoke Russian fluently and grew up speaking Azerbaijani with her grandmother.

Wherever Banine used an Azerbaijani, German or Russian expression in her memoir, I have preserved those words and added an English translation where needed.

The language of Azerbaijan is known as Azerbaijani, Azeri or Azerbaijani Turkish. Banine used the version *Azéri*, so in the translation I opted for the closest equivalent in English, Azeri.

Anne Thompson-Ahmadova

PART ONE

I

We all know families that are poor but 'respectable'. Mine, in contrast, was extremely rich but not 'respectable' at all. At the time I was born they were outrageously wealthy, but those days are long gone. Sad for us, though quite right in the moral scheme of things. Anyone kind enough to show interest might ask in what way my family wasn't 'respectable'. Well, because on the one hand it could not trace its ancestral line further than my great-grandfather, who went by the fine name of Asadullah, meaning 'loved by Allah'. This proved very apt: born a peasant, he died a millionaire, thanks to the oil gushing from his stony land, where sheep had once grazed on meagre pickings. On the other hand because my family included some extremely shady characters on whose activities it would be better not to dwell. If I get caught up in the story, I might reveal all, though my interest as an author is at odds with my concern to preserve the last shreds of family pride.

So, I was born into this odd, rich, exotic family one winter's day in a turbulent year; like so many 'historic' years, this one was full of strikes, pogroms, massacres and other displays of human genius (especially inventive when it comes to social unrest of all kinds). In Baku, the majority of the population of Armenians and Azerbaijanis were busy massacring one another. In that year, it was the better-organized Armenians who were exterminating the

Azerbaijanis in revenge for past massacres, while the Azerbaijanis made the best of it by storing up grounds for future slaughter. There was, therefore, something for everyone—except of course for the many who sadly lost their lives.*

No one would have considered me capable of taking part in the work of destruction, but I clearly was, since I killed my mother as I came into the world. To escape the bloodshed, she had chosen to give birth in an oil-producing area in the hope that it would be quieter there; but in the chaos of the time she ended up giving birth in dreadful conditions and contracted puerperal fever. In addition, the house was cut off from outside help by a violent storm, compounding the confusion into which we'd been plunged. Without the complex care that her condition required, my mother fought the illness in vain. She was lucid when she died, full of regret at leaving life so young and of anxiety at the fate of her loved ones.

My memories of conscious awareness begin with toys that my father brought from Berlin. It was through these that life was revealed to me: I first perceived the world through the purring stomach of a plush cat, the beautiful gleam of a maharajah astride a grey buckskin elephant, the bowing and scraping of a multicoloured clown. I perceived it all, felt it, marvelled and began to live.

My early years were the happiest; I was so young compared to my three older sisters that I enjoyed all kinds of privileges and knew how to make the most of them.

But, more than anything, my happiness was the result of my upbringing by a Baltic German governess—she was my governess, my mother and my guardian angel too. This saint (the noun is no exaggeration) gave us her health, and her life; she wore herself out for us, suffered all sorts of trouble because of us, and received little

---

* A brief summary of the history of Azerbaijan in the early twentieth century can be found at the end of this book.

joy; she always sacrificed herself and asked for nothing in return. In a nutshell, she was one of those rare beings who are able to give without receiving.

Fräulein Anna had fair skin and flaxen hair, while the four of us had brown skin, black hair and a markedly oriental, hirsute appearance. We made a fine group when we surrounded her in photographs, all hook noses and close-set eyebrows, she completely Nordic. And I should say that in those days—despite the prohibition of the Prophet, enemy of the image—we often had our photograph taken, dressed in our finery and flanked by as many relatives as possible, all against the background of a painted park. A harmless obsession that can be explained by the novelty of the process for the near savages that we were; an obsession to which I owe several hilarious and touching pictures that I preserve with great care.

But back to Fräulein Anna. Surrounded by a fanatically Muslim family, in a city that was still very oriental, she managed to create and maintain an atmosphere of *Vergissmeinnicht*, of sweet songs for blonde children, of Christmas trees with pink angels, of cakes heavy with cream and sentimentality. All of which proves that she had character despite her sweetness, and willpower despite her gentleness. It's true that in those days she had yet to be run ragged by us, and was better able to stand up for herself in an atmosphere that must have seemed, or even been, hostile towards her. Her influence was constantly counteracted by that of my paternal grandmother, who lived on the ground floor of our house. Grandmother was a large, fat, authoritarian woman, veiled and excessively fanatical, who preferred to sit on cushions on the floor, as every good Muslim did. She performed her ablutions and prayers with unfailing rigour and exulted in her abhorrence of Christians. If a plate had been touched by non-Muslim hands, my grandmother would refuse to use it, passing it to someone less discerning. If a white-skinned stranger walked by, she would often spit on the ground and shout insults, the mildest of which was 'son of a dog'. In turn, we disgusted her a little too, being brought up by Christians: so many caresses, so much contact from profane hands had impregnated us with a subtle odour of impiety, and her kisses, though affectionate, were often accompanied by a grimace of disgust. It certainly could not have been Grandmother who entrusted us to Fräulein Anna, and I can imagine the painful battles my father must have fought to gain acceptance for this heretical education. But the Russians had long since colonized us; their influence was everywhere and with it the desire for culture, for Europeanization. For the younger generations freedom was gaining precedence over the veil, education over fanaticism.

Having deposited us in the white hands of Fräulein Anna, with a confidence he never regretted, my father no longer had much to do with us. Besides, he was always travelling. As the eldest son he ran our oil firm, visiting its depots and offices along the Caspian Sea and Volga River, its flourishing subsidiary in Moscow, and even its concerns in Warsaw. Having got that far, momentum meant my father could not stop, and as Berlin was close by for someone accustomed to Russian distances, he often popped over to the German capital.

Before the war of 1914 Germany enjoyed enormous prestige among my compatriots, who had barely awoken to civilization: automobiles, Kaiser Wilhelm moustaches, pale governesses, music, pianos—they all came from Germany. My father would return from there, weighed down with all these things, including the martial moustache, which became more vigorous every trip, growing longer and standing up straighter. It should not be forgotten that Kaiser Wilhelm styled himself protector of Islam and the Turks, hence his prestige among us cousins of the Turks.

I think those years before his second marriage must have been the best of my father's life: young, rich, free, handsome, he excited considerable matrimonial interest and other, less honourable, desires. He had numerous affairs, but was in no hurry to get married, though he was encouraged to do so by all the family, who welcomed polygamy and disapproved of celibacy. Still, none of the suggested brides met with his approval: they were mediocre Muslims, barely educated, without elegance or charm, and my father would have none of them—he was firmly in favour of 'culture'. Other women, whom he met during his travels abroad and might have liked, were, according to my grandmother's definition, 'daughters of dogs', that is, Christians, and therefore not marriage material. The family had good reason to fear such marriages, and Grandmother a non-religious reason to hate them: her husband had rejected her to marry a Russian woman of dubious origin. After his marriage and until his death, when I was six, he lived in Moscow in a house cluttered with icons, mistreated by his wife and cut off from his family because of her. Did this example, so edifying for the faithful, make my father circumspect and prevent him marrying a Christian? In any case, he took a long time to choose a second wife.

We occupied the whole of the second floor in our town house, which compensated for the houses enclosing it on either side by stretching so far back that it reached the parallel street. This allowed for the creation of two identical apartments: twins with their backs to one another; twins separated by a courtyard but united by symmetrical passages running the length of the courtyard.

We girls lived with Fräulein Anna in the south-facing apartment that was always flooded with sunlight, while the other, north-facing, dark and quiet, was occupied by my father between his travels. It included what we proudly called the 'reception rooms', more simply the dining room and drawing room. Here was the grand piano on which, on holidays or when some governess too proud of her flock needed to be put in her place, Fräulein Anna would have my older sister Leyla perform a brilliant piece from her repertoire. A

Negro draped in gold, with a lamp held in his hand, stood upon a structure best described as a hybrid of pillar and pedestal. It was lit only on great occasions so it never ceased to inspire my admiration. It was in fact this statue that gave me my first, pleasurable sensation of wealth.

Ordinarily we rarely went into the drawing room. We would spend almost the whole day in the large, bright schoolroom. It had a piano too, an instrument of torture that dominated our lives; there was hardly a moment when one of the four of us children was not bashing it with our rough, impatient hands. It rattled out scales or arpeggios, or, even worse, a Mozart sonata mutilated with the best of intentions. To the off-putting sounds of this music we would laugh, cry, rebel and grow up, too quickly for Fräulein Anna's liking. She endeavoured to fight heredity, struggled against the prevailing atmosphere and had no fear of doing battle with nature itself, seeking to transmit to us her young German girl's soul, artless and loving. She hoped to see us turn into Gretchens with delicate figures and easy sighs. But our forebears were keeping watch. Under their guidance, our hips fleshed out, our noses grew longer, our breasts swelled beneath the sailor blouses that we wore in accordance with what was proper for 'young girls of good family'; and down, soft at first but quietly turning into thick hair, covered us in a dark shadow. What could poor Fräulein Anna do but simply observe the inevitable march of progress? All was well, more or less, as long as this progress was evident only in our physical growth. But the heart soon got involved, and the day came when Leyla, having reached the fateful age of thirteen, began to give due appreciation to the charms of a cousin who had sparkling eyes and a nascent beard. Fräulein Anna was dismayed and henceforth lost her peace of mind for good. At the cost of her health, she managed through recriminations and discipline to keep us on something of a leash, but fell martyr to suspicion and anxiety. As we grew up, we became resentful and beastly towards her, so unbearable was the brake she put on our instincts. More violent perhaps in oriental girls than Europeans of the same age, those instincts may partly excuse our beastliness towards Fräulein Anna; but she didn't suffer any the less as a result.

When we were small, we loved her unreservedly, at least I did. I don't think that love for a mother is any different. I thought her beautiful. In the morning, open-mouthed, I would watch her brush her long, blonde hair: her white skin shone in the morning light; her blue gaze would often rest tenderly on me; I was happy. My aunts were brown, as were my cousins and sisters, my uncles and aunts and I myself, as was everyone and everything. Only Fräulein Anna had come from another world, and to me she shone with a strange, precious exoticism.

Almost all that was lovely in my childhood was connected with her, or, rather, originated with her. Hence that unforgettable Christmas morning when, waking in the half-darkness, I thought I saw something shining next to my bed. I leant over slightly; not only did it continue to shine, but I noticed a subtle scent too. I stretched out my hand—I touched something prickly and realized that it was a Christmas tree, the Christian children's tree which, along with the frankfurters that Fräulein Anna would secretly buy us, was making a budding renegade out of me. It was perhaps the first time in Islamic history that such a heresy had shone so arrogantly in a Muslim child's bedroom. This happiness had been denied us for years; but one year my father weakened, or Grandmother did, or they both did at the same time, and the tree came to shine in our house. Captivated, mute with admiration and joy, I walked around the tree, touching and sniffing it. Everything about it was beautiful: the rich sparkle of the silver threads and colourful baubles; the delicate pink and blue candles; the winged angels and the white snow at the base of the trunk. It was a happy day: there was no German homework with its Gothic letters, no verbs to conjugate, no Mozart to play; only beauty remained, and ugliness disappeared from the world for a magical moment. To crown it all, Fräulein Anna promised to take us soon to the Frauenverein (Women's Union), an honourable, devout institution, where, in the company of a hundred German maidens, both young and old, we would devour superb sauerkraut washed down with beer. This would be followed with fitting psalms and hymns in praise of the Lord, songs that we four Muslims joined in with enthusiasm. We were delighted with this fine combination of earthly and spiritual nourishment. Prudently, nothing was said about this at home, as it was all forbidden by the Prophet. The honest Fräulein Anna was cheating; the poor woman didn't have the strength to deprive us of these pleasures, which she reasonably considered innocent. But if she didn't have the heart to refuse us some of the outward joys of Christianity, she took care not to influence us in her favour in a more subtle way. It would have been easy, though, as my father and the family, while holding firm to our religion, did nothing, or hardly anything, to explain it to us. I was never taught a single prayer and knew only one short verse from the Koran. I had been inculcated with so little religious feeling that my favourite time to play with my grandmother was when she was praying, sitting on the floor, the Koran open on a chair before her. That was when I would tease her: I would tug at her veil or her nose, jump around the chair shouting or pull terrifying faces; Grandmother would break off to cast a lazy insult in my direction, without a hint of malice, and then resume her mumbling.

Religious observance was often rather mechanical or simply a social affair, like for example the celebrations for New Year or the end of Ramadan. As for me, I enjoyed them very much.

For children, New Year, celebrated on 21st March (to coincide with the first day of spring), was a holiday that yielded great financial return. All day we would run from house to house to pay 'congratulatory' visits. First we would be force-fed; it was both awful and delicious. Everywhere tables bowed under the weight of all the food; one could judge the degree of civilization of a household by the variety of dishes adorning the table. The primitive families had only local sweets, plates of dried fruit and hard-boiled eggs, while the more evolved families had all sorts of dishes that owed their existence to the civilizing genius of the Russians: eggs were painted, marbled or drawn upon, reminiscent of Easter celebrations; cold turkey was not only a tasty white meat but also a sign of progress; fine chocolates made in Moscow brought us a breath of holy Russia.

Once we'd been force-fed, the head of the household—an uncle or aunt or grandfather or other relative, close or distant—would take from a purse blessed by Allah a gold coin bearing a Slavic profile. After feeling its weight, they would—somewhat regretfully—slip it into our hands, an act usually accompanied by a loud, sloppy kiss. So by evening we would consider ourselves rich, though plagued by indigestion.

The Ramadan holiday was quite different. In my childhood it always fell in high summer (it's a movable feast), so was celebrated in the country. We 'civilized' people did not keep the fast, except sometimes for the last few days. We did so entirely by choice; no one obliged us to fast. For my part, I didn't do it to please Allah, but to blackmail him: I made wishes in the hope that, touched by my piety, he would grant them all.

We were not to eat or drink during the day; it was even forbidden to brush one's teeth lest a drop of water spoil a dry palate. Smokers had to abandon their cigarettes that day. Husbands did not have the right to touch their wives (during the fasting hours, I should make clear). But the appearance of the first star of the evening heralded a gluttonous stampede for food; tremendous quantities disappeared down famished gullets. Then one would pause to allow for digestion. Then one would eat again. Then another pause for digestion. This would continue all night until the first light of dawn. Those who went to sleep would make sure they were woken up several times so they could fill themselves with as much food as possible.

At the end of Ramadan, sheep's throats would be slit and their innards cooked outdoors over a wood fire. We had sweet orgies of tripe—the best food memories of my childhood (though far removed from the sauerkraut of the Frauenverein...). Fat ran everywhere—we would lick our fingers and under our nails so as not to lose a single drop. The aroma hung heavy in the air. Oh, those fatty feasts!

I also loved another religious observance—the annual commemoration of the tragedy at Karbala where in 680 Ali's son Hossein and all his family were massacred. This was the point of departure of Shiism, enemy of Sunnism,* which my grandmother never failed to celebrate at home. That day the drawing room, furnished in the local fashion with only carpets and cushions, would acquire numerous additional cushions; they would be placed in a line along the wall, then, depending on the number of guests, they would form second, third and fourth rows. On the busiest days the entire floor would disappear beneath the cushions. A single chair, high and severe, like a throne, for 'Madam Mullah', rested against the wall in the middle of the room.

Swathed in *chadras* (called 'chadors' in the West), the guests arrived; their slippers clattered; their full silk skirts rustled; their shrill voices and the swirl of conversation were dizzying and the whole combined to create a considerable racket.

National costume, at its finest on holidays, had a stylish look and a richness that was wholly oriental. A low-cut jacket, worn

* The Shia support the family of the Prophet.

over a white blouse, revealed a veritable walking jeweller's shop: necklaces of pearls, necklaces of gold coins, gold chains, pendants, brooches of every kind. The jewellery was often of poor quality, but it shone, jingled, bobbed up and down and pleased the eye, which was enough for these ladies. The costume's *pièce de résistance*, if one can use that expression, was the skirt, or rather skirts, as they were layered, one on top of the other. Their quantity and their fullness were a sign of the wealth of the wearer: 'Show me your skirts and I will tell you who you are.'

The commemoration of Hossein's death, however, was a day of mourning: on this occasion ladies wore black and no jewels adorned their chests, which were in theory burdened with sadness. The women arrived and the cushions disappeared under the cascade of skirts. The chatter and shouting did not stop, though, until Madam Mullah, installed on her throne, began to read the Koran. She soon progressed from reading to holding forth in Azeri on the tragic subject of the death of Hossein.

Everything would go well at first as the women listened quietly. But soon one woman would start to cry, then another, then another, until the whole room joined in. There were terrible sighs, sobs, groans, cries of '*Yah Allah*', and the despair would grow more bitter, the grief become unbearable and the situation seem hopeless. Suddenly the Mullah's voice would fall silent and just as suddenly, without any transition whatsoever, the women would start to gossip, their eyes still full of tears. Armed with glass bottles, we children would circulate among the cushions, pouring rose water onto outstretched palms; the women would moisten their faces and wash their eyes; this was the interval. Then the reading and commentaries would start again, and with them the full gamut of despair, kept in check until the time came for release. How did the audience cry to order? I do not know. Professional mourners, sort of grief hostesses, would always be invited to these gatherings, and to burials too. They would be the first to cry; helped by the eloquence of Madam Mullah, the contagion would soon spread and the other women would follow their lead. These hostesses of a very special kind would ensure that the gatherings were suitably emotional. In truth, the grief was not very sincere, which perhaps explains the disconcerting swings in mood.

Be that as it may, my sisters and I were better attuned to the comic aspect of these brisk changes in mood than to the dubious charms of melancholy. So we had tremendous fun, all the more so since an elderly great-aunt, a veritable artiste of pain, was an inexhaustible source of joy for us. Her gestures, her shamelessly exaggerated cries, the alternation in her moods, in a word her hypocrisy, delighted us. When she would let out a sigh as powerful as a gust of autumn wind or pretend to rip her clothes, while taking care not to do so, rolling her mischievous little eyes to see the effect of her outbursts, we would choke beneath our veils, stifling our laughter. With our heads covered by these veils—obligatory at such gatherings—we were shielded from suspicion; when our shoulders shook with laughter, the women thought we were moved by noble tears. Ungodly though we were, we did not miss an opportunity to simulate devotion, which earned us the fond indulgence and support of our grandmother. So when Fräulein Anna came down to return us to our home and our beds, she would encounter the stern disapproval of the whole family and Grandmother in particular. She usually had to return alone, leaving us laughing beneath our capes, or rather our veils, and on those days we would go to bed deliciously late.

As a child I loved my grandmother very much; the things that were to separate us later did not yet matter to me. When they did become important, I cut myself off from her completely: she seemed to me to be from another world; indeed, she was from another world. Is blood thicker than water? I must confess that

I've never felt that about anyone. Is it an optimistic invention of humanity or am I a monster? Impartial observation seems to show that in families where interests diverge, hatred between relatives is constant and widespread; where interests are not divisive, affection sometimes exists. But most often there is only indifference mingled occasionally with a sense of duty towards the clan, which one could, with a little imagination, take to be love. To be honest, indifference appears to me to be the natural state between the members of a family. When one thinks of the number of people one must know in order to find some friends, to discover an affinity in the small group that is the family would be something of a surprise.

Over time, the differences between us and Grandmother grew ever more marked. The gap separating her, whose life was a continuation of that of the first Muslim women of the Hegira, from us was not one of a few dozen years but of fourteen centuries. She wanted to know nothing of the 'civilizing force' of the Russians, and did not even know the language, because it was not compulsory when she was young. She saw Russians only as colonizers, secular troublemakers, men of another race and another religion—in a word, infidels—for whom she felt hatred tinged with contempt. Her hatred is easy to understand: the life she loved was slowly disintegrating around her; her husband had abandoned her for a Russian woman; her daughters, whom she had brought up to lead a life similar to her own, gave up the veil as soon as they were married, dressed in European style and began to chatter in an astonishing mixture of Russian and Azeri.* Though this is as far as their innocent initiation into civilization went, it was too much for Grandmother and a cause of considerable distress. It was even worse with her sons: after a brief sojourn in a Russian school, where their father had enrolled

* A language of Turkish origin with a large contribution from Persian.

them, and especially after several tours that he made them take, they began to reject the tiresome constraints of religion, maintaining only the least restrictive. The discovery of oil wells in Baku greatly accelerated the liberation of the Muslims of the Caucasus: fortune suddenly put vast resources into their hands, allowing them to enjoy all the pleasures of civilization and taking away their taste for the strict, simple life of their forebears.

But if Grandmother wanted to monitor the effects of all these changes, she needed to look no further than us, her granddaughters. She had brought up her children herself; they had lived more or less in the Islamic style until their majority and this had left a clear mark. But we who were growing up in an atmosphere totally alien to hers embodied denial of the past. We scarcely spoke Azeri—though while lacking basic vocabulary, we did have an admirably rich repertoire of insults, thanks to her. I remember her most of all swearing, cursing and fulminating. Sometimes it was just for show and on those occasions Grandmother would merely mutter some half-hearted insults to maintain her prestige. At other times her ire was real and her imprecations would reverberate throughout the house.

Her enormous size, both in terms of girth and height, made it extremely difficult for her to move, which added to her majesty. The habit, already engrained, of commanding a whole army of children and servants combined with this extravagant corpulence to give her an air of grandeur which she never lost, not even when a torrent of foul insults escaped her mouth. She was a strange mixture of the imperious and the vulgar…

Although my relationship with her was fundamentally good, it was rather ambivalent and was easily drowned in a flood of insults and bad language. I would often try to tease her in a myriad ways or to beg something from her; she took teasing better than requests for material gain, as she was astonishingly mean.

We would go downstairs to see her almost every day, but she rarely came up to us. When she took it into her head to come, she would climb the stairs one by one, pausing for long rests after two or three consecutive steps. It was hard to watch as she clung on to the banister, puffing and panting. She would arrive in our rooms exhausted, struggle to squeeze herself into the largest armchair, put her chubby hands, palms and fingers painted with henna on her knees and watch our lives. She saw us busy doing things in which she saw neither purpose nor pleasure, listened to us speaking a barbaric tongue that she did not understand, nor wish to; instead she pitied us. Without analysing her impressions, she must have felt that her life and those of her peers, primitive and narrowly confined, left less scope for disappointment, while ours, rich in various possibilities, was thereby full of potential pitfalls too. She would have been right: liberty often comes at a heavy price.

Veiled women did not seem unhappy on the whole. I've never encountered so much merriment and laughter, so many dances and jokes (often dirty), as they enjoyed. Their life was simple and so were their desires. As for the oft-criticized polygamy, it was not a burden for a Muslim woman, to whom her husband was not a lover or even a companion, but a master who gave her children. She did not see much of him, and the fellow wives were her friends, home helps and childminders. I can tell an amusing story on this subject about something that happened in our own family.

My grandmother's brother, a man of around sixty, had only one wife, who was infertile to boot. She was troubled by the thought of dying in her solitary home, without a fellow wife or children. One day she decided she could bear it no longer and decreed that her husband would have to marry again.

One morning when Grandmother was colouring my hair with henna, Begum arrived in a fury and began to air her grievances.

'I said to Abbas: "Hey, Abbas, you have to take another wife." And do you know what he said to me?

'"I don't want to," he said.

'I could have killed him.

'"So that's it—you don't want to!"

'"That's it—I don't want to! One wife is enough for me. More than enough."

'"Now look here!" I said to him. "The Prophet (peace and prayers be upon him) had several wives, and you can't even have two?"

'"The Prophet does not oblige anyone to have several wives," he replied, proud of his wit.

'"Yes," I said, "but I do—I'm making you take at least a second wife. First of all, so she will give you a child. Second, I've had enough of always being on my own. You think it's fun having to run from house to house to find company? I am the only one of my friends who is condemned to solitude and boredom. I want you to get married, Abbas."

'He tried to make me pity him.

'"You know my declining powers..."

'"There'll be enough for the wedding night and to produce one child."

'Then Abbas got angry. "Leave me in peace, unbearable woman. I'm sixty years of age and master in my own home. I don't want to get married."

'Then he insulted me. I shouted: "You shall get married! You shall get married!"

'"Never."

'"You're a heartless eunuch, an apology for a man. He calls himself a man and can't manage two wives."

'I told him some home truths. Then Abbas marched out of the room. He tried to look proud, but that doesn't work with me. And now?'

Begum was close to tears.

'What can I do?' she asked Grandmother.

My grandmother continued her majestic application of walnut leaves to my head, which was already covered with a thick layer of henna. Then she said, 'Look for a girl that you like. When you've found her, I'll think of a way to force Abbas's hand. The stubborn fool! Perhaps he wants to imitate the Russians (may leprosy eat away their flesh). No children and just one wife! That's a fine state of affairs! Go and find yourself a companion, then we'll see. Wait a minute—you know Aslan the hunchback, whose sister married my cousin Mohammed? Well, he has a granddaughter who's just reached puberty. She's pretty and they say she's sweet; go and see her, I think you'll like her. She'll make an agreeable companion.'

Begum followed her advice; she liked the young girl. Grandmother summoned Abbas. At first he categorically refused to get married. There were endless talks, entreaties, discussions. Then scenes, lots of scenes, a huge number of scenes, and finally, his resistance exhausted, the poor man had to give in. He never had children, but his Begum had a companion and no longer pined away in an empty house.

So, polygamy sometimes had its benefits.

In the country where we spent half the year I could see Islamic life, still unaltered, close up every day. While in Baku the population was a rich mixture of Russians, Armenians, Georgians and some Europeans, in the country it remained more or less pure.

I loved this blessed countryside unreservedly. There we had less homework and more freedom; the weather was suited to games and a variety of amusements; but especially because there I lived with my cousins, extraordinary creatures about whom I will talk at length later.

So when spring came, I would be champing at the bit to leave the city life that disgusted me. Already by May Baku was hot, dusty and unbearable. Preparations for departure took an age, as our rural life was to last six months.

At that time we had yet to discover automobiles and we travelled halfway by train, then completed the journey by carriage. One sunny morning in May a rickety local train would take us to the places I had dreamt of all winter. Since this was the only train I knew in the universe's vast rail network, it seemed imposing and beautiful. It would give an expert whistle on departure, travel at a majestic pace through the stony landscape, duly stopping where it was supposed to and arriving habitually late at the terminus amid clouds of flies and dust. We were in the heart of the oil district, surrounded by derricks and cisterns, bathed in a pleasing smell of oil. I breathed in the air, enraptured. Born in one of these districts, I was a true child of oil and its smell delighted my nostrils.

At the exit from the little station, two carriages, gleaming in the sunshine, driven by two coachmen with near-identical names, Zeynal and Zeyni, would be waiting for us. There would be great salaams on both sides; Zeynal and Zeyni would look us up and down like the old fathers that they were, admiring how we had grown since the autumn. They would settle us and our hand luggage in the carriages as comfortably as they could. Then they would set off at a brisk pace, the walls around the oil wells echoing to the clatter of our gallop. Zeynal and Zeyni would clack their tongues and crack their whips and we would soon be hurtling down a rocky slope that led to desert land. We would immediately start to sigh 'It's so hot', 'It's so dusty', and this would go on for two hours, during which we were shaken and jolted on a road full of bumps and potholes. Everything changed after these two hours; well, not quite everything, as the road remained the same—a masterpiece of discomfort—but the view did. A green sea rose up on the horizon, a soughing, fragrant sea, a miraculous sea seen from the desert we were still galloping across. The sea would be cut off from view by the high walls that surrounded every property, while outside these enclosures the desert remained. But when the gate to our property opened at last, we were greeted by the stunning sight of a garden in bloom; it was stunning for us because on the other side of the wall we were still in the sad, grey desert. The carriages drove down a long avenue of poplars, around the stables and the small generator that provided us with electricity, and around the sheep's apartments (as I called them); then after trotting for a minute or two they would stop before the beautiful stone staircase leading up to the house.

Those first moments upon arriving in the country delighted me: the flowers never again appeared so large and fresh or their fragrance so penetrating; even when the air was still, the poplars seemed to rustle more than usual with pleasure, and the water in the pools was never so clear, nor the sky so blue.

I had plenty of hellos to say on my arrival—not only to the animal world, but also the vegetable and even mineral: like most children I was an animist and generously ascribed souls to objects and plants. What were inanimate objects to others, to me were full of feelings, and I would run to greet them. They did not play dead with me; they replied in a simple language, sufficient for those who knew how to hear. But not many people understood it, and when Fräulein Anna caught me in conversation with a tree or bench, she would take exception and threaten me with punishment. 'What for?' I would ask in surprise. Adults' blindness towards my world seemed to me a fundamental injustice. Half of my universe escaped them, while the other half remained mostly veiled. I pitied them, and their blindness filled me with contempt.

Almost all the poplars were my brothers, with the exception of the youngest. My relationship with them was constrained, mainly by their extreme youth, an age of intolerance and aggression. But the elders lavished their friendship and protection on me, and the games my cousins and I played depended on their assistance. Their leaves were our train tickets; when we straddled their branches, we had a horse; the smallest branches became whips used by our redoubtable cousins to frighten us; and we twisted the very smallest twigs into crowns for our coronation as king or queen.

One of the oldest poplars in the garden was my grandfather—I secretly wished that the grandfather life had given me was more like that poplar. He lavished me with loving names in his poplar language, caressed me with the rustle of his foliage, and when I told him my troubles he listened with all his leaves. The sympathy that I felt from him was all the more trustworthy in comparison with the human kind, as it was not expressed in gestures or articulated in words.

In the huge vineyard large rocks stuck their grey backs out of the sandy soil. One of them belonged solely to me, a fact acknowledged even by my cousins, who were usually none too particular where other people's property was concerned. The sun turned it into a radiator on which I loved to lie; I would imagine myself on a lost peninsula in Oceania, surrounded by sea rather than sand.

In the same vineyard at the edge of the property lived an old vine that was so large I could lie down entirely beneath her and feel as though I were in a hut of leaves. Resting my head on what I saw as the shoulders of the vine, I would tell her my most shameful secrets; but as an old philosopher who had seen it all, she was never shocked. Later, it was beneath her branches that I made my first attempts at smoking.

There was an abandoned well in the vineyard which I often visited. Humiliated at his comedown, he would complain and sigh. Though I could not see them, I knew that he had small, tearful eyes and red eyelids. His hot sides were a meeting place for lizards, the only friends left from his glory days. I would count them with satisfaction and be glad at their number—the old man had company and I did not have to worry about leaving him.

So, I had my favourites in every corner and avenue: here a pear tree, there a flight of steps, a box tree, a rose bush, a pool. I was happy with the friends I had chosen; unlike humans, I got back from them only what I gave them, and what I gave them was always to my benefit.

2

It was a large house, made up of two symmetrical wings with a dozen rooms in each. The two sides were separated by a large open passageway—the *dolan*—which remained cool and breezy even during the intense heat of summer. We had none of the comical fear of draughts suffered by those in temperate countries—on the contrary, a draught was to be sought out and harnessed as a free source of air conditioning. For this reason, almost every country house had a *dolan*.

Despite its size, the house struggled in springtime to accommodate the invading horde: my grandmother with her countless servants; her elder daughter with her husband; her younger daughter without her husband, not because she was widowed but because he was forever falling out with my father and scorned the enemy's country domain. To make up for this loss, his five children—liars, thieves, sneaks and the bane of Fräulein Anna's life—would come to spice up our blameless days. Then there was Grandmother's youngest son, the cheerful, childlike Uncle Ibrahim, who was still a bachelor; and to round off the list, the four of us and Fräulein Anna. Add to that each family's domestic staff, plus fifteen or so gardeners, coachmen and shepherds and we amounted to the population of a small village.

The property had extensive outbuildings, including henhouses, an enormous laundry and even a bakery, presided over by Grandmother, which produced the entire week's supply of bread. But the estate's finest feature, one that made us the envy of all our poor relations and covered us in well-deserved glory, was a large, magnificent hammam. Housed in a separate building at the bottom of the garden, it was more pleasure dome than utilitarian bathhouse for Grandmother and her guests.

We bought hardly anything: everything grew, so to speak, on the estate itself—bread, fruit and vegetables, and meat provided by the poor sheep.

While my father was still a widower, we all lived and ate together, and this communal life must have been most inelegant. At the table—and just imagine its length—there would be constant complaints, disputes, children crying and the clatter of crockery; all the usual goings-on of an ordinary, large family. Grandmother, who held court at the head of the table, ate with her fingers, more cleanly it should be said than did my aunts and uncles with their brand-new cutlery. Fräulein Anna, the only splash of blonde against a background of universally dark hair, eyes and skin, didn't dare tell us off when we ate messily. How could any reprimand not apply to the entire company? At the time this primitive atmosphere didn't bother me, but I can imagine now how much it must have troubled our more sophisticated governess.

The conversation flowed freely—a singular mix of scarcely intelligible Russian, children's German and Azeri. The Azeri spoken, or rather shouted, at this table sounded harsh and staccato; I didn't like it, which is probably why I've never been able to speak it properly.

How many innocent sheep were sacrificed for that table! We did eat other meat too, but not very often, as this entailed calling the butcher and, horror of horrors, watching actual, real, lovely roubles disappear into his pocket, which was more than Grandmother could bear. She controlled the purse strings for all the families staying here, and did so with unyielding strictness. She abhorred all excess, whether it cost money or not, and would even ration the property's own produce. Actually opening her purse to make a purchase caused her such physical distress that she avoided it with all her considerable might.

Her three daughters, my aunts, were fat brunettes, bearded and mustachioed, and very proud of their recent emancipation. To prove it, they jabbered away in an original blend of Russian and Azeri, smoked furiously and used the services of the most fashionable dressmaker in Baku. They loved jewellery and festooned themselves with it, even going so far as to stick brooches in their hair. They all had violent tempers, chattered non-stop and played poker with an unwavering passion. They couldn't talk without shouting and even the most peaceable conversation sounded more like a fight. Mudslinging was another passion, and they didn't have a good word to say about anyone, not even their own mother and father. As soon as one sister left the room, the other two would start to criticize their absent sibling, her children and husband. This didn't stop them loving one another in their own way, and they would be upset and miss one another when a family rift had separated them. More serious discord had come into their lives on the death of their father, as there was an INHERITANCE to be divided up. This became a source of bitter trouble, and the sisters lived permanently between a rock and a hard place. Their husbands urged them to claim their share from my father, who was head of the family and manager of the family firm. My father, for his part, did not want to share out the inheritance, as this would have robbed him of his importance. So when the unfortunate sisters finally did come to stake their claim, they would get a frosty reception.

'What do you need money for?' he would ask the sister who had voiced her grievance.

'My husband demands it.'

'Your husband is a worthless scoundrel. He wants to live off your money.'

'Your brother's a thief. If you don't get your share, I'll disown you,' her husband would yell when he heard the attempt had failed.

They were forever swinging back and forth between the wrath of their brother and the fury of their husbands.

In solidarity my uncles had no scruples about calling my father the worst of names in my presence. Strange though it may seem, this had no effect on the esteem in which I held him, and even increased his importance in my eyes. Thief, bastard, man without honour, crook—this is what his brothers-in-law thought of him, eaten up as they were by envy and greed at the thought of the unattainable inheritance.

My grandfather's second wife, the reviled Russian, for her part instituted legal proceedings over the division, which made things even more complicated. So complicated in fact that the situation became intractable: the heirs traded insults, hating one another; no one would give an inch, and jealousy and suspicion were the order of the day. And so the situation lurched from court hearing to court hearing, year to year, until the revolution, which managed quite impartially to bring everyone into accord.

My youngest aunt lived with her husband and three children in the neighbouring property, which was separated from us by a high wall. A gate had been made in the wall, which served not only as an ordinary entrance but, more interestingly, as a barometer of family relations. It remained hospitably open if relations were good, or angrily shut if they were not.

The oldest of the aunts, Rena, was my favourite. She was highly strung, suffered with numerous nervous tics and had a hot temper but a generous heart, which prompted her to spoil me shockingly on the pretext that I was an orphan. She had no children of her own. The only one of the sisters with cultural aspirations, she had piano lessons, and after considerable effort managed to bash out the tune of the era, the famous waltz 'A Life on the Ocean Wave', which became more of a slow march under her clumsy fingers. She read Gyp and Maupassant, not very quickly. My father claimed it had taken her seven years to read *War and Peace*, but he enjoyed teasing her. Later she had the audacity to hire a French lady's companion to teach her the language. Her studies didn't get very far. At most she would say of her husband, '*Comme il bête*' ('He very stupid'), using a foreign tongue to highlight the distance between her and her ignorant spouse. He had an admirable capacity to irritate her. I remember my uncle, a gentle giant who was hard of hearing, as someone who always had his hand cupped to his ear to hear better. Deafness and a phlegmatic temperament allowed him to remain on good terms with the most bellicose of his in-laws.

However, he very much irritated my aunt. 'He thinks I love him, but he really gets on my nerves!' she shouted at anyone who would listen, even in her husband's presence. This would be followed by more pleasantries in the same vein, only about a third of which my uncle would hear, allowing him to maintain his serenity. Thanks to his fortunate deafness, depriving him of half of everything that was said, he was the only brother-in-law to remain on excellent terms with my father, who fell out with people very easily. They would quarrel just once a season on average, a very moderate rate in such a disputatious family.

The youngest of the sisters lived with us during the summer; she had five children, the two youngest of whom were too little to interest me, but not so the three older ones! I was devoted to the eldest, Gulnar. Talkative, hypocritical and precocious, at the age of twelve she spoke about men in the tones of a woman of experience, giving me fascinating insights into our future dealings with them. She had already lost any illusions about male psychology: 'They are all selfish and will give us children if we let them. You have to lead them by the nose or they will take advantage.'

'You think so?' I asked, full of respect for her original insights and envious of her experience and subtlety.

'I don't think so, I know so!' Gulnar replied in a peremptory tone.

And she gave a passing gardener a haughty look.

She was entirely taken up with thinking about men, which stopped her getting down to her studies. And her lackadaisical mother, disinclined to be strict, left her in peace; only her father would give her a dressing-down from time to time, but the effect of his interventions was short-lived.

However, my admiration for Gulnar didn't come close to my admiration for her twin brothers, Asad and Ali, who were two years younger than her. They were my unrivalled teachers and professors, strict, unfair but magnificent. I eagerly sought them out, despite Fräulein Anna's protestations, losing a little of my innocence in their vigorous company.

Excessively liberal in morality, they lied, snitched, told tales and even stole whenever the opportunity arose. Their light fingers slipped into their pockets any money that was left lying around. 'We're all brothers, we're all one family. What belongs to one belongs to all,' they would say, pained to have to explain such an evident truth. They talked enthusiastically about the digestive system and its end product, discussing these things knowledgeably and making erudite comments, while Gulnar and I were thrilled to listen. While some people draw in red chalk, pencil or pastels, Asad and Ali drew with their dirty fingers on the whitewashed walls of the outhouses. They enjoyed spending time in one such retreat in particular, a rather romantic-looking turreted affair, and decorated its white walls with their almost lyrical creations, since they drew flowers just as well as obscene images. The outhouse was set up in Turkish style with the essential accoutrements for ablutions; it smelt of whitewash and humidity, which attracted a vast number of centipedes. Its walls were embellished with a variety of drawings—the genius of my cousins gave the outhouse a unique appearance. Its distinctive smell has stayed in my nostrils, and I cannot see a centipede without remembering it.

Needless to say, they taught me to smoke. Their loathing of the commonplace meant that my initiation did not take place in the outhouses, as convention requires, but beneath the great vines in the vineyard. There I would turn green and nearly expire to the merciless mockery of my teachers. Beforehand, Gulnar and I would empty the tea leaves from teapots, so we could chew them after the crime to get rid of the smell of tobacco that a suspicious adult might detect. After that we would combine business and pleasure by seeing who could spit them the furthest, a game at which the brothers beat us hands down, as usual.

They all loved card games, which they played with the greatest enthusiasm, due in part to their manual dexterity. Gulnar and I knew full well that they were cheating like mad, but this didn't stop us playing, as we'd been bitten by the bug too. Sometimes we caught the cheats red-handed, and then things would become heated and quickly descend into a fight which always ended in tears for us girls, now penniless. The brothers, though, would compensate us for some of our losses: very generously they would occasionally invite us to secret orgies of tomato and aubergine conserve, so rich and highly seasoned that we would be left stupefied for a good while. They bought the conserves secretly from a one-eyed, pockmarked pedlar.

But their most advanced skill was lying. They lied equally well out of necessity as for the fun of it, and even claimed that they lied out of kindness to spare adults the trouble of punishing them. They were confident, natural liars. I would even say they were graceful liars. They would take in the sharpest people with their air of absolute frankness that came more easily when they were telling the worst lies than when they were being totally honest.

They took it upon themselves to explain to me the inanity of the theory, dear to Fräulein Anna, that a cabbage was the procreator of the human genus. They considered the theory hilarious and dismissed anyone who tried to promote it. 'They think we're idiots. I'll show you a cabbage,' Asad would say, making an obscene gesture.

Dirty and scruffy by nature, they had a horror of water. But the lure of the pools was irresistible during the scorching heat of summer.

In this desert land where nothing grew without artificial irrigation, water had to be drawn from great depths, emptied into pools and then channelled to the plants and flowers that would otherwise wither beneath the cloudless sky. More than a dozen gardeners spent their days watering the vast, walled garden. Shovel in hand, they would stop up the mouth of one channel with earth to divert the water into another, open and close taps, clean the empty pools and fill up the others. These pools were dotted liberally across the estate and came in all shapes and sizes: large and small, round and square, long and rectangular. Some were surrounded by walnut trees, others by roses. In some, mildew covered the bottom and the green water smelt of slime; in others, the glittering clarity of the water was an invitation to dive in.

Nobody ever bathed in the largest of the pools, which was really a big, raised tank. It was too big for the gardeners to clean the bottom, so green slime built up there, smelling foul and giving the water a strange hue. The pool stood in the middle of a circle of poplars, which intersected the property's broadest and longest avenue. Rather than walk round it, we would climb a large ladder to the top, stroll around the very broad ledge and descend via a symmetrical ladder on the opposite side. But there were no railings! I still don't understand how Asad and Ali could hold frantic races in this dangerous place without ever falling, either on the garden side, where they would have broken a leg because of the big drop, or into the pool where they would have been drenched in delightful slime.

Walnut trees surrounded the pool with a thick green curtain. Two benches faced each other on the ledge, placed in the shade of the trees' highest branches. The ripe nuts would burst before our eyes and our indolent hands could gather them with no effort at all.

Far from the house, this solitary spot exuded an air of poetic serenity. The opaque, bottle-green water seemed to hide mysterious creatures and when no one was there to tell me not to, I would lie flat on my stomach, bend my head towards the water and stare intently, straining my ears, hoping to catch these aquatic animals unawares. I would stay like this for a long time, holding my breath, until my shoulders froze. I would end up giving myself a fright, finding two terrified eyes fixed on me. Forgetting they were my own and remembering the Hans Christian Andersen story in which a naughty girl is lured into the depths and tortured by sea monsters, I would run as fast as my legs could carry me towards more prosaic spots, where the shouts of children brought me back to a reassuring world.

We found our greatest aquatic pleasure in the Caspian, though. Just a few kilometres away, it looked very close and deep blue when seen from our estate, which stood at the end of a high ridge. Hundreds of squat, flat-roofed houses descended neatly towards the sea. They wallowed in sand, in which fig trees, mulberry trees and vines grew modestly. These small gardens and squat houses were not the property of proud Baku oil barons; this was where their poor relatives lived, ignored by fortune.

The Caspian Sea is said to be in slow decline: to be shrinking, evaporating, vanishing. Imagining the day when it would no longer be visible from the terrace, I would be overwhelmed by sadness.

At this tender age I was already troubled by the thought of the changes that befall everyone and everything in this world. But while awaiting its disappearance in a distant future, the blue sea shone magnificently and I would spend long periods contemplating it. We often saw tankers sailing by; sometimes they were ours and would greet us with a sonorous voice as they passed.

Trips to this nearby sea were made complicated by the tediously bad roads. The sand was so deep on the road to the sea that it was passable only by cart, mule or pedestrian, taking two hours to reach the coveted beach. However, our intense longing for seawater meant we made this miniature expedition several times. The carts would be hitched up and covered inside with old, threadbare carpets. The party would take their places there, surrounded by bundles of linen and piles of bread and fruit. Off we went while those who stayed behind called Allah's blessing on our burnt heads. The carts' high wooden wheels would creak on the uneven rocks, then plunge into bottomless sand, throwing it spinning into the air. Since Asad and Ali preferred to walk, I did too, and we would follow the carts, hurling insults and making fun of everything, easily pleased as we were. The rocks hurt our bare feet and the sand burned them—but neither the rough rocks nor the burning sand, nor the prickly dry plants that managed to grow in this terrain, could stop us. Luckily our feet were used to all the hazards of the ground. My father had an impressive number of health rules, one of which was to give up shoes in summer. So we lived barefoot and the soles of our feet were permanently scratched, cooked by the heat and battered by the uneven ground, becoming as tough as those of savages. But however much we suffered on this arduous route (and we did, especially towards the end of the road), none of us would seek salvation by getting into the cart. As the oriental saying goes, 'It's a disgrace to get on a donkey, but a great disgrace to get off it.' So, since we had chosen the thorny path of endurance, there was no getting into a cart for us.

Our estate was located on a ridge: a steep slope led down to a valley, beyond which was the sea. As I've already explained, this valley was populated by non-oil barons, a good race but a little contemptible to our oil baron eyes. The differences were immediately apparent: the houses were smaller, the walls around the gardens lower, and in the gardens themselves were only fig trees and vines. No deep wells skilfully sunk, no artificial irrigation and its corollary, dozens of sweaty, labouring gardeners. A small, hand-operated well provided only enough water for the animals (including the humans) to drink. Houses were no longer lit by electricity but by oil.

The race of non-oil barons was very kind, though: our journey would be punctuated by cries of welcome, and we had constantly to fend off invitations shouted over a wall or from the flat roof of the house. If their cries wore us down and we stopped at the home of a relative, we would be plied with cool water and force-fed grapes or figs, but also subjected to a barrage of gossip, rattled off at a remarkable rate in order to get everything out in as short a time as possible. 'This is what Aghabaji did,' and, 'This is what Bahar Khanim said,' and everyone would be shouting and laughing at once and, sometimes, cursing.

Despite these visits to my grandmother's cousin's sister-in-law or my great-aunt's son-in-law's great-uncle, we would eventually reach the sea. Our bodies could sense its proximity before we saw it; our ears heard it, our noses picked up its indescribable smell, and breaking shells hurt our feet. Then we would turn a corner and it would suddenly be revealed to us in all its fresh, blue beauty; small, frothy waves hid modestly in the wet sand and a gentle breeze (as though from the evaporated sea) revived us after the twists and turns of the sandy road.

The 'civilized' among us decked themselves out in the extravagant bathing costumes of the day: great black, shapeless sacks, made only more comical by their supposedly pretty ruffles. But those who remained faithful to Allah bathed in their undergarments: a long-sleeved shirt and long bloomers, an ensemble similar to modern pyjamas.

Hardly any of these ladies had good figures, the price perhaps of a sedentary life, most of which was spent sitting on the floor. Sagging breasts and bellies were everywhere; it was a competition to see who was the hairiest, who had the shortest neck and the biggest buttocks. I often thought they had pretty faces but ugly bodies, may Allah forgive me. Fräulein Anna, in her smooth whiteness, seemed to me to be an exotic beauty and I couldn't help both admiring and envying her.

Leaving my heroic cousins to their maritime exploits, I lay in the shallows and let the little waves like white horses ripple over my body and withdraw, revealing me to the sun's rays, before they washed over me again. I could have stayed like this for hours, but Fräulein Anna was on guard; she too was armed with an arsenal of health rules. She claimed that the Caspian, saturated with salt, was debilitating and after twenty minutes or so beneath the wavelets I would hear the German command to come out. Why did I always have to do as I was told? I thought with longing. Would it be like this all my life? I wondered, anxious and with a presentiment of the truth. Tedious duties would sadly always stretch time out into infinity, relieved only by meagre interludes of small pleasures. I sighed and as consolation for woes, both present and future, stuffed myself with fruit and bread, then bread and fruit…

3

My astonishing grandmother dominated the clan which gathered around her every summer. Her dimensions alone set her apart. When she rose to her feet, she looked like a giant from one of Perrault's fairy tales. Looking like this, it would have been absurd for her to be meek and gentle, and she certainly wasn't. All day long she could be heard giving orders, making demands and hurling insults, shaking the house to its foundations.

Almost immobilized by her monstrous weight, like Louis XIV she found it practical to spend much of her time on a commode, a jug for ablutions within reach. Sitting regally on this throne, she received her supplicants, including men, before whom she modestly covered her face, as became a good Muslim woman. It should also be noted that she looked not only very grand but also perfectly respectable, since her traditional, richly pleated skirt fell all around her chair. Thus installed, Grandmother would reduce to dust some trembling, grovelling gardener.

Her daughters, her sons, her sons-in-law—in short, everybody—submitted to the same strict treatment. Even when my father became head of the family on the death of his father, this made no impression on her. Really, he did as he liked but he nevertheless always sought to please her. It was only us, her grandchildren, who escaped her tyranny. We were her weakness, and we exploited this to extract a thousand and one favours. She plied us with her famous nut jam, the best in the world, hid us in her generous skirts when Fräulein Anna came looking, gave us pieces of cloth for our dolls, and loved us so much that she would even bestow a few kopeks on us from time to time. One of her most sought-after favours was, however, admission to her famous hammam parties.

On those days an eager crowd of poor relations—the women from the valley, who constituted Grandmother's regular retinue—would turn up with their babies and bundles of linen under their arms. Since morning the gardeners would have been at work heating the hammam, which consisted of an anteroom, a room for undressing and, finally, the hammam proper. The hammam contained two large pools, surrounded by stone benches; one pool held hot water, the other cold, liberally dispensed from the numerous taps protruding from their high sides.

Many were the pleasures to be had in this blessed place. Hair was washed with a type of clay; massages were given and received; body hair was removed using thread, a method unknown to Europeans, and depilatory creams, which were forerunners of the Taky brand but even fouler smelling; henna was applied to every possible part of the body. At other times, there would be a massacre of lice; for reasons that remain a mystery to me the poor women were often infested with them, despite their conscientious weekly washing.

But these corporeal concerns still left room for matters of the spirit and, while they bathed, the women would chat, gossip and tell stories. The dense steam went to their heads like wine. Between washing their hair and depilating their thighs, they would on occasion be bold enough to arrange a marriage, which only increased the prestige and renown of the hammam parties.

I stopped at nothing to gain admission to these celebrations of body and soul. On one occasion, Grandmother had refused me entry to paradise for no good reason; feeling most aggrieved, I decided to get my revenge. I waited until all the women had gone into the hammam, then locked them in with the key that was kept outside and hid it. This cunning trick accomplished, I went off to play with the other children and forgot all about it.

When the ladies had finished their complex cleansing rituals and wanted to leave the hammam, to their surprise the door wouldn't budge. They started banging on the door and shouting, but nobody passed that way. The windows were high up in the bathhouse so the women couldn't reach them; they were shut in. An hour of banging and shouting met with no response. They fell into tragic despair. Another hour passed of hunger, steam and increasing commotion. At last a gardener happened to walk by the hammam, which was set apart from the other outbuildings, and heard the racket. He went up and listened through the door to their catalogue of woe, interspersed with hysterical sobs. He discovered that the key was missing and raised the alarm. Another key was easily found and the poor women were freed, half-baked, suffocated and totally drained of emotion.

I nearly fainted from terror when I realized the enormity of my crime. I took the coward's way out and didn't own up, letting suspicion fall on Asad and Ali, whose vehement protestations of innocence were not believed. Their punishment was light, for lack of proof of their misdemeanour, but it seemed harsh to the innocent boys. Once my fear had passed, I revelled in the comedy of the situation: for once my cousins were not lying, just for once… and they were not believed. What just injustice!

On other days the poor relations came to do their laundry in the frog pool under Grandmother's watchful eye. The frogs had made the pool their headquarters, hence its name; when evening came, a fearful, deafening racket started up. 'Those frogs,' everyone would say in tones of disapproval, shaking their heads, but the frogs couldn't care less and just croaked more loudly.

The pool was low with a broad rim, two features that made

it the ideal spot to do the weekly laundry. The murky, even dirty, water did not deter the washerwomen. This was where ablutions were performed, babies bathed, and a wide range of other things washed, from feet to Grandmother's dishes.

One day Asad and Ali came to find me, bringing some good news: they were planning to play a trick on a great-great-aunt three times removed by the name of Amidostu, whom we hated for reasons that were obscure: she had never done anything to us. So I followed my beloved cousins as we headed for the frog pool, looking as though butter wouldn't melt in our mouths.

That day a dozen washerwomen were sitting on the rim of the pool, furiously pounding their laundry. Their veils fluttered behind them like banners, as the women didn't bother to cover their hot, sweaty faces—they knew that no man of the household would come near the pool on the weekly washing day. Brown hands, fingers and palms dyed with henna beat, rinsed and wrung the laundry. The water in the pool became choppy, large waves rippling from one side to the other. But manual labour in no way impaired the women's verbal capacity. The greater their physical exertion, the greater their need to give vent to their feelings. The conversation was, therefore, intense, rapid-fire and riotous. Only when Grandmother spoke did the women fall into an immediate, respectful silence. Grandmother didn't do any washing, but kept her beady eye on the laundry's progress while dropping words of wisdom into the choppy waters of the pool. Grandmother didn't really address anyone in particular; her words were intended as much for the mulberry trees as for the birds, for the water as for the women.

Grandmother was speaking as we approached, but stopped for a moment to look us up and down suspiciously.

'What are you doing here, creatures of *Shaytan*?'* she asked.

---

* 'Devil' in Azeri.

'Nothing, Grandmother, nothing at all. We've come to keep you company,' we replied sweetly, keeping up our performance by kissing her cheeks, damp with perspiration in the sweltering heat.

Grandmother was not convinced and continued her mistrustful scrutiny. She knew from experience that nothing good ever came of Asad and Ali looking demure. But we sat down quietly around her, and Grandmother turned away, sighing.

Asad and Ali had not yet reached the fateful age of thirteen, which would bar them entry to feminine society. While they were not yet fully fledged males, they did not miss out on the intoxicating and pleasurable atmosphere of the weaker sex. These ladies left their streaming faces uncovered before them; their veils continued to flutter on their shoulders like banners and they beat and rubbed and wrung out their laundry with an ardour that even the sun could not extinguish.

'Yes,' Grandmother continued where she had left off. 'Then Farida said she didn't want to marry Akbar because he was sixty. That's where those dirty Christian dogs are taking us, *ay Allah*!'

'*Ay Allah!*' ten mouths declared in unison.

'Where are we going?' our enemy Amidostu asked grandly.

And the emotional Amidostu screwed up her little piggy eyes as though she were about to cry.

'Where are we going?' she asked again, looking at Grandmother as though she might find salvation in her.

Grandmother made a vague gesture in the air and her large emerald and ruby rings caught the sunlight; then she majestically rested her hand on her thigh, crossed in oriental style.

'Only Allah is wise,' she pronounced finally.

And the ten women immediately repeated, 'Only Allah is wise.'

The sun shone fiercely in a cloudless sky. Long beads of sweat trickled down the brown faces, dropping into the pool or onto the laundry, but not one of the women bothered to wipe them away; it would have been a futile gesture, a waste of time and energy. Wipe away ten drops and another ten will take their place… What's the point of wiping them away, *ay Allah*?

The women all went back to talking at once; each one firmly believed she had the most interesting thing to say so shouted as loud as possible to be heard. They made such a din that the night-time croaking of the frogs seemed a gentle chirping in comparison. In the still air of the dog days their chattering reached the far ends of the garden and the gardeners would shake their heads, laughing… The frog pool had earned its name twice over.

'Do you know,' Grandmother resumed, and all the women fell instantly silent, 'do you know that Ginger Ahmet, my niece's sister-in-law's great-uncle, has serious heart disease? He might die. There's no… Only Allah is eternal.'

'Only Allah is eternal,' the washerwomen's chorus replied immediately.

And for several moments the splash of the water was punctuated by appropriate sighs. Amidostu sighed more loudly than the others and a tear appeared in the corner of her eye. But Grandmother returned to the subject close to her heart.

'Can you imagine that Farida, who is only sixteen—she was born in the year of the great Surakhani fire—doesn't want to marry Balaja-Giz-Bibi's uncle, because, she says, he's sixty. As I was saying, this is where the Russian pigs are taking us. My children are mad to bring up their children the Russian way. They'll be sorry one day. But nothing happens without the will of Allah.'

'Nothing happens without the will of Allah,' the chorus responded.

'That is true,' Asad interjected firmly.

He got up and walked over to Amidostu, taking a small flask out of his pocket and splashing its contents on the old woman's veil and clothes. In open-mouthed fascination she watched him do it. Ali in turn took a box of matches out of his pocket and looked as though he was about to use them.

'What are you doing, children of dogs?' Grandmother shouted, sensing trouble.

'I've told you a hundred times that you insult yourself when you insult us like that,' Asad said coldly. 'Our parents may be dogs, but don't forget that they're your children. Anyway, we've decided to burn Amidostu, as she annoys us. I've poured petrol over her and now we're going to set her alight…'

Amidostu gave a wild cry. She leapt to her feet, threw aside her veil and undid her skirt, which fell to the ground, revealing long white bloomers. She was taking off her jacket which had also been sprayed with petrol, when Ali brought a burning match close up to her, or rather appeared to do so. Amidostu jumped down from the pool's rim and charged down a long avenue, calling for help at the top of her piercing voice. Grandmother rained curses down on us, and the other women followed suit. As for me, I rolled on the ground laughing. Amidostu fled through the garden in bloomers and without her veil, despite the gardeners or other men she might encounter; Asad and Ali, still brandishing his box of matches, were hot on her heels. Hadn't it occurred to her simply to jump into the pool?

When Grandmother wasn't busy with one of her five daily prayers or on her commode receiving visitors, she held court in the kitchen, which served as her drawing room. Crowds of poor relations swarmed around her, but rich relations came too, as did poor people who were not even related. One of this last group stood out in particular: an old woman called Fatima who was said to be a hermaphrodite and descended from the Prophet—though the only benefit this ancestry brought her was to increase her vanity. Even marriage had eluded her, and she was the only celibate Muslim woman that I knew; perhaps because her hermaphroditism posed sexual problems that were difficult to resolve; perhaps because her divine ancestry frightened the men, rendering them unable to be at ease with her; or perhaps simply because she was so ugly that even the usually imperturbable Asad and Ali found her disturbing. She had a large face like a dog, deeply wrinkled and covered in hair. Were it not for her breasts, which hung loose and banged together like two squashed mortadellas as she walked, she would have been taken for a man. Another of her distinguishing traits was her passion for the hookah, which Grandmother, with uncharacteristic generosity, offered her during her visits. I loved Fatima despite her ugliness, as she was Grandmother's only visitor who never tried to kiss me with her wet lips and damp cheeks.

Those revolting kisses were the bane of my childhood. As soon as one of the poor relations spotted me, she would inexplicably make a beeline for me and cover me with kisses that were a dense mixture of sweat and saliva. Knowing from experience the impossibility of escape, I would let them get on with it, clenching my teeth and nursing hatred in my soul. As soon as the woman let me go, I would demonstratively wipe my face with a handkerchief or, failing that, the hem of my dress. But this eloquent performance didn't stop them starting all over again. Tact was not their forte.

The vast kitchen was always overflowing with visitors, most of them accompanied by children of all ages. It was impossible to go in without seeing one of them breastfeeding an infant, or even a child whose nursing days were long since over (if there's milk there, then of course someone has to have it). These lousy, snotty-nosed, screaming children repulsed me and I didn't try to hide it. The assembled company took exception and decided I was a child of *Shaytan*. Obedient to my reputation, I lived up to it with even worse behaviour: I would stick out my tongue at one woman, pull another's plaits and pinch a third woman's child.

Asad, Gulnar, Ali and I made frequent incursions into the kitchen, where from seven in the morning to nine at night something was always cooking. Wanting to be seen more than to satisfy hunger, we would stick our fingers into boiling jam then lick them, snatch a morsel of mutton simmering in its sauce and eat it half-cooked, choking on it and burning our mouths. Grandmother would threaten us with a rolling pin or meat skewer; knowing that she couldn't get up quickly enough, we would continue to ravage the dishes until she told one of her visitors to throw us out without ceremony, which the latter would do with obvious pleasure.

Sometimes, though, we would sit quietly on the straw mats scattered over the floor in place of chairs, and listen. We listened with delight to a storyteller's nasal twang (all the storytellers had a nasal twang—tradition demanded it). The children suckled, the women fanned themselves with raffia fans or quietly twiddled their thumbs while the storyteller told the tale of Ahmad and Surayya or Mohammed and Leyla. Love stories were popular with us all, though the women rarely experienced them themselves. They always began with the words: 'Someone was and someone was not; apart from Allah no one was.' As the story unfolded, the milk curdled in the large earthenware bowls, the mutton gently roasted and the jam boiled in the enormous red copper vats, watched over by one of the women.

The sloppy kisses were not the poor relations' only drawback. They were eaten up by curiosity and unrestrained by any scruples; they would burst into our bedrooms while we were still asleep, opening all the drawers and cupboards to look at our things, feeling our dresses to work out the cost of the fabric and our breasts to see if they were growing well. They wanted to know everything about their rich relations and fired questions at us. Which of us was already menstruating and since when? Which of us was our father's favourite? How many dresses did we each have and how much were the 'Christian women' paid to look after us? They listened behind doors, pressed their faces up to our windows and were amazed at everything: the piano, the mechanical toys, tennis. They envied us these things with a childlike candour, but were suspicious of the progress they represented; their simple life must have seemed more peaceful to them. Sometimes they irritated us so much we slammed the door in their faces, telling them to go to the Devil, but they wouldn't take umbrage and would start up again later.

Grandmother loved them and took their side against us, because she liked to surround herself with a biddable entourage. The poor relations were her courtiers: servile, fawning and backbiting. They brought her all the local gossip, making it up if need be to entertain her. Grandmother would invite them to the hammam parties, give them some leftover mutton or a length of cotton for their trouble. Of course, she could be very rude about them when she felt like it, but the women did not flinch: her courtiers were unencumbered by pride.

4

Quarrels and rifts were a dominant feature of family life, for two reasons: one was the fiery tempers and fractious dispositions of all the members of the family; the other was the INHERITANCE. The famous, elusive inheritance that had to be shared out on the death of my paternal grandfather. I'll say it again—the INHERITANCE! The word merits several exclamation marks, not just one, as it spawned endless discussions, arguments and hatred. Three sisters and their husbands, two brothers (and later, their wives), their mother and their father's second wife spent much of their lives haggling over it, each fiercely defending their share. The children of these brothers and sisters were dragged along the rocky road as well. Their parents would forbid them to play with those cousins whose father, or mother, or both, were out of favour. Nobody escaped involvement in these intractable disputes that went on year after year, court hearing after court hearing, until 1917. No explanation needed...

We children were upset when we had to break off relations with our cousins, stopping our games to satisfy the passing whims of adults. Sometimes we continued playing in secret, and those games were doubly exciting, as they had the allure of forbidden fruit. But often Asad and Ali, belligerent and foul-mouthed at the best of times, used the opportunity to heap undeserved abuse on us with impunity—breaking my young heart, ignorant as I was of the fickleness of human sentiment.

I've already said that their father, Uncle Suleyman, never came to the country house because of the semi-permanent rift with my father. But he let his wife live with us, on the sole condition that she have the occasional row with my father. And when she did, a cloud hung over relations with my amazing cousins, whom I loved so much; but they loved their father more and followed his instructions to the letter. They were so much in his thrall that, typically, it took just one word forbidding them to play with the children of the 'thief', as he usually called my father, for them to fall into line. When the paternal rift had passed, they would be friendly towards me again in their own way.

I could understand their love for their father, with his powerful personality. Wagging tongues said he was syphilitic, a murderer and a thief, but if we believed every malicious rumour, we would have nothing to do with anyone but ourselves. Handsome, violent, a shrewd businessman, he had come from nothing and managed (I wonder by what sleight of hand) to marry a daughter of the Family and build a town house that inspired the admiration of all its visitors. The house had an inner courtyard for elephants (who never did take up residence) and a roof where jasmine could grow (but never did). Other things remained unfinished too, but, even as it was, the town house filled me with awe, especially the inevitable Moorish reception room with a fountain, and the boldly decorated Renaissance room. Not forgetting to mention a room covered entirely in mirrors and a bedroom with twin beds separated from the rest of the room by a fretwork panel that created the strange effect of a cage.

Despite all this splendour the whole house was untidy, even dirty, most likely due to the residents themselves. I am sure that Asad and Ali would have managed to turn the Élysée Palace into a similar mess: a strong personality leaves its imprint everywhere.

But let's get back to the eternal rifts that wrought havoc in the family. The state of affairs with the other sister and her husband would be quickly made apparent—the barometer door between the two country houses would be bolted shut, so it would be impossible to see each other; though both sides could hurl abuse over these two-metre-high ramparts, which they did sometimes when a storm was brewing and spirits sank.

All this was child's play, though, in comparison with what happened one disastrous day when my grandfather's second wife took the ridiculous idea into her head to come and visit us in the country. We were shut up in a distant room—still not far enough away, however, to stop the cries, or rather howls, from reaching us. All the adults of the family were gathered on the terrace; hard feelings forgotten, those who had not been on speaking terms that morning were united against a common enemy. From what I learnt afterwards, the second wife feared neither God nor the Devil. Standing up to the lot of them with admirable courage, she repeatedly went on the offensive. I don't know exactly what went on during this historic encounter, but the wicked stepmother did not stay the night, returning to the city the same evening. When we were allowed out of exile, we saw shocked faces, dishevelled hair and eyes smouldering with a dangerous fire. At dinner the conversation was exclusively in Azeri, as was always the case when passions were running high. With the enemy gone, the sides regrouped and resumed their quarrels with more vigour than ever. The racket grew ever louder during the meal, and after dinner moved onto the terrace, where discussions between the interested parties were resumed, redoubled, quadrupled, and so forth. It ended in a grand battle; everyone was angry that evening, and for around a week all the factions within the family broke off relations with one another. It was a painful time. When we saw a member of an enemy faction, we had to look away and make it obvious by our demeanour that we had become deaf, blind and dumb and saw no one but ourselves. We would go on our haughty way, in a silence that spoke volumes or rather spoke nothing at all.

We were not the only ones to suffer from the loss of our games: the three sisters would be stricken, as the rift deprived them of their daily card games. They had a burning passion for poker, perhaps using it as a receptacle for all their repressed feelings. Sometimes they would start playing in the early afternoon, only breaking off to gulp down a few mouthfuls, as though they scorned base dietary concerns in favour of purer pleasures, then resume their game and not finish until dawn. And estrangements meant they had to give all this up! When peace was restored, how they would race to the green baize table! And we celebrated too. During those endless card games we would take up position at the four corners of the table, preferably near whoever was winning (and this required intuition). Intoxicated with victory, the winner rarely forgot the smart nephew or sweet niece sitting quietly at her side and would give them a rouble, sometimes more, depending on the size of the winnings and the mood of the moment. Though Fräulein Anna objected time and again to the practice, no one took any notice of her virtuous indignation: neither the generous donor who laughed at her anger, nor the recipient who was motivated by love of money. We secured substantial revenues for ourselves in this way, and went on to lose them too as we already shared the passion for the game. Only Asad and Ali ended up in profit—they always won, by cheating or through their greater skill and intelligence. What noble boys they were!

Let's go back to the last get-together around the frog pool, when Grandmother talked about pretty Farida, sixteen years old and sentimental at heart, who baulked at marriage to a man of sixty. Not long after that conversation the young girl gave in to her authoritarian father, as was only to be expected, and agreed to marry the man they had chosen for her. Veiled and kept well away from young men, how was she to find a fiancé herself? (Later, when revolution had conquered the Caucasus, she cast off her veil and her husband and married a man her own age. History does not say whether she was happier with the former or the latter.)

The wedding was set for mid-June. Though scornful of the sentimental dramas surrounding the marriage, we children were delighted, as a wedding was a gift to those who like to enjoy themselves. And my cousins and I really did enjoy ourselves at that wedding. We were too young for gender distinctions to be applied, so we could spend as much time as we liked at the men's wedding party or the women's. Like the house of any good Muslim, Farida's parents' home was divided into two: one part for the women, the other for Them (the husband and his guests).

In one part, people ate, sang, danced and drank rose water; in the other people ate, sang, danced and drank rose water. You might think it would have been simpler to eat, sing, dance and drink rose water all together, but the gentlemen did not think so and, as for the ladies, nobody asked their foolish opinion.

The exquisite young Farida sat regally upon a chair in the middle of the room reserved for the women's wedding party; but we couldn't see her, as she was covered by an impenetrable red veil. As was the practice, she sat very still and said nothing. The poor thing was not meant to enjoy herself; she must have been very bored, especially since no one seemed to pay her the slightest attention, which I would certainly have found annoying in her shoes. It surely was no fun for her.

My cousins and I, however, really enjoyed ourselves, as I've already said. Cheeky and scruffy, as was their wont, Asad and Ali inspected the whole house, having something to eat in one room, a drink in another, teasing one person, annoying another, while Gulnar and I followed in their wake. With their customary brilliance they knew how to make the most of a situation and turn it to their advantage. Would it be too much to say that they forged their destiny, rather than followed it? They chose their seats, gave orders to the servants, who circulated barefoot and wearing the traditional fez, and wouldn't let anyone tell them what to do, especially when they were in the women's quarters, where they felt like masters; as the only males, they knew how to profit from the situation. Their mother had only to make an innocent remark for them to belittle her and put her in her place as a woman. So she didn't push her point too hard.

Under their protection and tipsy on rose water and buttermilk which we imbibed in unlikely quantities, Gulnar and I became daring too. Fräulein Anna was a long way away as no one had thought to invite her to this Islamic wedding; Grandmother, however, was there, but she still had a weak spot for us and restricted herself to throwing us a gentle 'children of dogs' or other unmentionable insult when our bad behaviour got too much. But even then we had only to plant a kiss on her permanently damp cheeks for our misdeeds to be forgotten. A smack for fun, a supposedly angry look, a few harsh words and it was over—we could start again.

There was lots of dancing at those weddings. All the women, except the very old or the very weak, showed off their moves to the accompaniment of oriental instruments and rhythmic clapping.

The gentlemen were even more spoilt. Professional singers and energetic dancers were invited. I hated the local singing, and when I saw a singer raise his hand to his cheek, a gesture that heralded a song, I was out of there in a flash. Brought up on Mozart and Bach, I loathed those strange songs, a sort of lament that continued indefinitely on two or three notes but seemed to fill the audience with rapture.

As for the dancers, they were always effeminate young men, and dancing was not their only weapon with which to charm the gentlemen. Pretty by and large, with plucked eyebrows and wasp waists, they would slay a roomful with one killer look. Render to men what is men's!

I was starting to fall for one of these Adonises, whose sinuous grace seemed to me extraordinary, when Asad whispered in my ear in tones of utter contempt, 'Yuck, that's not a man, it's a *goetveren*. When I'm older, I'll...'.

'Is it?'

I didn't really understand, but pretended to know all about it.

'Come on, a doll like that isn't made to be a man. I'll be an *ushaqbas*.' This literally means 'a lover of children', while the word *goetveren* translates as 'giver of one's behind'.

The two sorts of pederasty—active and passive—flourished in Baku among men condemned to the company of their male peers. The former, more or less respected, was practised by almost all men, at least until their marriage, and considered to perform some kind of public service. The second, on the other hand, was practised only by young, effeminate boys for mercenary ends, and held in deep contempt. It was an insult to call a man a *goetveren*, but no one found fault with a respectable gentleman belonging to the brotherhood of the *ushaqbas*.

I haven't introduced the groom yet: he was a handsome man, with a youthful appearance and dyed hair. Smartly turned out, he was admirably preserved by his marriages to young girls. Farida was to be his fourth wife.

Of course, the three other wives attended the wedding. They sat near their young rival, casting her solicitous glances from time to time; they were the only people present who appeared to show the least interest in her, prompted by the solidarity of fellow spouses.

It was obvious from looking at the old young groom that the marriage would be consummated in the proper fashion with no hesitation on the groom's part. His attractive demeanour boded well, so I don't think it occurred to anyone to pity his future wife. In fact, the wedding night went admirably, according to the rule book. Farida was taken to her husband's house in a carriage, escorted by horsemen who fired rifle shots into the air in honour of the newly weds. Deposited into the hands of wise women, Farida was undressed and prepared for the wedding night. This done, it was time for the groom to demonstrate his *savoir faire*. While the youthful sexagenarian was doing his job as young groom, a woman waited in the neighbouring room. What was the eavesdropper waiting for? The prime exhibit—a sheet with the marks confirming the young girl's virginity. Her parents were waiting anxiously to see it—only then could they give a sigh of relief and glorify Allah. If not, everything would be ruined: cheated over the merchandise, the husband might return his bride to her parents, covering her in shame and dishonour. But to general satisfaction Farida proved herself to be immaculate. You might think I was too young to keep up with it all; indeed, had I been the young girl Fräulein Anna imagined me to be, I wouldn't have understood. But make no mistake—that would be to forget both oriental precocity and the lessons of my cousins, who already knew everything about sex. If they were not yet having it, it was only for lack of opportunity, not knowledge.

Though having only just developed, they tried hard to be men. I didn't know until later about their activities in this regard, when a playmate chose to confide in me.

Tamara was a product of two enemy races—Armenian and Turkish. Her father was somehow related to the family, while her Armenian mother had converted to Islam to please her husband. An only daughter, spoilt by her parents and taken good care of by a German governess, Tamara should have had a carefree childhood. But Allah decided otherwise when he sent her to us. Her father bought a property not far from ours and her governess became friends with Fräulein Anna; her age meant she was destined to be our playmate. It was more than enough to make Tamara our regular visitor.

She was the prettiest girl in the world, with beautiful almond eyes, a straight nose, clean, firm lips and long silky tresses. When we happened to stop tormenting her, she would immediately start to smile and show affection to the whole world; she was as gentle as she was beautiful. Such a successful product of the two races should have encouraged Turco-Armenian rapprochement, but not a bit of it—fanaticism raged on.

Tamara paid a heavy price for having an Armenian mother.

'You're a vile, salty Armenian, Tamara,' Ali said, pinching her arm. (When attached to 'Armenian', the word 'salty' was an insult, for reasons that remain unclear.)

Tamara gave a cry of pain, then lowered her lovely head, sighing in defeat.

'Come here, Tamara, and I'll straighten your dirty, crooked Armenian nose,' Asad shouted. He ran up and twisted her perfectly straight little nose.

She had tears in her eyes but kept quiet. She put up with everything with courage worthy of a better cause.

On holidays we played at massacring Armenians, a game we loved above all others. Heady with racist passion, we would sacrifice Tamara on the altar of our ancestral hatred. First we would make arbitrary accusations against her of murdering Muslims and shoot her on the spot, doing it several times in succession to savour the pleasure. Then, when we were drunk at the sight of her blood, we would revive her for the good of the cause before massacring her once more, this time in the prescribed manner. We would tie her up and throw her to the ground; then we would cut out her tongue and cut off her limbs and head; we would tear out her heart and guts and throw them to the dogs to show our contempt for Armenian flesh. When we had finally sated ourselves with our ferocity and there was nothing left of the poor girl, we would dance around her corpse, waving our wooden guns in the air and uttering savage cries. If a governess or other adult appeared in the distance, we would promptly pick up Tamara, frightened out of her wits, take her by the hand and begin dancing in a friendly circle, singing nursery rhymes.

It didn't occur to Tamara to complain; she would have been called an informer, a traitor, and once again a dirty Armenian, and been deprived of all contact with us; even though she was humiliated, mistreated and massacred at regular intervals she could not do without our company. Anybody else would have been dull by comparison.

'You know, Asad and Ali forced me to play with them without you and Gulnar,' Tamara told me several years later, 'in secret.'

'Really?'

I couldn't get over it and bitterness pierced my heart.

'That's disgusting. What did you play at?'

'At rape,' Tamara murmured.

'At rape? Oh!'

I felt even more deprived.

'Yes, at rape, at rape the Armenian.'

I was an exclamation mark.

'Yes, it happened during the afternoons on the hottest days, when everyone was having a nap. Asad and Ali would come to find me and take me to the vineyard near the Devil's house.'

The Devil's house was a derelict cottage on the edge of the vineyard, abandoned to the spiders and lizards. An air of doom emanated from its unglazed windows, wholly justifying the house's name. Even those people who seemed to laugh at the Devil were none too keen on going anywhere near that ruin. One can never be sure.

'You know I don't really like that place,' Tamara went on, 'but they made me go there, saying that I had nothing to fear from the

Devil when I was with them. They said they had seen worse. Can you believe it?' she exclaimed admiringly. 'They took me to the fig tree there, you know, the large fig tree to the left of the house. Then they told me to take off my bloomers. I didn't want to at first but you know what they're like; they started to hit me, so I took them off. There I was without my bloomers and they stood behind me and did things, first one, then the other; sometimes they started all over again. I got so hot!'

'But what did they do exactly?'

'I've no idea. I was just so hot. I would start off in the shade of the fig tree, but you know how quickly the shade moves. So I was left in the blazing sun. It didn't bother Asad and Ali. They could have a rest under the tree, but the sun was beating down on my head and the sand was burning my bare feet and Asad and Ali didn't finish. It was no fun. They said they were doing it to punish me for being a bit Armenian.'

'I'd still like to know what exactly they were doing.'

'Well, I think... You won't tell anyone, will you?' Her eyes wide in fright, Tamara whispered, 'I think they put spit on that thing that they have and we don't and tried to push it in my back.'

'Goodness,' I said. 'If the Fräuleins had found out...'

'But they couldn't have found out. I wasn't going to tell them, was I?' She sighed. 'Do you think it was bad?'

'Yes, I do, I think it was bad.' Then I shrugged my shoulders and said philosophically, 'Bad, good; good, bad? Happy the person who can tell the difference.'

Then Tamara blinked and lowered her gaze, flushing. 'You know, I have to say... it wasn't unpleasant all the time, rape.'

But it's time I said something about my own love life, which began very early and was rich and turbulent throughout my childhood. Began very early? At least I think so, since I was ten when I experienced my first love.

You already know that we had many gardeners. They were indispensable in a desert land where nothing grew without plenty of watering. One gardener was extraordinarily handsome, I thought at the time. He had the fine name of Ruslan, which added to his attraction. I became aware of this love during a humdrum walk together to the vegetable patch where Grandmother had sent me to find a ripe juicy melon. When Ruslan passed me the fragrant yellow fruit, I felt the first pangs of this celebrated malaise. It was to remain essentially the same for me, irrespective of the variety and number of people who would be its object in future. I came back carrying my melon in my hands, but it weighed less than the freshly blooming love in my heart. On that day I became a different—I was going to say woman—a different child.

I swooned whenever Ruslan passed by, so great was my emotion when I saw him; I dreamt of him day and night. I knew it would take a miracle for me to marry him, so I made up scenarios that would have allowed me to become his wife one day. For example, my father would be ruined and I would be left penniless. This also required the ruination of my maternal grandfather, from whom I would inherit, and I destroyed him with cruel skill for the good of the cause—nothing could stop me. I never imagined then that my dream would one day become reality by a twist of history. So I became desperately poor. I led the life of a beggar. I lived in a garret, mending my rags (which were clean despite my new social status). I gathered pieces of wood on the beach to feed the mean fire in my attic on which I cooked my equally mean soup. I was glad to be utterly destitute as this brought me closer to paradise—possible marriage to the glorious Ruslan. One day when I was sadly wandering the streets of Baku, barefoot and the wind in my hair, though not without a touch of vanity as my rags were still clean, I met Ruslan. Struck by my beauty and dignity, he took me by the hand and led me to his home to make me his wife. I imagined what followed with a beatific, knowing smile. The opposite miracle involved making Ruslan fabulously wealthy after the discovery of a distant relative in Persia or Turkey. He was given a rapid education, taught good manners, inducted into the ways of polite society, and his providential relative considered all the possible brides in Baku and chose me, the most beautiful and accomplished. Ruslan showered me with sumptuous jewels and built me a palace entirely in black marble—I was very keen on it as a child—and became the most infatuated of husbands. We floated along in perfect happiness and had many children.

This passion was extinguished when Ruslan made the blunder of marrying the daughter of one of our gardeners—a large, coarse girl who wasn't even pretty. At first I was indignant at the worthlessness of my victorious rival, but then found consolation in it: if this was Ruslan's taste, I was better off without him.

After this bitter disappointment, which was to be the first of many, I fell for a Russian boy, a friend of Asad and Ali but a few years older. Spotty, with a tendency to sweat and a shock of artfully tousled blonde hair, he seemed, despite this or perhaps because of it, the archetype of the classic foreigner and intellectual. He could say 'I acknowledge that fact' better than anyone else in the world, which to me was the height of erudition. Having 'acknowledged the fact' that I admired him desperately, he would swagger before me and even try to court me by pinching my arm, leaving me breathless with emotion. This romance came to an abrupt end when his heartless parents took my spotty knight away to another city.

My third love was divided in two, as its object was two brothers. They were both radiantly handsome, and that wasn't blind passion speaking; I still have photographs to prove it. It was an agonizing love, as I loved them both equally, but differently. All the more agonizing as I was very virtuous at that time and could not conceive of love outside the well-worn path of marriage. I didn't know how to reconcile the double demands of my heart. When I finally settled on one, the image of the other would appear before my eyes, stopping me from making a definitive choice. I could see no way out, as there was no polyandry in Islam, only polygamy. I spent sleepless nights imagining myself reaching marriageable age and having to choose between the divine brothers, whatever the cost. Scenes of tragedy gave way to scenes of pathos, but everything remained up in the air. When I could no longer deny my powerlessness to cut the Gordian knot, something happened to distract me from amorous thoughts about men, at least for a while.

5

My father had gone to Moscow, where his brother, Uncle Ibrahim, joined him. On his return ten days later, my uncle made an astonishing announcement at the dinner table that stopped the daily race for mutton in its tracks.

'Your father is getting married,' Uncle Ibrahim said, addressing us girls sitting at one end of the table, 'and he wants Leyla to come to Moscow with me to attend the wedding.'

There was silence for a moment, followed by an explosion of shouts, exclamations and questions.

'Who's her father? Who's her mother?' one of the aunts asked hysterically. 'How much money have they got?' shouted a second aunt, while the third wanted to know, 'What does her father sell?' Grandmother must have been in the know, at least to some extent, as for the moment she maintained a scornful silence.

'She's poor,' Uncle Ibrahim replied.

'What? How?' cried the aunts, receiving the news like a stab to the heart.

Every reply spelt equal calamity. At least 'She' was Muslim; her family were Ossetian (a people from the North Caucasus) and in the bosom of Islam; Allah be praised, but that said...

First on the list of misfortunes: her father didn't sell anything. His failure to belong to the merchant caste (it didn't matter whether they sold oil or watermelons, as long as they sold something) was already deeply suspect. So, her father sold nothing and wasn't at all rich; he was an ordinary engineer, may Allah forgive him! A railway inspector, neither more nor less; an employee—a government employee, true, but even so, he was still a common employee. When his first wife, the mother of Amina (my future stepmother) died, he married a Jew.

'That's nothing to be proud of either, but at least it's better than those Christian dogs, may Allah curse them,' my grandmother interjected judiciously at this moment in the story.

We hung on Uncle Ibrahim's every word, hungry for news.

This strange family lived in Moscow, where the father had raised his two daughters in the European fashion, or, to be more exact, what passed for the European fashion. At this point Uncle Ibrahim cast a look presaging doom around the whole assembly—I knew he loved to try and terrify his audiences and enjoyed himself enormously when he succeeded. From this moment on his account was constantly interrupted by sighs, more in keeping with a burial than a marriage announcement.

He (the engineer who sold nothing) had not been content with a Muscovite education for his daughters and had later sent them to Paris. They lived there on their own, completely on their own (there were no more cries now, just a terrified silence). Uncle Ibrahim was not qualified to say how they had lived there, but his expression gave us to understand the worst. For example, he knew that in Moscow they had moved in artistic circles (general amazement mixed with incredulity) and gone out alone at night with men (here Grandmother let out vehement cries of '*Yah Allah*', seconded by all her daughters at once). Amina had married a Muslim from the Volga at twenty ('So old!' exclaimed the aunts), but had divorced six months later and returned to live with her engineer father and Jewish stepmother. My father met her at a soirée at the home of some mutual friends and catastrophe soon followed—he fell in love with her. Now he was determined to marry her. Amina had hesitated for a long time before agreeing to marry him. 'What?' Bitter laughter rang out on all sides. The daughter of a 'nobody', a poor man, an employee, had hesitated to marry the eldest son of an illustrious family, one of the richest in Baku? 'That's the funniest thing I've heard in years,' said the women, on the verge of tears.

A love match with a penniless girl! It was unthinkable, contrary to good sense, good taste, reason, even common decency, but was going to happen because the poor man (my father, of course) had lost his mind. The world of my grandmother and aunts was already showing cracks, but this would bring it crashing down. They knew who to blame, reserving their hatred for Russia and Christians, the destroyers of their world.

Ignorant of the feelings of the older generation, we children were overjoyed, delighted. We were going to have a young, civilized stepmother, with fair skin and almost blonde—as was confirmed by Uncle Ibrahim, who had a recent photo of Amina. We devoured that picture, finding her dazzling.

My eldest sister Leyla became unbearable. She was going to Moscow... No, not only Moscow, maybe even Paris, the omniscient Uncle Ibrahim declared. Amina wanted to go to Paris before coming to Baku, and since business stopped my father from accompanying her, he was going to send Uncle Ibrahim in his place, and for reasons of propriety Leyla was to join them; to put it in political terms, it would be 'a unilateral honeymoon, taken within the family framework'.

It was infuriating that Leyla would have the good fortune to see Paris! Wasn't it enough that she was sixteen with voluptuous breasts and a dozen suitors? To reinforce her crushing superiority over us, she would travel to Europe! My heart ached at my dreary fate. I remembered my unhappy romances with Ruslan, the Russian boy and the two brothers; the hollow word 'injustice' was imbued with tragic meaning... off I went to shed unseen tears beneath the leaves of my friend the vine.

Two long months passed, lit up by burning arrows—postcards from Warsaw, Berlin, Paris. The cards seemed imbued with a hidden magic power that I tried to decipher; I fingered them, turning them over and over; I sniffed them, trying to picture where they had been chosen and posted, how they had crossed all those distant countries to reach us. I couldn't get to sleep at night as I constantly imagined a glittering life with Amina; an eventful life, full of joy and pleasure; the kind of life one can only dream of. Following Amina everywhere—to Paris, Nice, Rome... I had completely forgotten my love for the two brothers and was now indifferent to their charms whenever I happened to see them.

That memorable summer I was obsessed with dreaming—an obsession, moreover, that has never left me. I sought solitude so I could dream in peace; only in this escape from the tedium of daily life could I be sure of finding happiness, independent of everyone and everything.

But I needed the guile of an old Sioux to find this solitude, throwing off the scent of sisters, cousins, aunts and governesses, and especially those bloodhounds Asad and Ali. When I managed it, I ran to my vine in the heart of the vineyard, lay down on sand softer than the softest skin, my friend's leaves all around me, closed my eyes and plunged into the story of my love for Amina. I saw myself at her side in Paris, instead of the loathsome Leyla with her enormous cow eyes and bulging breasts. 'She' showered me with presents and tenderness, while I adored her unreservedly, with all the generosity of a child who hasn't yet learnt how to hold anything back, despite the tough school of my cousins.

The day that I would meet her, a day impossible to imagine, finally arrived. At dawn we set to work with garlands and paper lanterns and thousands of fresh flowers, until the house was resplendent and aromatic. Then we dressed in all our finery. Towards five in the afternoon, the entire Family, except for Grandmother, gathered beneath the large portico at the main entrance to await the arrival, all quarrels set aside.

Overcome with excitement, I shivered despite the blazing sun; I had had a lump in my throat intermittently since morning and could drink only water; my heart was pounding violently. I imagined every detail of the great love scene: as She got out of the car, I would be the first person She saw. She would walk towards me, arms outstretched and eyes glistening, and say something dazzling, such as: 'My little angel, love me.' The next part of the scene was vague, as my happiness was beyond expression.

We sat on the stone benches beneath the large portico, eyes fixed on the empty road. Whenever a cloud of dust appeared in the distance, I was at breaking point. Everyone got on my nerves. My aunts were gossiping at full volume as usual, criticizing their sister-in-law—whom they had yet to meet—at a rate of three hundred words per minute; excitement racked up the speed of their utterances from impressive to prodigious. My sisters and female cousins, presided over by the governesses, sat in a separate group, all 'good little girls' together. Enormous powder-blue ribbons sat on top of their well-brushed hair; the same blue bordered the collars of the eternal sailor suits they had to wear, with nascent moustaches the finishing touch. Their feet elegantly pointing inwards and their hands casually resting on their thighs, they seemed to be waiting for the click of the camera.

My male cousins were as scruffy as usual, despite the efforts of the whole family. They pulled each other's hair and punched each other out of the blue, as a kind of game. That day, for the very first time I despised them, rather than admired them.

A cloud of dust appeared in the distance—was it them? As they came closer, all doubt disappeared: we recognized our horses, our coachman, our father. The carriage made rapid progress and pulled up at the portico. My father was first to emerge, swarthy as usual but expansively content as never before; next came Leyla preceded by her breasts like a herald's trumpet, and finally 'She' stepped out…

My heart wasn't beating, it was jumping up and down. More than that, my internal organs had been rearranged. Instead of one heart, I now had several: one in its usual place, one in my head, another in my throat and more scattered all over. They all pounded together, making me shake terribly. And not without reason. Amina was more beautiful in the flesh than in photographs. She was touched by the freshness of dawn; her very slightly snub nose seemed to me to be the height of originality; her lips were red, full and smiling. The sun illuminated flecks of flame in her chestnut hair, which I studied in fascination. As she approached, her fitted dress hinted at a fine waist and long, slim thighs.

My father did the introductions. According to my fantasy, Amina should have recognized me herself among the laypeople, chosen me, favoured me straightaway, sensed my all-consuming love for her. But she embraced the aunts, the sisters, the cousins, even the insolent twins who were staring at her rudely. All the family were introduced—I was the only one left out. They were about to walk down the grand avenue towards the house when my father became aware of my presence behind an aunt and pointed me out to Amina: 'And there's the littlest.'

Only then did she turn her light-brown eyes towards me, kiss my forehead and pat my cheek.

'Oh, what a black little thing!' she said smiling, and turned her back on me, taking my father's arm.

It was a bitter disappointment, but even children are capable of compromise. I bravely choked back my sorrow and got acquainted with the chasm between dreams and reality. I found a thousand and one justifications for Amina's behaviour towards me and my love remained as strong as ever, but less demanding. Amina, though, was indifferent towards me; or, rather, she was kind when she saw me, but forgot all about me when I wasn't there. She had other things on her mind than her relationship with a lovesick little girl. The poor thing was like a fish out of water. Young and used to her freedom, she found herself surrounded by veiled women, malicious sisters-in-law and wild brothers-in-law for whom virtue was no laughing matter. What was to become of her among all these strange people? And what good was the celebrated oil in these impossible conditions? The oil that could take the form of jewels, dresses, furs and other frivolous things? What use were they in this milieu? Even to possess them seemed pointless, absurd. Dress in Parisian creations for the mustachioed sisters-in-law, put on make-up for the suspicious brothers-in-law? With the exception of some old engineers from the family firm, respectable, bearded, long-serving employees with armies of children, any male who was not part of the clan was automatically suspect; it was considered indecent to invite a man to call. My tolerant father, known for not giving a damn, wouldn't have minded, but the Family, strong, united, jealous and strict, was on watch.

At least at the start, Amina's life was far from cheerful. Besotted with France or, rather, with Paris, or even with a particular aspect of Paris, she found herself forced instead to live an almost miserable, enclosed existence.

Not sharing her suffering, my three sisters and I were happy and proud to have her with us and learnt much through her presence. Amina had brought back a lot of music from her latest trip to Paris.

À la Martinique, Martinique, Martinique,
C'est ça qu'est chic, c'est ça qu'est chic...

we would sing in delight, imitating the sounds without understanding the words. Tangos, the 'Apache Dance', Mayol's songs and all the popular tunes of the era were strewn across our magnificent Bechstein concert piano. It was only much later that I learnt of composers such as Ravel or Debussy. The same could be said of the literary genius of France which was revealed to us through *La vie parisienne* with its captivating pictures. Emancipation had begun.

Some time later, though, and thanks to the good-natured Amina, whose idea it was, we had more useful contact with French culture through the intermediary of a charming demoiselle, Marie Sarment, who came from France for our benefit.

Also thanks to Amina, an Englishwoman arrived from England at almost the same time in order to teach us the language of Shakespeare and social graces from across the Channel. From day one she astounded us with the excellence of her table manners; instead of eating corn on the cob by grabbing it with both hands, as we usually did, Miss Collins would remove the kernels meticulously with a knife and fork; she would stab each kernel separately with her fork and convey it to her mouth; it was attractive to watch but took far too long. After humbly admiring the grace and skill of her performance, we would grab our cobs again with both hands and devour them in the Caucasian manner.

Fräulein Anna was justifiably resentful at the arrival of the new governesses. Her situation remained privileged; she was in some ways part of the family, but her authority was diminishing and we admired only one woman now: the dazzling Amina. All her ways impressed us: how she spoke French, how elegantly she wore her dresses by Poiret, how beautiful her chestnut hair was (I now found poor Fräulein Anna's blondness dull in comparison), and her intelligence (ah, what intelligence), and her culture (ah, what culture), and so on and so forth… I was sick with admiration.

I didn't want to play our usual games very often now; I thought it was boring to pretend the apricot tree was a train and we were passengers, drivers and stationmasters, and found it childish to play at 'the ruling family'; even the 'massacre of Armenians' had lost its spice for me. No, I wanted to play at being Amina. I would imitate her; mimic her voice, her walk, her gestures; I would wrap myself in a blanket that was meant to be one of Worth's creations, declaim French words and pretend I was strolling down the grand boulevards of which Amina had so often spoken.

Asad played the part of my father—and with considerable talent, I have to say—while Gulnar, Ali and Tamara were the extras—servants, doctors, merchants, police officers, whatever the game demanded.

To me, Amina was France, and this was the start of my love for the country that was later to become mine. As a result, I wanted everything to be French or at least everyone to speak French; I even wanted to teach Grandmother the language. I went to find her, sitting majestically as usual on her commode.

'Grandmother,' I said in Azeri, as she didn't speak any other language, 'say *"Bonjour, petite fille"*.'

Grandmother would start off with a few insults and then meekly repeat '*Bondjouptitfil*'. I would make her repeat it, then teach her other words until she lost patience and gave me a good smack, accompanied by one of the tremendous swear words she had made her own. So I would leave her to go and teach French to more receptive souls.

Amina's arrival turned our whole life upside down, materially as well as spiritually. In the autumn we would move to a new house, for which furniture had been ordered from Moscow. Our former apartment would gradually disappear from our ungrateful memories; a piece of our lives would fall into oblivion. Farewell to the five of us together, farewell to cream tarts, farewell to pink cotton angels. The era of Germanic sentimentality, transplanted so strangely to Azerbaijani soil, was over—a new era was beginning: the era of Amina.

6

Everything amazes me when I go back to the past. I'm surprised to realize that this part-oriental, part-German and, later, Russian childhood is my own; that the dreamy, withdrawn and rather naughty girl is me. All these dredged-up memories seem borrowed: it's hard to believe they're mine. I walk through them like a tourist, not a resident; Baku seems to be a distant dream and the family my own invention. Sometimes I enjoy going back, but more often I am apprehensive. I was happy until around the age of ten, but then withdrew into myself, feeling lonely among my older sisters. The change began when my father remarried; maybe Amina embodied the dream I had thought would always be out of reach. At that time a new horizon opened up before me: I realized there were other worlds, not just my small world with Fräulein Anna at its centre and our country house at its boundary. Convinced that Baku was a splendid city, my family irreproachable and our life desirable, I was surprised and saddened to discover that Amina did not share my opinion; Amina despised Baku, loathed the family and rebelled against our existence. I had 'to reconsider my position' and came to see Baku as a filthy backwater despite its millionaires, our family as dangerously barbaric and our life as pitiable from all points of view. I dreamt of crazy things that I knew were impossible to attain. I would have been dumbfounded to hear that I would one day have the free life of which I dreamt, abroad, far from all the oppressive constraints which Amina chafed against; that I would possess Paris in all its beauty, in all its poignant beauty; that I would cross the Place de la Concorde almost every day and regularly visit the Louvre. I didn't know that a long, hard war and a long, hard revolution would one day open up to me the land of my most cherished dreams. No, I knew none of this then. I was preparing for a very different life that I thought I already knew. I would marry one of Baku's oil barons, decked out in dazzling jewels that would attest to the importance of my fortune, and would have many children. With a lot of luck, my husband would be handsome and inspire me with love, a hope that never left me. Having dreamt of love from a very early age, I wanted to know it.

There's nothing left of the Baku of my childhood, and who regrets it, other than a few old émigrés who parade their vigilant nostalgia around the world? No one will be moved by the memory of the sordid millionaires; it is right that they disappeared. Islam had ceased to be true Islam, thereby losing its function. Engulfed by modern life, it no longer brought peace to the soul, only a list of constraints that were thrown off without regret. Is gambling forbidden by the Koran? The whole of Baku played cards, staking enormous sums into the bargain. Is wine forbidden by the Prophet? People made up for it by drinking spirits—vodka, brandy—on the false pretext that it wasn't wine. Reviled too was reproduction of the human image, but the photographers were overwhelmed with customers and the Muslims had their pictures taken in profile and full face against the background of a painted park or riotously draped curtains.

What a strange childhood! I know that every childhood feels far away. Mine, though, seems even more unreal because of this complete fracture, both geographic and social. Nothing connects me to it: neither religion, which I abandoned, nor language, since today I think and write in French; neither my nationality, which has changed, nor the lost millions; nothing and no one. My past seems like a previous life. Unlike Baudelaire in his poem 'Former Life', I didn't live 'beneath vast colonnades', but in places that seem equally unreal to me, like a dream that arose in response to some forgotten tale.

7

We returned to the city and did our best to settle into our new, half-empty house. As we watched the furniture from Moscow arrive, our admiration for Amina's taste reached fever pitch. We thought the furniture triumphantly luxurious, as the furniture of rich people should be, and so original! To please our oriental taste, there was the inevitable Moorish furniture, all carved wood and fretwork and covered in sumptuous ornaments in all the colours of the rainbow; long, narrow divans stood on a dais separated from the rest of the room by an elaborate wooden balustrade. I think the divans were supposed to be soft and voluptuous in the oriental style, but they were neither—they were hard and uncomfortable. But this was probably the will of Allah! The stucco on the salon's walls was shaped into wonderfully painted and gilded arabesques. The whole was meant to recreate the Alhambra…

There was also furniture for two other salons, inspired by Versailles. As far as I remember, this was much simpler and, perhaps for that reason, more beautiful than the Moorish furniture. Then there was yet more furniture for a small room that was to be Amina's 'boudoir'. This room had an alcove with a large divan, which shocked the aunts and uncles; they claimed that the divan in the alcove, the low chairs and shaded lights created a coquettish atmosphere.

The house's *pièce de résistance* was without question the huge, flamboyantly Gothic dining room, where the pointed tops of the cupboards attacked the ceiling, cathedral-style. The walls were covered in a fabric of golden fleur-de-lys and the oak doors were studded with leather nails. Alas, where was the armour of our medieval ancestors?

Amina's bedroom was yet more modern Alhambra, with chairs to match.

Oh, what a fine apartment we had! And everything else changed in keeping with it. Instead of the maids-of-all-work that we used to have, we now had a chef, valets and lady's maids. Amina also asked my father to buy some motor cars, so we became the owners of two Mercedes-Benzes, which had to be used; this was not as easy as it might seem at first sight. Baku was still a very small city, so any distance could be covered in a few minutes and the car would have only just got going when it arrived at our destination. This did not encourage motoring. There were not many places for excursions outside Baku. There was really only one in winter and we made that trip again and again until we were sick of it. We went to Bibi Heybat, an oil-producing suburb that ended in a narrow spit of land plunging several kilometres into the sea. There, the derricks, waves and wind gave off their distinctive tang and it all had a terribly melancholy air.

But I would sit next to Amina, and squashed up against her I soon forgot the sadness inspired by the gloomy landscape, cliffs on one side and the stormy sea on the other.

In spring we would add an alternative destination for our excursions: we went to the Nobel Gardens, which the Nobel family had laid out close to Baku in an area, like all areas close to Baku, where oil was produced by hundreds of derricks. It was an enormous public park, inserted between the Nobels' industrial workings, a location that gave it a special charm and turned it into a sort of floral jewel:

it had an abundance of trees, including fruit trees, flowers in greenhouses and flowers in flower beds. We would return laden down with branches of cherry blossom, and decorate Amina's boudoir with them, bringing the beautiful spring into our home afresh.

My father's marriage had turned our lives upside down and was gradually to disrupt them even more. Amina weathered storms and tempests, success and failure, in order to keep open house, not only for men who had one or several wives, a double or treble chin and a clear family tie to us, but also for bachelors, sometimes young and handsome, whose parentage was not known. To that end, Amina made frequent use of the word 'cultures'; even if she misused it, making it serve other ends than those that might be implied, we benefited from this state of mind. We were enriched by influences other than Fräulein Anna. We were enlightened not only by Amina, but also by the new governesses.

Mademoiselle Marie Sarment was a woman of character, in the best sense of the word; she was lively and an excellent teacher. Physically, she had an aquiline nose, bouffant hair and breasts that took up a lot of room, which irritated her since she was small and didn't really know where to put them. I can still remember clearly that first, colourful lesson: Mlle Marie spoke only colours: red, blue, violet, and so on, again and again... Despondent, I thought we would have to learn their English equivalents next, and if our linguistic studies continued in the same vein, I would end up in ten years' time knowing twenty languages. I was depressed at the thought of all that hard work. But Mlle Marie gave me a shake, lifted her aquiline nose and cried in triumph, '*C'est un crayon rouge!*'—waving in front of my nose the irrefutable proof of her assertion. 'Repeat after me.' I felt she would have rather died than give up the truth of her assertion.

'*C'est un crayon rouge,*' I repeated half-heartedly, out of politeness.

My lack of conviction upset Mlle Marie.

'My dear, one has to be sure of what one learns. It is a red pencil, after all. So repeat it.'

And I repeated it, but couldn't help thinking of the girls my own age whom I had met at Grandmother's; true, they were veiled, or at least they would be one day; true, they had lice in their hair, and oriental slippers on their feet, but no conscientious governess came to torment them by teaching them a new language every year. Lucky things, I sighed to myself, while repeating out loud, *'C'est un crayon rouge.'*

Pencils of every colour marched before my eyes for an hour, at the end of which I knew colours as well as millions of Frenchmen did. Then Mlle Marie gave me two kisses, one on each cheek, and assured me in charming, eccentric Russian that I was a lovely person. I believed her implicitly and set about loving her in return.

Later I had plenty of reasons to love her; one in particular disposed me favourably towards her. Studying me one day, she said, 'You will be famous.' I was impressed, flattered and thoroughly delighted, especially since I was beginning to suffer from an incurable inferiority complex. Dear Mlle Marie! Such a lovable person and such a skilled teacher! Even if your prediction was never to come true (and there are good reasons for thinking so), I am nevertheless very grateful to you. It is good to believe those who believe in you.

A few days later I found myself sitting opposite Miss Collins and learning 'white', 'red', 'blue'... even more half-heartedly than with Mlle Marie, and thinking with even greater longing of the ignorant, lousy girl I would have been if emancipation hadn't become the order of the day. Lousy, but speaking only Azeri; lousy, but not forced to play scales for two hours a day; lousy but not wearing myself out over the geography of countries of no concern to me; in a word, lousy but happy. To me, lice became a symbol of a simple, but happy life.

Miss Collins lacked Mlle Marie's charm. Too reserved for my taste, she intimidated me; on top of that I held her personally responsible for the disconcerting fact that almost all English words consisted of refashioned French or German words. One letter was removed, another changed and the job was done—badly, I thought. '*Bleu*' became 'blue', '*rot*' became 'red', '*Hut*' changed to 'hat', and so on ad infinitum. Those sad Englishmen with no imagination took words from everyone, made the slightest of changes and flattered themselves that they had their own language and enjoyed universal respect. But they certainly didn't have mine. I thought resentfully that if they had had the courage and honesty to adopt French or German, I (and a quarter of humanity) would have been spared the task of learning an amalgam of mutilated words. And I put the English in the same category as the Armenians and Greeks: a category reserved for people I considered underhand and wicked.

For me, one of the greatest advantages of our new residence was our proximity to Aunt Rena, who came to live on the floor above ours. This closeness was very beneficial for me. First of all, because she would often invite us to eat the most delicious apple tart in the world, which was the speciality of her Russian cook; second, the aunts and uncles often played poker there, games at which my sisters and I garnered a much appreciated, steady income. The biggest advantage of all, though, was that during her husband's frequent absences Aunt Rena would 'borrow' me from Fräulein Anna, who was none too keen on the arrangement but was obliged to 'lend' me. The faint-hearted Aunt Rena could not bear sleeping alone. Fräulein Anna suggested she have one of the servants sleep in the neighbouring room, but Aunt Rena replied that this would solve nothing; she needed to have someone in the bedroom itself, in the bed of her travelling husband, and I was her preferred choice. So I went upstairs to sleep at Aunt Rena's quite often. Sometimes this arrangement lasted one or two weeks, to my unfettered delight. And for good reason: Aunt Rena often visited one or other of her sisters for the indispensable game of cards and during that time I was alone in the large apartment and master of my own fate, taking the opportunity to read whatever I liked for as long as I liked. A small room next to the bedroom housed a huge carved-oak bookcase, full of books that were mostly translations of French authors. There were the complete works of Maupassant and Flaubert; I found Loti, Mirbeau and Zola. During my solitary nights there I read all these books, some of them several times. I would go up at nine, supposedly about to drop off at any minute; carried away by enthusiasm, Aunt Rena would usually return between three and five in the morning, so I would spend all this time reading. The reading went to my head like wine. From three o'clock onwards, though, I would remain alert, listening out while I read. When I heard a car pull up outside the house, the main door slam and footsteps coming up the staircase, I would throw the book back onto the shelf, put out all the lights and hurry into bed. Aunt Rena would find a girl asleep in her husband's bed and would hardly dare breathe for fear of waking me. I would magnanimously decide to put her at her ease and pretend to wake up; I would enquire pleasantly who won the game, and Aunt Rena would be delighted to be able to talk and make as much noise as she liked. And she made a lot of noise as she went to bed: she would let out oohs and ahs of pain as she got into bed, would murmur in satisfaction or groan in displeasure, endlessly rearranging her many pillows and blankets, tossing and turning and invoking Allah and his Prophet, before finally lying still, exhausted. But not for long. A few minutes later she would be on the move again.

'*Ay Allah*,' she would invariably say, 'I think I have to wee.'

Then she would make a dash for the chamber pot, placed between two cupboards at the far side of the room.

'What can I do? I've got a weak bladder,' she would say quite unnecessarily.

I wasn't really bothered, as I would be half-asleep by now.

I was sometimes horribly frightened during the long hours in the large, deserted apartment. I remember one such night, when I was reading Maupassant's 'Le horla' and terrors assailed me on every side: the furniture creaked in sinister fashion, the curtains seemed to move for no reason, the wind whistled in the chimney, but most of all I was terrified by the shadows that surrounded me. I thought they were going to materialize into horrible, hairy, slimy phantoms and suffocate me with their soft flesh. I froze in my chair, blood pounding in my temples, covered in cold sweat and scarcely able to breathe. Sometimes I would stay like this for a long time in the greatest mortal fear, expecting to be attacked by nocturnal monsters at any moment. Nevertheless, I would be as happy as ever to return to Aunt Rena's the next evening, so great was my passion for reading. Breathless, I read and reread Mirbeau's *Torture Garden* and *Diary of a Chambermaid*—if poor Fräulein Anna had known! She had no idea, though, and was downstairs, sleeping the sleep of the just. I got through the whole of Chekhov; I read Gyp, Hugo and others, many others. This went on for years, and I had the time to read and reread everything. I didn't mind if I understood only half of what I read—I was happy with that half, which was more than enough to introduce me to the wonderful world of the imagination, more intense than the real world. I would be the different heroines in turn: wicked or good, treacherous or brave, magnanimous or cruel. I was all things, ever changing. I lived through fever, enchantment and horror.

Daydreaming brings such wonderful memories! A little later it would be the groans of Aunt Rena and the dash for the chamber pot; but this was dull and lifeless in comparison to the hours I spent in other people's shoes.

Who can tell the importance of dreaming? And of reading!

8

Spring came astonishingly early the first year that Amina lived with us; warm breezes blew constantly, making the sparrows sing and the blossoms open. With the change in season came the question of where to spend the summer. Here too everything had changed: Amina did not want to go to the country with the entire Family as usual—she couldn't bear the prospect of prying cousins all over the property, poor, lousy relations in every corner of the garden, aggressive brothers-in-law and touchy sisters-in-law. She wanted to go to France, but France was denied her. After much discussion my father decided we would go to the North Caucasus to take the waters in Kislovodsk, the most elegant of a cluster of spa towns. My maternal grandfather agreed to put one of his villas at our disposal, so that even when my father was away, we would be in a decent family atmosphere, not a showy hotel full of hazards of every sort for weak women and children.

At last I was really going to leave Baku, and on a proper train, not the ridiculous slow coach that took us to the country every spring.

Amina took personal charge of selecting the many dresses we had made; she wanted us to be well dressed, as she insisted on having an atmosphere of elegance around her.

I was captivated by my new dresses. One of them in particular kept me awake at night: it was made of white lace with short, puff sleeves and rosebuds all over. I would lie in bed, my eyes wide open, imagining myself in this dream of a dress promenading with Amina. I also thought my stepmother might love me more when she saw me covered in rosebuds and submerged in lace. I had to face the evidence: I had made no progress whatsoever in winning her love. She was utterly indifferent towards me. I looked for the reason for her indifference and eventually found it: I was too ugly, too ugly to be loved.

This idea stayed with me for some time, and I suffered cruelly as a result. I didn't like anything about myself; the more I looked at Amina, the more I found myself repulsive. I thought her beauty perfect… and realized with a growing despair that all my features were the exact opposite of hers. In desperation I prayed long and hard to Allah, begging him to make me beautiful right away. I thought the miracle would happen as a result of my prayers and I would wake up one morning, transformed into a diaphanous blonde, all pink skin and clear eyes.

For the first time I was going to take what I used to call a real train, a big train. Amina had already left with Leyla and my father; Fräulein Anna and we three 'little girls' were to join them.

The heat was stifling on the day of our departure; a dust-laden wind blew over a dazed Baku. I wandered from room to room in the dark, shuttered house, among furniture covered in white dust sheets, but couldn't settle. All three of us were in the same state of excitement and could not eat a thing at lunchtime. Seeing this, Fräulein Anna suggested that instead of having dinner at home we go for a bathe in the Caspian, followed by milky drinks in one of the cafes on the Boulevard. From there we could go straight to the station without returning to the house. We greeted this brilliant idea with enthusiasm.

The famous Boulevard occupied a prominent place in Baku's social life. It was a long stretch of asphalt next to the sea with many seats and few trees. One went to the Boulevard to see and be seen, to keep up with the latest news, to eat, drink and listen to music. In the open-air cafes *zurnachi* (the *zurna* is a kind of fife) played and singers sang themselves hoarse in Azeri, their leader sporting a fez. Buttermilk, yoghurt, kumis and other dairy products were consumed. Sometimes the municipal orchestra played with excessive gusto in a bandstand in the middle of the promenade. And those weren't the only attractions on offer: there were the landing stages, where boats would be moored and others would be docking or setting sail; and, finally, there was the bathing area, which was reached via a long wooden jetty projecting out into the sea. There wasn't a public beach system in Baku: for a few roubles every bather acquired exclusive use of a cabin that opened onto a minuscule square of sea, bounded by wooden planks dug into the sand.

I was astounded at the opulence of the sleeper compartment, where our luggage was already waiting for us. Everything was rich and gleaming: the mirrors, the wood, the lamps all shone; we had plush carpet beneath our feet, velvet at the touch of our hands. The restricted space concentrated all these riches, condensed them in some way: what was contained in a square centimetre there would have embellished a square metre anywhere else.

Fräulein Anna settled me on a couchette. The others went to bed in turn and soon everyone was asleep; only I tossed and turned on my borrowed bed. The red night light reminded me of the icons I had seen in our Russian maids' rooms. My thoughts hopped from one subject to another: I relived that evening's dip in the Caspian; I imagined the marvellous life the next day would bring; I reviewed all my new dresses, lingering with tender satisfaction on the one with rosebuds. The next moment I wondered why Fräulein Anna and Amina had such white skin, while we were all so brown. My elder sister Zuleykha's upper lip had already acquired a covering of light down. The next eldest, Surayya, had a much thicker covering.

As for Leyla, the eldest of us all, she already possessed a real moustache, which she removed regularly. Having so many older sisters was such a bore: I could see my physical destiny in each of them; I knew what I would be like in four, five or eight years. At that age I didn't give a thought to the day when we would be not just adults, but older than that; when I would see what the 'ravages of time' would inevitably wreak on me.

I woke up at dawn and remembered with pride that I was travelling.

As I got up, I could see the sky, then a wood, something I had never seen before. Trees, hundreds of trees, thousands of trees, standing on a thick, grassy carpet; grass that grew lush and green, and appeared entirely natural—what a marvel! If only our gardeners could see that, I thought; for all their artificial irrigation they could not turn the sandy earth green.

The train stopped suddenly in the middle of the countryside. The spot wasn't completely deserted, though, as there was a house for the crossing keeper. He emerged from inside and walked over to the locomotive; I heard him talking to the driver, then silence returned.

The silence that follows a train stopping in a deserted place is always so troubling. Why? There is more than silence in this silence, there is a sort of waiting, an enchantment that is both delicious and sad at the same time.

A bird sang. In front of me was the crossing keeper's white house, surrounded by a little garden. Shutters opened beside red geraniums on a windowsill; a woman appeared, young, blonde and glowing. The woman opening the shutters in the fresh, pink calm of morning—a morning that was as radiant as her beauty; the red geraniums, the wood touched by the first rays of sunshine, the magical silence: all this beauty, which in a few moments would melt into the past, is still within me. I have only to close my eyes and I can see the colours and objects again; I can hear the silence, punctuated only by the refrain of a bird. I can see it all as it was, at one precise moment, centuries ago, and though all that harmony has vanished, it remains as alive as ever.

The dark, dank house that Grandfather Musa* had allocated to us was covered in ivy outside and inhabited inside by centipedes, cockroaches, spiders and other monsters. What we lost in comfort as a result, we gained in animation and movement. It was a bizarre surprise to find a toothpaste-scented centipede in your tooth glass, to discover a spider resting in your bed or a cockroach settled in your shoe; it was open season on insects, the richness of the haul depending on the luck of the day; there was the satisfaction, too, of never feeling completely alone or abandoned. As I had the bad luck to catch mumps as soon as we arrived in Kislovodsk, I came to appreciate the presence of the insects. I spent a whole month in bed, where watching their lives was my only diversion.

I had some sad times in that gloomy room where half the window was covered in ivy. Outside, in a world inaccessible to me, the sun was shining for other people, the birds were singing non-stop, hundreds of people were out promenading. My rosebud dress hung limply in a wardrobe that smelt of camphor. Beneath the dress, where legs and feet should have been, my black patent leather shoes shone in the emptiness, for nothing and no one. The world was getting on very well without me: people carried on being happy or sad, loving or hating one another, and I even learnt from Fräulein Anna that the Russians had gone to war against the Germans and our brother Turks. It left me unmoved, though: it was my mumps that had acquired historic importance for me.

Widening the circle step by step, I could at last get out of bed,

* Musa is the Arabic form of the name Moses.

out of my room and then out of the house. When I was at the stage of leaving the garden, I went to pay my respects to my grandfather, who had arrived in Kislovodsk in the meantime. I found him sitting in an armchair beneath a large plane tree.

Grandfather wasn't handsome, and he wasn't at all affectionate towards his granddaughters either. So I didn't love him very much, or at least felt no affection for him. This courtesy call that I had to pay, now I had recovered from the mumps, really irked me, but there was no getting out of it: it was better to get it over with quickly, like a purge.

I strode towards the plane tree where Grandfather Musa was sitting and planted a kiss, lighter than a dragonfly, on his rough cheek, above his fine, black-dyed beard. Then I sat down nearby on a bench and studied the sky and the clouds, which I rightly found more attractive than my grandfather. He said nothing, but we both had the reassuring sense of doing our duty: Grandfather by putting up with my presence and me by sitting close to the person to whom I owed the greatest possible respect. When I felt that a suitable period of time had elapsed, I got up. Then Grandfather, aware too of his duty, started to rummage in his pockets. This took a long time: he thought the coins he found too valuable. At last he made some choking sounds that seemed to indicate satisfaction and furtively slipped into my hand a ten-kopek coin. It was the custom in our family of realists, who knew what life was about, to make gifts of money. I had nothing against this practice, quite the reverse, but I thought it humiliating to accept ten kopeks. I had to take them, though, and even feign delight.

At that moment, however, fortune was smiling on me: my grandfather's second wife came up to us and kissed me. Spying the ten-kopek coin in my hand, she cried in indignation: 'Agha Musa' (she always used the respectful term Agha when addressing her husband), 'give her more than that. What do you expect her to do with ten kopeks?' A pained expression on his face, he started rummaging in his pockets again. He found a rouble, and handed it to me reluctantly, then turned away, disgusted with me and his generosity.

My grandfather was one of the richest men in Baku, but also the most parsimonious. Though his miserliness is still notorious in the annals of our city, it was shot through with a host of bewildering contradictions. Suffice it to mention just one to give some idea of the complexity of his miserliness. On days when people were out in the streets of Baku selling artificial daisies, a symbol of some charitable society or other, Grandfather would not go out, lest he fall victim to one of these vigilant souls who would promptly pin a flower on his clothes and invitingly rattle a small collecting tin. But when he died, we were amazed to learn that he had given out enormous sums of money, sometimes to people he didn't know and always without publicity. He also set up numerous bursaries for poor boys.

He was kidnapped twice in his life and both times emerged unscathed after paying huge ransoms. I am proud to say that Baku was many years ahead of America in all that concerned kidnapping, only our gangsters were called *qochus*. Like their American counterparts, they knew how to operate quickly, effectively, discreetly and with the help of the Russian police, who took care not to impede an activity that was so profitable for everyone—except the victims, that is. The *qochus*, moreover, enjoyed not only impunity but also a well-deserved reputation for generosity and daring. Unfortunately, very little was known about the stays imposed on their clientele: the victims remained silent on the subject, it was assumed by order of the *qochus*. One could deduce, though, that they had been well treated and, especially, well fed; when they returned from their enforced sojourns they would almost always look in the best of health and have put on weight. It was only right that they should pay for their board and lodging!

Another act of munificence by this real-life version of Molière's Harpagon was the erection of an opulent edifice built in a rather bizarre architectural style. Dedicated to the memory of his son Ismayil, who died of consumption, the building was known as the Ismayilliye. It was later the seat of the ephemeral parliament of the ephemeral independent Republic of Azerbaijan.

I will mention in passing that the name Azerbaijan in Persian means 'Land of Fire', from the fires sometimes ignited spontaneously by the sun shining on oil slicks on the ground.

9

Kislovodsk was a pretty town surrounded by lush countryside. I was enchanted by it all—the verdant grass, the woods dark with ivy and dense foliage, the humidity beneath the trees and even in the houses, which penetrated my whole body, accustomed as I was to the dry climate of Baku. And beyond were the snow-covered peaks of the Caucasus Mountains; in good weather Mount Elbrus could be seen above them all, awakening in me a longing for the unattainable.

That summer, though, I learnt that dreams do sometimes come true: decked out in rosebuds and a hat with the most seductively frilly brim, I went out promenading with my dear Amina. I would be stiff with pride when people turned to look at her in the park, gazing until she disappeared from view. Beautiful women were not in short supply there, it should be said. Today, no longer blinded by passion, I realize that Amina wasn't physically beautiful, but possessed charm, which like all charm is difficult to analyse. She had a sparkling freshness and a good figure, and dressed elegantly, but that is not enough to explain her powers of seduction, so great that almost all the men who came into contact with her courted her. How well I understood them, and how I envied them! If only I were one of those free men, able to please Amina—a man and not a little girl, still condemned to governesses and castor oil.

That year, the fatal year of 1914, Kislovodsk was full of Russians, who usually went abroad but had been forced by the war to remain in their own country. The spa towns of the North Caucasus were full of the carriages of princes, millionaires and celebrities of all kinds. Balls, concerts, ballets and excursions filled the eternal leisure time of this idle society. Far away from Baku and decent Islamic ways, Amina could lead the free, society existence she had always been used to. Greatly helped by Leyla, my father's favourite daughter, who ardently hoped for emancipation too, Amina obtained practically all she desired; and since she desired a lot, she obtained a lot.

Leyla had become a marriageable young woman: the warning signs could not be denied. All the requirements were in place: her age, her physical development, her behaviour. On the advice of Amina, who had an excellent influence on her appearance, Leyla removed her grenadier's moustache and trimmed her eyebrows, so thick they took up a good third of her forehead. Instead of wearing dresses of watered silk (*taffetas shan-jan*, as it was pronounced in Russian, from the French *taffeta changeant*), set off by gold lace and pearl embroidery, she dressed in an understated manner, which the aunts, however, considered poor and unworthy of the daughter of a rich family (one of the richest in Baku, as they liked to point out). Leyla was extremely plump and decided to lose weight by following a brilliantly simple and effective regime of her own invention: she would secretly eat chocolate an hour before meals, after which she would no longer be hungry and could watch us eat with the haughty disdain of an ascetic floating above earthly concerns. As well as these meals of chocolate, she drank vinegar by the glass, also in secret, of course. The effect was striking: Leyla melted away—her generous hips disappeared, her breasts, which seemed destined to feed an entire tribe, deflated; her face, round as the full moon, became oval, and Leyla could at last cross her legs, something she had previously found difficult to do. How her health withstood this regime is another matter, and one worthy of some concern. But withstand it it did, and beneath the kilos of melted fat emerged a splendid girl: 'a real beauty', as families love to say, proud of their output. Her eyes especially were an astounding size and the deepest black. Amina's father (the engineer who sold nothing and had no fortune) would say in distaste: 'In the Caucasus even the dogs have beautiful eyes,' but he could not help admiring Leyla's.

She was a girl whose fancies sometimes touched on madness. She was a mass of manias; perhaps the most noticeable was tearing out her hair. The phrase 'tearing out her hair' brings to mind an image of despair; that wasn't the case with Leyla at all. She would tear out her hair very calmly, or better still, methodically. This is how she did it: my sister would sit at a table, on which she would place a book with a light cover, then pull out one hair from the middle of her head, and hold it up in the air for several moments, studying it carefully with her enormous, wide eyes; then she would place it on the book and examine it for a long time. When she had examined it to her heart's content, she would begin the operation again with another hair. One might think I'm exaggerating for the sake of the story, but I'm not inventing anything. She started to go bald from tearing out so much hair; she carried on anyway, despite being forbidden to do it. She would lock herself in her room and give herself up to this pleasant pastime, so often and so thoroughly that she became completely bald and had to have a wig made, which she was very proud of and wore with panache. She presumably did not give up this mania so easily: she must have continued it at night when she had taken her wig off, as her hair was not regrowing. It was only many years later that Leyla stopped this absorbing activity and her naturally thick hair grew back on her head.

But I am in no position to mock: I had manias to match my older sister's. For example, I would play with my eyebrows and pull them out. I derived hours of pleasure from fiddling with them; I twisted them and tugged them, making them hurt. I wasn't trying to pull them out, and actually would have preferred them to stay in place, but, unfortunately, I played so much with the hairs that they ended up in my fingers and my brow became as bald as Leyla's scalp. But I had only to leave them alone for ten days for my eyebrows to grow back in all their fullness. This mania troubled me for many years: though I resolved to cure myself of it, it proved stronger than me and would control my restless fingers, always on the lookout for something to fiddle with. Later, I found a name for it in the medical dictionary—'trichotillomania' (I'm not sure of the spelling).

Another of my manias, more of an obsession, was the obligation to touch an object: the corner of a table, the back of a chair, an electric switch. I could be about to drop off, snug in my warm bed, when I would suddenly feel this obligation: 'You must go and touch the corner of the table, you must.' I would try to resist, pretend I hadn't heard, but the command would return, pounding incessantly until I got up to go and touch the corner of the table. Then I would go back to bed, hoping to get to sleep. But often it would begin all over again, several times in succession, and every time I had to get up... But let's get back to Kislovodsk.

We had hardly been there three weeks when the Family turned up. First Aunt Rena, then the two other sisters with their broods; then Uncle Ibrahim with his young wife.

'What?' they must have said. 'Amina's in Kislovodsk; Mirza* (my father) and his children are in Kislovodsk? What about us?' Weren't they civilized too and just as capable of travelling and staying somewhere other than the country? So the whole Family, minus Grandmother, assembled in this spa town.

---

* In France, the boy's name Mirza, meaning 'master' in Persian, is most improperly given to dogs and, even worse, bitches.

Amina wept. Was she doomed to rot away surrounded by all these relatives? Fortunately for her, the aunts had to stay a long way from us, for lack of accommodation, but we met them constantly in this small town, centred on the park and casino. Buoyed by my father's support, Amina decided to ignore the opinion of her in-laws and continued to lead her society life, criticized, spied upon and covered in opprobrium. She met up with friends from Moscow and made a host of new acquaintances, some of them deemed 'undesirable' by the aunts. As for Leyla, intoxicated by her growing beauty and a sense of freedom, she flirted furiously and indiscriminately: any man over the age of sixteen and below the age of sixty was potential prey. A watchful eye had to be kept on her, but half a dozen pairs of eyes were not enough for the task. 'She has to be married, ay Mirza!' the aunts cried to my father, who wasted his breath explaining to them the new ideas about women's freedom. And they too wasted their breath giving him advice, calling him mad and a bad Muslim. Each side remained convinced of their cherished rightness. Leyla had no lack of suitors, quite the reverse: offers of marriage flooded in once her marriageability became public knowledge. Every free Muslim of sound mind sought the honour of becoming her husband, but all were considered unworthy of such a treasure.

When we returned to Baku in the autumn, Amina and Leyla continued their triumphant offensive under the banner of 'Progress for All'. Faced by these two redoubtable forces, my father ceded more and more ground. Powerless and trembling with horror, the family watched these changes. There were soirées with an orchestra at which women danced with real men. There was even a masked ball, at which Leyla dressed as a pageboy, wore breeches and scandalized 'the entire city', to listen to the aunts. Instead of talking, eyes lowered modestly, with young Muslims who were respectful of their family and their millions, Amina and Leyla would take their languorous ease (still in the words of my aunts) on the faux-luxurious divans of the Moorish salon, and flirt indiscriminately with infidels who were considered suspect, since the family knew neither their father nor their mother. As for alcohol, which was forbidden by the Prophet and had never passed our lips before my father's second marriage, it became the daily bread of this house, henceforth condemned to the just wrath of Allah. 'The champagne flowed freely,' to use the classic phrase. Thus our world marched towards disaster.

10

One dark winter morning, Fräulein Anna was surprised not to see Leyla up and about, so she went and knocked on her door. No reply. Fräulein Anna opened the door and gave a cry. The room had clearly not been used the night before: the curtains were open, the bed made, there was a complete, total, unmistakable absence of Leyla. Fräulein Anna's knees started to tremble and her heart pounded. Where could she be, the dreadful child? Fräulein Anna spied a letter on the table, pounced on it, read it and collapsed. 'I am leaving with the man I love, without whom I cannot live. Do not look for me. Forgive me. Adieu.'

An hour later the entire family was gathered around my father, shouting, crying and cursing. It was an unbridled triumph for the Muslim traditionalists. 'I told you so,' one of the aunts shouted; 'It could only end in shame,' another screamed; 'You've got what you wanted,' a brother-in-law declared; 'That will teach you,' hissed Asad and Ali's father, who had come, despite a recent estrangement, with the sole aim of witnessing my father's humiliation. After every shout, every scream, Aunt Rena's husband, alone in his deafness and with his hand cupped around his ear, would ask anxiously, 'What's he saying? What's she saying?'—garnering in return only impatient cries of 'Leave us in peace.'

A total victory for the other side. My father aged, in despair.

How could his Leyla, his beloved daughter, have gone off with a man? A young girl from the best Muslim family in Baku, such a rich and respected family. Who could this man be? Certainly not a Muslim: such infamy could come only from an infidel (curse them all). 'Were it not for their influence, such shame would never have befallen us,' Grandmother cried.

The event had been christened: it was 'the Shame', 'the Great Shame'. From now on, the family would talk of it in the same way they talked of an earthquake or a great plague.

'I'll kill her like a dog,' my father shouted with conviction.

While the men approved of this drastic decision, the women burst into tears of anticipation and regret.

Leyla had to be found before the threat could be carried out. One of Russia's many inconveniences was its vast size. How could they find the fugitive there? Where should they look for her? Action was required, however: the police were alerted, telegrams sent to various stations on the railway from Baku. My father decided to head towards Moscow: he calculated it was the most likely route for their escape. Amina was, to quote the Russian proverb, 'lower than grass, quieter than water'. Crushed by the avowed hostility of the family—and worse, the silent reproaches of my father (hadn't she been the promoter of Progress for All?)—she asked to go too, claiming it was to stop him doing anything excessive. The family approved. 'He is capable of anything,' she declared, not without a touch of pride, it should be said. At the last minute Uncle Ibrahim went as well, 'to keep them company'; really because he loved travelling and sought any pretext to do it.

They left and silence fell on the house, not a calm silence but one of anxious waiting. Were they going to kill Leyla or 'Him', or both of them? I wondered, terrified. How would they punish her if they didn't kill her? She could not be forgiven: such things were not forgiven. My heart weighed heavily that night: it was full of questions, of pity for my father and fear for Leyla (mixed with an insidious, unacknowledged satisfaction: she who had been so dazzling, so envied…). A host of possible dramas might play out at any moment.

The next day a telegram arrived: 'Leyla found, returning with her tomorrow evening.' The drama was already subsiding. Leyla was clearly still alive, if she was to be brought home.

She was brought back the next day, but we could only glimpse her from afar walking towards her bedroom as though to the scaffold, between sobbing Fräulein Anna and my louring father.

Only later did I learn that Leyla had been found in some small hotel in some small town; that she had been torn from the arms of a Russian aviator, beardless and amorous, whom she had decided to love until death; that said beardless, amorous aviator swore he had not 'dishonoured' Leyla and fell to his knees, begging permission to marry her; that my father almost killed Leyla; that Uncle Ibrahim almost killed the aviator, but that without anyone killing anyone they led Leyla away in tears, abandoning the aviator with his broken heart in the small hotel in the small town.

As soon as they got back, my father issued an order: we were forbidden to see Leyla, who would remain in her room until a new decree resolved her fate once and for all. A few days later the crackdown intensified: we learnt in sorrowful amazement that the three of us, all innocent, were also to be punished—in anticipation of our future misdeeds, I thought. We were not going to continue our studies: the two governesses, the Englishwoman and the French, were sent back, while the dancing, painting and even music lessons were suspended. They (my sisters) had only to grow up quickly; then they would be married to decent Muslims whose fathers and mothers were known, and the great Islamic peace would descend upon them. As for me, I was to be sent to the only school for Muslim girls, where the language of instruction was Azeri and most of the pupils were veiled. My older sisters were probably considered too contaminated by civilization to benefit from the illumination of this venerable institution. Only I, still fresh and pure, could hope to be enriched by good moral precepts.

Oh, that school! I was so unhappy there I cried every day for two months. The schoolgirls came from poor families (the rich did not send their offspring to that establishment, preferring a more European education). Rough and hostile, they felt class resentment towards me, of which I didn't understand the cause but felt the effects. In one way or another almost everyone made me feel out of place: they either laughed at me or avoided me. The teachers were Muslim women, mostly from Kazan, where women were not veiled and were often educated. They were ugly, with accentuated Mongol features, and shrill voices. They were mean with it, too.

I had lunch at school—what dreadful lunches! The awful smell of one dish in particular, a forbidding combination of gelatinous dough, pieces of fat and dishwater, has pursued me down the years. The finishing touch to my apprenticeship of martyrdom was sharing a desk with a girl who was always streaming in sweat. Saturday gave my olfactory senses a rest, as she would go to the hammam on Fridays. By Sunday (the school was open on Sundays and closed on Fridays, as befits a good Muslim establishment) the smell had returned and followed an ascending curve until its apogee on Thursdays, when it reached an overwhelming intensity. Dragged along in this smelly slipstream I was incapable of following what the teacher said; she took my depression for congenital stupidity and gave me one bad mark after another. I ended up looking a complete idiot, which greatly pleased the entire class—apart from me of course, who became only more miserable. I didn't complain to anyone and this moral isolation only made me feel worse. Then, when I had decided that death would be preferable to this life, my father took me out of the disastrous school where I had spent the two most depressing months of my childhood.

It was all change again: our instructresses and governesses returned to us and dancing and music were re-established; Leyla was free to leave her room and had the run of the apartment, while Amina was ordering new dresses.

For the good of us all, my father had decided that the punishment had lasted long enough and it was time to marry off Leyla, thereby passing responsibility for her behaviour on to someone else, and everything would return to normal. However, the suitors who had been rebuffed might now prove less enthusiastic, despite the lure of the millions (especially since three more prospective brides were coming up behind Leyla with as many millions and without the Shame—it was just a question of having a little patience). My father, therefore, summoned a relative who wasn't very rich and told him he was soon to marry Leyla. He didn't ask the relative's opinion, so sure was he that the chosen one would be deliriously happy. This relative was both my father's cousin and brother-in-law: a cousin through his mother and brother-in-law through his brother, who was my Aunt Rena's husband.

He was, therefore, going to be: 1. my father's son-in-law; 2. my father's cousin; 3. his brother-in-law too. It was a fine example of accumulation.

The cousin lived in Moscow, where he managed his father's firm. This had the advantage that if Leyla should dare to behave badly, distance would soften the effect of her exploits. Moreover, the future husband, twenty years her elder, had only 'to lower his ears' (an oriental expression meaning 'to listen carefully') and to 'sew his eyes onto her' ('to keep a close eye on her') and all would be well; in other words, he was being relied upon to do the job of a warder.

Leyla accepted her fate gracefully: she was indifferent towards the marriage itself, but was glad to be going to live in Moscow, especially since she knew Amina envied her. (My stepmother hated Baku more than ever and longed to leave the city.) She was also pleased at the thought of her future independence: the husband and double uncle would not bother her, she was sure, as the husband–double uncle's role in this world was to be at her feet, ever grateful, admiring and humble. Which he was, as it happens.

11

Amina and Leyla brought sons into the world at almost the same time. My father could not contain his joy, as he had thought himself condemned to female succession. He gave presents to anyone and everyone, and as soon as Amina was up and about after her confinement he held receptions to honour the arrival of a male heir. The house was constantly awash with flowers and truly tasteless gifts sent in congratulation by the whole of Baku.

But all that didn't really interest me much. I wasn't too bothered about the birth of a brother or a nephew, though I was pleased about the arrival of the latter as it made me an aunt, a status that conferred authority and brought me closer to adulthood. No, what interested me at that time was a new romance that was lighting up my life.

Little by little I had grown tired of loving Amina; she continued to ignore my love and it wasn't in my nature to love indefinitely without hope. I did need to love, though, and this time I fell in love with a man—an officer, a Georgian, a prince: a real prince at that. He was one of those men who frequented our house after our liberation, whom my aunts so fervently maligned and condemned to the torments of hell. He was handsome, slim and, apparently, spiritual (I knew nothing of that and relied on the views of those more competent than me). Of course, he courted Amina and took no more notice of me than he would of a paving stone as he walked down the street.

I wasn't the only one who was in love with him: Surayya and Zuleykha were in thrall to him too. Our romances were a collective enterprise from then on, until my sisters went abroad. My two sisters… I've just realized that I haven't said much about them; I haven't described them and should do so for the good of the story. I can hear the reproaches: 'My dear, you should be composing an *oeuvre*, not just writing any old how,' and so on. Too bad, too bad; let those who can, compose—I will not.

So, my two sisters: the elder was called Surayya and the next Zuleykha. Surayya was reserved, quiet and polite; Zuleykha, on the other hand, was volatile, talkative, aggressive and as rude as possible. She always knew everything and considered herself the most intelligent and talented person in the known universe. Although she was the elder, Surayya lived in her shadow and submitted to her ascendancy without demur. Disinclined towards obedience, I chafed at her peremptory orders, while her rigid opinions annoyed me in the extreme. She had little influence over me except in matters of the heart, for she always gave the signal for us collectively to fall in love. If Zuleykha had doe eyes and simpered when she talked about a man, I was hooked and would prepare for this important event; we would love in concert.

Zuleykha sighed deeply when she talked about Tengiz (that was the Georgian prince's name) and I immediately sensed her interest in him. Within a week, my feelings had deepened into passion.

Tengiz lived on the same street as us, in a house that we could see from the Moorish salon if we strained our necks a little, which is precisely what I did as I watched the door through which Tengiz would pass. If for a few fleeting seconds I glimpsed my beloved's long greatcoat, my heart would race in time to the turmoil within.

One day I had been watching out for him for more than an hour in the freezing salon when I saw him come out of his house and head in our direction. If he were going to town he would have to turn his back to us, so I deduced that Tengiz was coming to our house, especially since it was the time of day for visiting. I wasn't mistaken: Tengiz walked up to our house and came in. I ran straight to the hall and as I heard steps on the staircase opened the door. Tengiz stood before me—handsome, slim, so neatly fitted into his greatcoat that it seemed part of his physical person. His helmet, worn slightly at an angle, looked at me with the same mocking air as his clear eyes.

'Oh, hello,' I said hypocritically, 'I was just going up to see my aunt. Would you like to see my stepmother?'

'Yes, if that's possible,' Tengiz replied. He took off his greatcoat and I showed him into Amina's boudoir. I explained to Tengiz that I would go and fetch my stepmother, who must be in her bedroom.

'You are very kind, Mademoiselle,' Tengiz said, this time in French.

As he talked, he took my hand and kissed the tips of my fingers, frozen with emotion. For the first time he took notice of me and for a moment I stopped being a paving stone. Then he became ironical. Had he sensed my emotion, noticed my look of adoration? The fact remains that he inclined towards me and said, still in French: 'Allow me to kiss your cheek.'

Half dead with confusion, delight and shame, I turned my cheek towards him and Tengiz kissed it: then he turned his towards me and I touched it with the tips of my lips, quivering with joy and fear; if anyone caught me in this act of refined depravity, I would be lost for ever!

'And now,' Tengiz said, 'be good and go and find Amina Khanim.'

He smiled at me again and I found myself tiptoeing out of the room, as though caught up in a mysterious, secret pact.

When I next saw Zuleykha and Surayya, I looked at them pityingly. If they only knew! I thought. If they only suspected that Tengiz had kissed my hand and cheek, and that I had kissed his in return! There was no doubt that Tengiz liked me, or why would he have kissed me and had me kiss him? The perceptive Zuleykha realized from my air of superiority that something had happened. 'What's up with you?' she asked, but I remained as dumb as the sand in our vineyard.

After that, whenever I saw Tengiz I thought of our exchange of kisses: we were united by a delicious secret. I could already imagine myself abandoning everything for him—my religion, my family, my fortune; becoming Princess X and leaving with him for the other end of Russia, Siberia if necessary, despite my horror of the cold. I was already counting the children he would give me...

As always, when I loved passionately (and I only loved passionately), I couldn't sleep, and these sleepless nights were the heaviest price I paid for my sentimental adventures. I was defenceless against this insomnia and it wore me out. Fortunately, Tengiz left Baku in early spring and I recovered my inner peace, for some time anyway, until my next love, impossible as ever.

At about the same time the subject of marriage was raised with me for the first time. To be more exact, it was a marriage demand.

I've stopped talking about my cousins, because after Amina's arrival they played less of a role in my life. My admiration for them was largely replaced by my admiration for Amina, and then by my infatuations, which left little room for cousins in my fickle heart. I had always seen much more of them in the country anyway; I saw them less often in town. About once a week I went to their very unusual house to see them, and we would play all our old games and make up others. Asad had definitely become the leader: he gave orders with such authority that it was impossible to disobey him.

We marched in unison to his commands, and under his direction our games acquired a martial air, recalling the parade ground.

Asad's father was extremely fond of him and dreamt of a good marriage for him, which in the language of Baku meant a very wealthy marriage. He did not delay in advancing his advantageous marriage project and thought that I, endowed with Grandfather Musa's millions, would make an excellent wife for his son. At first I was oblivious to the tender looks that Uncle Suleyman would give me when I came to see my cousins. Just as other adults pinch children's cheeks in a gesture of goodwill, when he saw me he would pinch the place where my breasts would grow one day and shake his head in a knowing way, saying '*Memesi, memesi*' ('Titties, titties'); or he would pretend to catch and kill a nit on my head, the whole performance accompanied by the delighted laughter of his children.

These hints of interest did not strike me at first; I was still naive and didn't know how to put two and two together and draw the right conclusions. One day, Uncle Suleyman took me into his study and sat me on his knee. I should say in passing that this study was half-Renaissance, half-Moorish and full of books that no one had any intention of reading.

This is the dialogue that followed his opening gambit:

UNCLE SULEYMAN: Would you like to get married?

ME (*struck dumb in astonishment. This question was of the greatest interest to me; I thought about it passionately and constantly, but knew that at my age I should feign a lack of interest.*)

UNCLE SULEYMAN: Answer me. Would you like to get married?

ME (*lowering my eyes*): I'm too young to think about it.

UNCLE SULEYMAN (*touching my future breasts*): They'll come soon enough. Young—what does that mean anyway? Huh… Cock and bull stories from those anaemic Christians. Both your grandmothers were married at thirteen, my mother at fourteen and your aunts at fourteen and fifteen. You haven't got long to wait. So, would you like to get married?

ME (*making evasive, non-committal sounds, avoiding an actual reply*)

UNCLE SULEYMAN: Because I've got a fiancé for you, you know. You won't find his like again.

ME (*with interest*): Who?

UNCLE SULEYMAN (*giving me a good smack on the bottom*): Asad!

ME (*disappointed*): Oh...

UNCLE SULEYMAN: What does that mean, 'Oh'? Asad is handsome. He'll be tall and strong. He's healthy and got rosy cheeks. He's intelligent. And he'll shower you with gold. (*Warming to his theme*) He'll shower you with diamonds. He'll build you a palace unlike any in Baku, even that pretentious Taghi Ruslanov's place. With marble everywhere... goldfish swimming in pools. (*Getting even warmer*) You'll eat from golden dishes, you'll drink from crystal. (*With sudden inspiration*) Your aunts will be your lady's maids; your uncles will be your valets. You will be their mistress and give them any orders you wish. I'll make them cringe before you like dogs. Answer me.

ME (*without much enthusiasm, but not wanting to cause any upset*): We'll see.

UNCLE SULEYMAN (*giving me a loud, sloppy kiss*): We'll see. Stay for dinner this evening. I'll order the chocolate ice cream that you like. When you're Asad's wife, you'll have chocolate ice cream every evening. And in summer you can watch me eat ice cream with flies in it, you know... (*and he winked at me*)

I've forgotten to mention that during Uncle Suleyman's rare visits to us in the country in summer, he always had his own way of eating ice cream: with one masterly hand he would catch the flies that buzzed around us in clouds, poke them into the ice cream with his finger and tuck into this dessert with a show of pleasure, smacking his lips and making groans of satisfaction. The governesses would feel queasy; the aunts too would seem disgusted, but we children would watch this feat open-mouthed. Nothing seemed more heroic than to eat flies in ice cream.

And Uncle Suleyman's belches!

They were excellent belches, the best that I knew. They had the resonance and power, the distinctive rumbling and echoing of thunder. These belches delighted us (I'm talking about the children), but terrified the governesses. When Uncle Suleyman had met someone more than twice and liked them, he would belch as was his wont, that's to say, frequently and with the obvious desire to amuse; even the people most resistant to this kind of amusement would put up with it in the end, if not actually acquire a taste for it. But for educational reasons, the governesses persisted in finding these manners horrible and thought they constituted a dangerous example to the children. And it's true that we were often tempted to imitate Uncle Suleyman, to no avail of course—didn't I say that his belches were inimitable?

I loved other things about him. Didn't he once pay tremendous fines to the Berlin police because he felt the urge to spit all day long in the streets of the German capital, though this was explicitly forbidden? Another time he commandeered a hotel lift, obliging the lift attendant to go up and down non-stop a hundred times. He sang our songs in the foyer of the Paris Opera, urinated from his hotel balcony and emitted his thunderous belches at Maxim's. When he came back from his frequent foreign trips, he brought not only presents, but also items pilfered from the most elegant hotels. He brought back cutlery, ashtrays and other small objects, stolen for fun, and would share them out among us. We loved them much more than the finest toys—the mystery of human nature… All this eccentric behaviour gave him a unique aura in my eyes and it's easy to understand why he was my favourite uncle.

Uncle Suleyman knew my weaknesses and used them to seduce me. Despite the wonderful picture he painted, I didn't find this marriage project very attractive. Accustomed to loving princes, I thought a marriage between cousins rather dull, even if the cousin was the gallant Asad. Uncle Suleyman did not give up his idea, though. He shared it with all the family, receiving only limited support, but consoling himself with thoughts of how young I was. He was committed to recommencing the attack as soon as the time was right.

12

Next came one of those storms that spell delight for history professors and disaster for humanity.

Russia's dramatic story is well known: the tsar abdicated, then Kerensky too renounced his position of power; the October Revolution erupted and civil war set Reds against Whites. The empire broke up.

These disturbances allowed the border regions, whose populations did not share the history, ancestry and religion of the Russians, to break away and form independent republics. In the Caucasus, Georgia, Armenia and Azerbaijan claimed their right to self-determination and set about exercising it.

Baku, the capital of Azerbaijan, grew restive too. Several political factions emerged with the inevitable consequences: rivalry, unrest, confrontation. Under the guise of saving the country from the communist threat, an organization of Armenians with socialist sympathies managed to install a military dictatorship; but it was whispered that the leaders were really Bolsheviks.

Be that as it may, they inaugurated their rule with a massacre of Muslims, who were unable to defend themselves. As always, it was primarily the ordinary people who fell victim to the 'stimulant of militant nationalism', as one English writer put it. The so-called upper classes, or rather the wealthy classes, Armenian or

Azerbaijani, often connected by mutual interests, would provide reciprocal protection during these massacres, which would be carried out by whichever party was the more powerful or the better organized at the time.

It should be emphasized that while one-sided massacres of Armenians by Turks had occurred in Turkey, in Azerbaijan the Armenians had also massacred the Azerbaijanis (Christians against Muslims) before the indifferent gaze of the Russian authorities, who may have been thinking that the famous colonial formula 'divide and rule' made effective politics.

At about two o'clock one dark night, Fräulein Anna came to fetch me from my bed: snatched from my dreams, I fell into a state of anxiety.

With the electricity cut off, the house and entire city were plunged into darkness, pierced by whistling bullets that whizzed out of nowhere. Machine guns could be heard in the distance. We expected at any minute to see the Dashnaks (that was the name of the members of the Armenian nationalist party) storm the house and demolish everything, including the inhabitants. The telephone didn't work and the house had become our desert island surrounded by an uncharted sea.

Confined in the gloom of Amina's Moorish bedroom, we had nothing to do but wait, so we waited. Around four o'clock in the morning violent blows at the front door sought to demolish the house and our last hope with it. We thought it was the Dashnaks come to massacre us. My father grabbed his revolver and left the room, followed by Amina, who, for a woman with such a frivolous air, was to display unexpected courage and devotion from then on. We were already preparing to die but it was premature: a few moments later Amina and my father returned, almost elated, bringing not armed Dashnaks but Armenian friends: our neighbours opposite, who had come to offer us their protection and their house. Need I say that both were accepted gratefully?

We each quickly packed a small suitcase and went down the stairs. All we had to do was cross the width of the street, but since bullets were flying freely there, even this short distance could prove fatal. We were told to run to reduce our time crossing the shooting range. A battle was under way at the other end of the dark street: gunfire crackled intermittently, interrupted by long blasts on a whistle.

Lily-livered as we were, we had to force ourselves to run to the house opposite, stumbling over the uneven cobblestones because of the darkness and our fear. Only my father, who was carrying my brother in his arms, walked slowly lest he fall over with him. But Allah was guiding him.

Once we were inside the front door our neighbours greeted us with a very touching welcome for such a moment. Then we had to go to bed, which proved difficult: there were more people than beds. Some of us had to be content with a mattress on the carpet; I was given one in a small room where Fräulein Anna was to sleep on a narrow divan with my brother; between the intermittent cries of the latter and the gunfire there could be no question of sleep.

In the morning, we were dismayed to witness the following scene: men with cartridge belts slung across their bodies were throwing a wide variety of objects from the windows of our house into lorries parked outside, gradually filling them up. Dressed in filthy uniforms of diverse provenance, the men had a martial air that did not bode well, and we were glad that we were only spectators. Had we been on the other side of the street, we would probably have been subjected to the same defenestration. The household flew past: forks rained down, then laced corsets took to the breeze followed by a Louis XIV chandelier and a flying cashmere shawl.

'My blue velvet dress,' groaned Amina, while Fräulein Anna sadly watched the descent of a cushion that it had taken her more than a year to embroider.

'My beautiful, brand-new dressing gown,' Zuleykha sighed in turn. And still incorrigibly animistic, I whispered to my favourite coat, trimmed with fox fur, which was tumbling into one of the lorries, 'Poor coat, look how they're treating you. Adieu.'

That same afternoon my father and Amina left us. Our residence wasn't secure enough for a man wanted by Armenian terrorists, so an Armenian friend took my father to a secret location where he would be out of danger. Moreover, the situation promised to get even worse: as often happens, the leaders were losing control of their men, who were pillaging, rampaging and slaughtering.

The night after my father's departure, we were woken around three in the morning by a band of armed men, who began to search for him everywhere. They climbed onto the roof, opened all the cupboards and wardrobes, poked under the beds with their bayonets and anywhere else that might possibly contain a man. When they didn't find him, they drank all the wine in the house, swore repeatedly and left in a fury.

In the morning, soldiers of unknown allegiance came to install a machine gun on the roof of the house where we were staying and began to pepper the one opposite (ours) with avenging but useless bullets—a gratuitous act but one that must have given the soldiers a sense of power.

We lived like this for two weeks: mentally restless but physically immobilized. We led a cloistered existence and even the shutters of the house were kept closed most of the time to shield us from prying eyes and the bullets of the ragtag army.

When night came, we trembled in concert with the candles, which we had to use sparingly; it was impossible to buy more, so we were burning our capital. It was the same with our food: we had to munch lentils for two weeks; we munched them for lunch, we munched them for dinner; we began again the next day and did the same the next. It was a flood of lentils, an avalanche. 'Help yourselves, have some more,' our hosts would say kindly. 'Don't worry, we've got sacks full of them...' they would assure us graciously. Strange to say but I wasn't put off them for life; I still enjoy them today, remembering those faraway Armenian lentils.

Our meals were poor in provender but rich in sighs and tears. The three old ladies in our saviours' family would weep and sigh one after the other, or even all together.

Death was such a sad prospect! The oldest especially, who was a very sensitive soul, could not look at us without thinking of our misfortune and bursting into tears of compassion. She had white, silky hair and touchingly soft black eyes in a face smooth and pink despite her age. Her benevolence was directed at everything and everyone, and in turn everyone was well disposed towards her. When the good soul saw me rigid and trembling with fear, she would take me in her arms and try to make me feel better. But it wasn't easy to make me feel better: I was too afraid. I was also lonely, due in part to my character and in part to circumstance. I no longer saw any children of my own age. The few years that separated me from Zuleykha were a gulf at that age; my relationship with her was that of an inferior to a superior with all that that implies in resentment and impatience for the bullied. My cousins, my unspeakable, brave cousins, lived a long way away and the older I became, the more I was to be kept apart from them. The virtuous will say, 'So much the better,' while others may think it a shame.

There was always Fräulein Anna with her loving heart. But I rejected her affection through misplaced pride; moreover, as she had replaced my brother's nurse, she was busy with him all the time and had no choice but to neglect me somewhat. I still longed constantly for Amina's affection, but I was beginning to realize the futility of my feelings. So I withdrew into myself.

Sometimes, during slight lulls in the confusing battle taking place in Baku, our hosts would receive visits from some of their relatives. One of them, a handsome young man with blonde hair (yes, Armenian but blonde) and blue eyes, aroused the boldly declared interest of Zuleykha-the-artist and the not so boldly declared interest of Zuleykha-the-woman. When he visited, the two conjoined Zuleykhas would throw themselves upon him and install him in a glassed-in balcony, and, notwithstanding the ongoing crisis, one would set about painting him, the other flirting with him. As for me, I knew what an object of painterly zeal should look like, and I would study this young man carefully to see if he was worthy of our love. I was already preparing to acquiesce to it.

I met this handsome young man later in Paris, where I still see him often. The years have perhaps made him a little less handsome, but he has the same eyes and the same blonde hair. When he is cross with my sisters and me, he never misses an opportunity to say, 'To think I was stupid enough to save these women from the massacre.'

I didn't have the leisure to love him, nor did Zuleykha to complete his portrait; the two weeks of lentils, fear and intermittent lulls soon came to an end. Someone came to tell us to get ready to leave the same evening to join my father. Our preparations didn't take long, but what did take long were our touching farewells to our saviours: the hugs were mixed with tears and the tears with sighs; then we had to part all the same. A car driven by an employee of the family firm came to collect us and we jumped in, blessed and sprinkled with the tears of our elderly hostesses. I talk about this now in a light-hearted way, but at the time my attitude was quite different: I didn't know then what I know now, that it would all end well, and I was paralysed with fear.

For two days the gunfire had almost stopped entirely: it was possible to move about the city again until seven in the evening, the time of the curfew.

The city was pitiful: the ransacked shops, upended paving stones, broken windows and bullet-riddled facades gave it an air of desolation that would have depressed braver men than us. Even the aggressive Zuleykha became gloomy and fell silent.

Our car slowly descended towards the harbour avoiding the main streets; it soon stopped outside a small house near the docks. We got out of the car and the driver took us inside the house where we saw Amina sitting at the table with a worker in overalls—it was my father! Amid more hugs and tears, we learnt that we would be leaving for Persia, where my father hoped to escape the perils facing us in our native city, which was as troubled by the revolution as elsewhere in Russia. At least we would be foreigners there and could hope to go unnoticed.

The house belonged to one of our tanker captains, who was keeping his ship ready to sail. We boarded that evening without difficulty, but the departure checks made by the Dashnaks could end in disaster if my father were recognized. It was decided that he would work as a stoker in the engine room, while we would be presented as the captain's children; Amina and Fräulein Anna, both veiled as circumstance dictated, would pass for good Muslim wives.

Everything went swimmingly: the Dashnaks who came aboard were very lax, due in large part to the glasses of vodka proffered by the captain. They didn't even go down to the engine room, where my father, shovel in hand and cap rammed over his eyes, was struggling to identify with the world that he had hitherto exploited. Peering through a light veil of alcohol fumes into the dining room, full of the captain's alleged wives and children, and probably seeing double, they expressed mild surprise at their number but left without taking their investigations further. A few moments later, the dark mass of Baku, still without electricity, began to recede.

It was then that we became familiar with the state that I will call, for want of a better term, 'post-fear'. It's a well-defined state that deserves a special designation. When fear paralyses you, forces you to curl up on yourself physically and psychologically, when internal spasms shake your bowels and your jaw starts to ache because of your spasmodically clenched teeth, when you keep waking up in terror, and then suddenly you enter a world where your fears stop abruptly and are no longer relevant, that's when this state begins for which I would like to find a special word. It is total deliverance: your body becomes supple again; you can breathe deeply, released from constant anxiety; your spirit becomes lighter. You are free at last! The sensitive weep for joy, believers thank their God, atheists are jubilant; but for everyone the immediate, material result is an enormous appetite.

As soon as the ship reached the open sea, we threw ourselves on the table that was sagging under the weight of magical dishes, or at least that's how they seemed to us after two weeks of lentils. There was fresh caviar and sturgeon pilaff and chicken pilaff and almond cakes... We ate the caviar with spoons and the chicken with our hands, as this was quicker. We ate in silence, forgetting everything. A chicken leg roasted to perfection took the place of the revolution and a golden slice of sturgeon replaced the massacres. But instead of the profound well-being that I was expecting, a malaise took root inside me, at first imperceptible but then violent. I turned from pink to green, from joyous to nauseous... And it all ended in the lavatory bowl.

My violent seasickness lasted throughout the voyage. The fear had disappeared, but horrible nausea raged in its place. Since everyone else was fine and I was suffering alone, solitude in misfortune made my misery even worse. When the boat arrived in Enzeli, I was a wreck ready to surrender my soul.

We stayed in Persia for six months—or was it longer? My recollections of that disastrous period are very hazy; maybe my subconscious consigned them to oblivion, as this time seemed to me a morass of boredom, heat, mosquitoes and malaria.

In Enzeli we lived in an awful house by the side of a canal—or was it a branch of the Caspian? Later my father decided we would move to Rasht, which was then an ugly little town where a single house of stone stood on a deserted square; all the other buildings were constructed of some indeterminate material, but certainly not stone.

Hardly had we settled in before war broke out between the patriots—called, I think, Kichik Khan—and the British, who were in Persia as conquerors. The patriots sported great beards, which they swore not to trim until the invaders had left the country.

Aeroplanes bombed the town, the rattle of gunfire could be heard in the streets, and here we were again, caught up as victims in historic events that we could well have done without. We stayed shut up in the ugly house, which was built of some porous material that wouldn't have withstood a well-aimed bullet.

When the liberation war was suspended, we stayed shut up at home; I mean to say we, the female gender. To be honest, we didn't have anything to do outside, and we could only go out swathed head to toe in a *chadra*, the cursed veil that we had never worn before, thanks to progress. It took a degree of practice to wear one without getting tangled up in it or losing it altogether; with one hand one held the *chadra* in front of one's face with only one's eyes emerging from the prison, and with the other hand one held it against the body. An inconvenient covering that certainly wasn't Islam's best invention. In Baku at least the *chadras* could be any colour of the rainbow, but in Persia they were all black, so the country seemed to be swarming with crows.

Another inconvenience in Persia: I've forgotten to mention that Azerbaijan, as a former province of Persia, was Shiite. Now, Amina came from the 'Sunni heresy'. In Persia this deviance had to be hidden like a shameful illness and Amina took umbrage, although she took no more interest in Islam than in the snows of yesteryear. She suddenly discovered principles and felt she had become a renegade. She longed to go back more than the rest of us did.

Rumours reached us that gave us hope and my father decided to return to Enzeli, from where Baku seemed within easy reach.

We moved back into the same ugly house next to the Caspian, agog for news. While we waited to return, though, we were struck by malaria, which picked us off one by one. I still have a vivid memory of our intermittent fevers, which shook us with the force of a merciless hurricane.

Several months dragged in this way until we heard that the Turks, the real Turks from Turkey, the Osmanli, or Ottomans,* had occupied Baku and re-established order in the Caucasus. From that day on we could think only of our return, but we still had a long time to wait; the occupiers feared revolutionaries and were protecting the entry to Baku with boats. This wait became all the harder when we heard enticing reports that calm and plenty had returned to our city.

The day finally came, though, when the same captain who had brought us to Persia and was unrivalled in all the Caspian in terms of skill, daring and jollity, took us back on board his boat and set full steam ahead for Baku. After a short time pitching on the

* We were sometimes called Turks too. In reality we are more Turco-Persian. For centuries Baku was part of a Persian province, half of which is still part of Persia and bears the old name of Azerbaijan.

capricious waves, during which I again surrendered the contents of my stomach, we were reunited with our beloved city and our house, which had been wrecked from top to bottom. Only the large furniture was left standing, though much of it was damaged; the arrowheads of the cathedral-cupboards had been targeted and badly damaged by bullets; the carved wood had been scored by knives; a Louis XIV writing desk had been upended and its large decorative china medallion, depicting Cupid and Psyche reunited at last, was lying on the ground, smashed into tiny pieces. Poor Cupid and Psyche, separated again by the violence of men… But we were so happy to be back home that everything seemed wonderful, from the disembowelled furniture to the broken washbasins.

After eight months of silence we at last heard news of the other half of the family: having made a long, dangerous journey across revolutionary Russia, Leyla, her husband and son, and Surayya had finally reached Odessa, where they had already been for two months, waiting for a boat to Batumi. Their wait might be prolonged as the Black Sea had been mined and was still a battlefield between different nations and sides.

The Turks restored calm in Baku by hanging some poor wretch almost every day. The gallows had been erected in a public park and in broad daylight the hanged men swung back and forth in the wind for general edification. It has to be acknowledged that the method was effective: thefts, armed robberies and all the other accompaniments to troubled times soon stopped and calm was restored.

When they arrived in the Caucasus, the Turks naturally took revenge on the Armenians, massacring them on a large scale, and once again it was the ordinary people who had to pay for the unleashing of nationalist fury. Our friends and saviours had been spared and we found our old hostess's white-silk hair and the kindness of all her family unharmed. We laughed at the memory of the innumerable kilos of lentils and the fears we had shared. After all, our troubles were limited to material damage, which was of little import to us: compared to the irreparable harm that could have been done, it didn't count.

Some time later, the Turkish occupation was replaced by a British occupation. The Turks, who were allies of the Germans, were defeated in 1918 and forced to return home, while the victorious British, oil-lovers as ever, took their place in the oilfields.

Our house became the meeting point for the British army. Amina received them, now seconded by the ever more simpering Zuleykha, whom I loathed and envied, especially for her age, her freedom and her intimacy with Amina. She grew more self-assured by the day and was even brazen enough to smoke in public.

Baku was turning European before our eyes. As happens during troubled times in history, morals were relaxed, and tradition and religion, already badly shaken, fell further into decline. The family had lost interest in Amina's behaviour: all the events surrounding the Caucasus, in vast Russia, our former mistress, convinced them that there were more important problems than Amina's excessively low neckline or even her flings. As for my father, his only passion was politics, and he left Amina to do what seemed right to her. There was talk of an independent Azerbaijan, Armenia, Karelia, Kazakhstan and I don't know what else: Independent, Autonomous, Proud, Free and Happy. Epithets accompanied by Republics and Republics combined with epithets rained down on the astonished peoples. Soon it was the turn of the British to leave the Caucasus, and our good city with its minarets and oil barons became the capital of an independent Republic of Azerbaijan. The new Republic had its own parliament, where there were as many parties as parliamentarians. It also had its army made up of poor devils who had never held a rifle in their lives (during the time of tsarist Russia the Azeri population had been exempt from military service). There were, nevertheless, military parades and reviews, followed by patriotic speeches, followed in turn by a national anthem composed in haste by a young patriot, which at least partially excused the song's ugliness. There was also a president and ministers of all kinds, as befits a well-organized republic. My father became minister of commerce and—striking, visible proof of the fact—two *askaris* (soldiers) were posted permanently at the entrance to our house, now that it was a ministerial residence. Our concierge, a hideously ugly man whose sole attractive feature was his name, Aflatun (Plato), was dressed in green livery, and my father bought a magnificent tan leather briefcase, which never left him until the disappearance of the independent Republic of Azerbaijan and, with it, his ministry. But in the meantime our hearts swelled with joy.

Not long after the British had gone, my sisters were able to leave Odessa, where they had languished for a long time, and return to Baku. They too had had strange adventures, which they were amazed to have survived. But these adventures had left their mark: they were gaunt, weary and dressed in an extraordinary fashion. Surayya wore an outfit of some kind of sackcloth, which she had made herself; the outfit was completely shapeless and, consequently, so was Surayya. Considering herself very well dressed, she was extremely hurt when Zuleykha bluntly disabused her. As for Leyla, she wore a dress made from woollen curtain lining—multicoloured wool, which didn't help matters. Leyla, though, did not let sartorial considerations get her down: she remained cheerful, exuberant and more resolved than ever to 'lead her own life'. Since for the time being she liked living with us all in her father's house, she decided that her husband was a hateful man, though the opposite was blindingly obvious to everyone, and that she could not live with him any longer. Neither the uncle-husband's heart-rending prayers nor his threats—pretty feeble, it's true—had any effect. Exasperated in the end by this persistence, which she considered unseemly, Leyla took it into her head to get divorced, especially since this solution gave her every right to live with her father. She returned, therefore, to the room she had had as a young girl, settled her son in a nearby room and henceforth treated her husband like an annoying old relative who has to be humoured in order to obtain a favour—divorce, which the poor man, still in love with Leyla, refused to give her. The unfortunate husband, forced to live with his mother, came every day to see his son, whom he adored, and to try and cajole cruel Leyla. In vain! When one 'wants to live one's life' nothing gets in the way more than a husband—any woman will confirm this. So she was firmly resolved to get rid of him.

While some women dispense with husbands, others acquire them. Surayya and Zuleykha were clearly at the latter stage. A young Muslim man from a good family, 'almost' a doctor or engineer (as a general rule, he would claim to have interrupted his studies one or two years before the end), would ask for the hand of one of them in marriage, it didn't matter which: the suitors would leave the choice up to my father's enlightened judgement. And since the suitors weren't stubborn, they would agree, if necessary, to wait a few years until I came of marriageable age.

13

The independent Republic of Azerbaijan was getting into its stride. Though still a babe in arms, the country sent a delegation to Geneva, gaining recognition for the Republic *de facto* if not *de jure*. Baku was nationalist, extremely chauvinist even, as behoves the capital of a country newly emerged from its cocoon. Some parties were fiercely traditionalist, while others sought 'Progress and Emancipation for All'. The latter demanded education for women and decried their exclusion from public life. This exclusion sometimes took surprising forms: for example, at the National Theatre of Baku, which often staged operas in Azeri, a muscular Desdemona would tread the boards, her face blue from a stubborn beard and her eyebrows bushy; she would reply in a vigorous male voice to Othello's passionate declarations, while only the curls cascading over her shoulders and the artificially generous breasts made an exaggerated attempt to compensate for the lack of femininity.

The very young capital was cheerful and lively. A flood of emigrants from revolutionary Russia contributed to the atmosphere. Everyone who had connections to the Caucasus, and plenty who didn't, came to take refuge until the revolution was over, which they thought just a matter of months. 'When the Bolsheviks have gone' was the stock phrase of all these far-sighted people, a phrase that would be followed with a description of what they would then do. While waiting for this imminent event, they borrowed as much money as their credit would allow and enjoyed themselves as much as possible.

Our house was now open to many people and became a reception carousel. Among the many young people received there, we always found an object worthy of our collective devotion. When falling in love we rigorously followed the same well-established order: first Zuleykha, then Surayya and, as soon as I picked up on it, me. In one season our flock was in love with a Russian musician, a Baltic lad and a Swedish engineer. Our tastes were eclectic, our hearts fickle.

Towards spring we made the acquaintance of a young officer who eclipsed all our previous loves; he boasted a huge chest, already decorated, surprisingly thick eyebrows and a vicious temper that made everyone afraid of him. How could so much charm be resisted? No one did resist and we fell in love with him one after the other, like skittles.

Though he was Persian, he had studied at St Petersburg's most aristocratic school, having gained admission by virtue of his noble descent. At this school the future stars of the military learnt their profession from books they held in gloved hands 'to avoid touching them and getting dirty' (books and studying representing effort, which is good for flunkeys but not for young lords). They wore their mistresses' silk stockings wrapped around their necks, frequently got drunk and applied their, often sharp, intelligence to devising fiendishly complex, cruel and crazy initiation rites for young pupils seeking to rise up the ranks. Murad had volunteered for the army when he was sixteen and fought courageously, receiving honours several times. When the revolution disrupted military life, he came to Baku with his parents, who had many relatives there. That is how we met.

My, or rather our, passion was violent—and fruitless for two-thirds of our amorous collective, that is to say, for two of the three sisters. Of the three of us, I had the least hope, or no hope at all, and was well aware of it. I loved to no avail, as usual, but did not love any the less for that. I had no reasonable chance of being alone with Murad and had to be content with a poor trick to assuage my passion: when he was visiting our house, I would slip into the entrance hall, quickly pick out his officer's cap among all the hats, clasp it to my thirteen-year-old bosom and cover it with fervent kisses, especially the lining, which had a light scent I found intoxicating in the full sense of the word.

'Dear cap,' I would say, treating it as a living thing, 'tell Murad I love him. I would make him happy, if he wanted.' I said other things to him too. Perhaps it sometimes conveyed my declarations to him, because to Murad I wasn't the paving stone I had been to the Georgian prince. He looked at me sometimes, even spoke to me, but in the caustic way that frightened and attracted me at the same time. He must have known that all three of us were enamoured of him and enjoyed it, I think. But he didn't often talk to me—Zuleykha was on watch and would always monopolize him. If she happened to let go of him for a moment, Surayya would be waiting. I would fade away in my corner, without hope. If we gave grand receptions, I was not allowed to attend, while at more intimate meals I was relegated to the far end of the table. I was like Cinderella—everything was denied me: liaisons, love, hope.

Today I look back on that time with distaste: my age did not match my physical or moral development at all, but since I was several years younger than my sisters, everyone treated me like a child. I was practically put on a level with my brother and nephew, and hated them both equally as a result. If they rushed up to me in their childish eagerness, I would look away in disgust, so painful was it to me, who had read the whole of Mirbeau and Maupassant and had studied at my cousins' school of freedom, to be equated with them.

One thing in particular made me suffer: having to go to bed early, especially since I had persistent insomnia. Snatches of music, voices and laughter carried from distant reception rooms, as I tossed and turned in my bed, sometimes crying in rage, tiredness and vexation. I thought it ridiculous to be shut away alone in this sad room instead of partaking of adult pleasures.

So, I suffered all alone while Surayya and Zuleykha acted like adults. To make matters worse, I did not follow any regular studies, maybe because of the turbulent times or just negligence, and I felt disjointed as a result. I was fortunate to have a consolation that I turned to with greater frequency—my piano. I divided my days between studying the piano, daydreaming, which was exclusively sentimental, and reading.

I might have felt less isolated if I had confided in Fräulein Anna, whose affection for us never wavered but which we disregarded. Not only did I not take my troubles to her, I began at this time to hate her. She had long since lost all authority over us. Leyla, wife and mother, thought it an insult if she were given advice; Surayya and Zuleykha were still fascinated by Amina and found Fräulein Anna old-fashioned, her moral precepts thoroughly annoying. They couldn't give a damn about the domestic virtues that the poor woman had tried in vain to inculcate in us. Fräulein Anna disapproved of their behaviour and appearance, but could do nothing about it since the example came from on high and was part of the famous 'emancipation for all'.

She could not get used to all these innovations, which exacerbated the distance between us. The past few years with us had been difficult for her; she had been relegated practically to the rank of a servant; no one was interested in her opinions and when they were, it was only to be sarcastic about them. I may have been the worst; shut up with the babies, their *nyanyas* (the Russian for children's nannies) and Fräulein Anna, who kept a close eye on us all, I saw her—cruelly and illogically—as the symbol of what I most detested at that time: childhood. I was rude to her and was glad when I managed to make her cry—sadly all too easily done, as the poor woman was extremely sensitive. Sometimes, though, I felt bitter remorse and my heart would be overcome with tenderness. I was aware of how much I owed her. These moments of kindness usually came during my sleepless nights when I couldn't settle in my bed; I relived the scenes with Fräulein Anna and it was my turn to cry, from shame, and I wanted to run and tell her of my affection, which always lay dormant beneath a crust of superficial feelings… but I did nothing of the kind and the next day would once again exercise the full gamut of my spitefulness.

Poor Fräulein Anna was so unfairly treated by fate and man. In return for twenty years of devotion, she received disappointment and humiliation; only Allah could explain to us the mystery of injustice.

Let's return to Murad. While I was moping in the company of young children, his intentions were becoming clearer. Signals, initially weak but growing stronger, made it clear that Surayya was his chosen one—his chosen one for life, as Murad was Muslim and nothing stood in the way of this marriage. The engagement was celebrated and Zuleykha and I, both equally piqued, had no option but to fall for another man; which we promptly did, setting about loving a Russian colonel.

While my father saw no difficulty in letting Murad marry Surayya, the Family disapproved of this marriage with their customary vehemence. On the one hand, Baku people did not like marriages to 'foreigners' and, on the other, my father's youngest sister, the one whose property was separated from ours by the wall and barometer gate, had long cherished the hope of seeing her son Mirza wed Surayya. My relatives had a marked preference for unions between cousins, since these kept money within the family.

I haven't mentioned my cousin Mirza, as the big age gap between us meant we were not close. From my early childhood he always associated with the Zuleykha–Surayya clan, not my Asad–Ali one.

He belonged to the least honourable section of the family. Like the whole of our generation, he could have, or rather should have, enjoyed the benefits of civilization. Despite the consistent, determined and costly efforts to civilize him even just a little, nothing came of it. Worse, he lacked a sense of humour and the kind of spirit that made spending time with Asad and Ali so attractive. He had a crude manner, and his wild appearance and almost permanent air of gloom were equally off-putting. Even as a small child he frightened his governesses, who were unable to calm his attacks of rage or control his indiscipline, which proved incurable; after a short time trying they would give up and leave. Later, he was expelled from several schools and ended up abandoning his studies and leading a life of idleness, pleasant but unedifying. His parents adored him—he was their only son—and spoke of his faults so tenderly that they transformed them into good qualities. The mysterious power of love…

So his mother nursed the hope he would marry his cousin Surayya, but neither my father nor the interested party had ever approved of her intentions. Nonetheless, when Surayya's engagement became official, my aunt made such fervent protests that one might have thought her wronged or robbed, though my father had never promised her anything. The whole family was in ferment: some—the minority—supported marriage to Murad, while the others—the majority—opposed it and were not sparing in their threats to the fiancé and his family or their invective about my father. Their rage did not bother my father, who maintained his usual composure.

One night as Murad was leaving our house a revolver was fired in the darkness, but the bullet missed him. No one had any doubts who was behind this attack, but precisely because of this the incident was smoothed over and not taken any further.

For his part, Murad found it all highly amusing and laughed at the 'natives', who were a revelation to him, raised as he was in the aristocratic circles of the capital. He would happily mimic others, had an eye for the slightly ridiculous and enjoyed himself immensely at the expense of his new relatives. He paid visits to all the members of the family, taking delight in the most colourful. His visit to Uncle Suleyman was the high point.

'I arrive by car,' he told us, 'and get out to walk to the door when I see your cousin Gulnar on the balcony. I greet her as one should. Instead of replying, she shouts at the top of her voice, "What do you want?"

'I reply: "Nothing, Mademoiselle, nothing. I simply crave the honour of presenting my respects to your mother."

'"What?" cries Gulnar who seems to have mistaken the meaning of my words. She studies me with a dubious, angry air, then shouts, "Very well, wait there," then disappears into the depths of the house.

'I wait. I wait so long in the street, on the pavement, that I start to wonder if the pretty but rude Gulnar has forgotten me. No, she hasn't forgotten me. She herself eventually opens the front door and tells me in a mocking tone to follow her. She leads me to a strangely furnished salon, where the whole family has gathered.

'"You know," Uncle Suleyman shouts at me, "I'm not impressed by uniforms and all that. We don't have any, but we have something better—money."

'And he strikes his chest in the place where wallets are usually kept.

'After this noble introduction, everyone starts asking questions designed to make fun of me; as they ask them, they look round at each other to make sure their wit is appreciated, and the children snigger into their hands and nudge each other with their elbows. What a delightful and original family! And why the devil do they never speak but shout all the time? Is it a custom?'

Surayya flushed in shame for her relatives. Unlike Murad she had no khans or ambassadors in her family, only poor millionaires of whom she had no cause to be proud.

Murad had an uncle who was president of one of the new republics of the north Caucasus, freshly Free, Proud and Happy, which he was representing in Paris at this historic moment. As there was nothing to keep him in the Caucasus, Murad decided to join him—a trip that could be most agreeable if combined with a honeymoon, 'while waiting for the Bolsheviks to go…'.

This sentence was still repeated, but with qualification. Of course, *they* would go but perhaps not as quickly as had been expected. There were even people who did not think they would leave Russia at all; others, clearly irresponsible, claimed that instead of leaving they might come to the Caucasus once the civil war was over. Many things were said, but no one knew anything, other than that all was uncertain.

Murad's plan made Amina sick with nostalgia. It was inconceivable to her that anyone should leave for France while she remained in Baku. She convinced my father that she should go to Paris as well, accompanied by Zuleykha. She found new reasons to make the trip: she had an illness that could be treated only in France; Surayya, a young wife, would not feel isolated in a foreign country; Zuleykha, who definitely had a talent for painting, should perfect her skills in a Parisian academy to become an Azerbaijani Ingres (the beloved homeland so needed one!); and both of them really had nothing to wear and lacked the most essential items.

They definitely had to go.

My accommodating father eventually agreed to the trip but on one condition: he wanted Amina to take my brother with her. He thought, not without good reason, that during these uncertain times a son should remain with his mother. Amina was ready to make any sacrifice.

There was no question of my going—and more than ever I felt like Cinderella. There may have been reasons for leaving me in Baku, but I have never understood them and a great sense of injustice has remained with me.

Surayya and Murad were first to leave, on a gloriously sunny day. The air was warm and the compartment from which Surayya sent us her last smiles was overflowing with flowers; Surayya thought her future would be flower-strewn too and so did we. She was wrong. None of us knew we had years of uncertainty ahead, and it was better that way.

Then it was time for the others to leave. I thought against all reason that they might change their minds at the last moment and take me to Paris too. The day came closer, though, and there was no change of plan. Their travelling clothes were finally ready, the suitcases buckled, and the day of departure arrived.

The train left at nine in the evening. At quarter past eight we began to say our goodbyes. I cut them short on some pretext or other and, not wanting anyone to see my sorrow, I went up to the Moorish salon, from where I could hear them leave.

In the total darkness of that large room, I pressed my forehead against the windowpane; I waited, listening. The main door opened downstairs, I heard voices, the door slam and the car move off. Then it was the silence of the end.

The inconceivable had happened. Amina and Zuleykha had left without me for something too radiant to name. They had gone and I was left behind in the darkness with no way out. I imagined with unbearable clarity the life that awaited me: grey and joyless, a life where hopes were always dashed and an overwhelming sense of injustice reigned. While there, in Paris, in that city that had lost all geographic meaning for me and become a fairy-tale land, more dream than reality; there in Paris, Amina and Zuleykha... and I finally began to cry; I wept a flood of tears. Why couldn't I dissolve into tears, become a stream and disappear, escaping life and its sorrows? Like all naive fools, I asked myself what I had done to deserve such injustice. But tears dry up, leaving you wrung out, a rag only fit to be thrown to the winds.

I was wrong to imagine a grey future. My life was to be many things but it was never grey.

A month later my grandfather Musa died. He left us, his four granddaughters, a vast fortune, even by the standards of Baku, where there were dozens of millionaires. This ironic legacy made me a multimillionaire at the age of thirteen, but only for a few days, for I was soon woken at dawn by 'The Internationale' sung in the street. I got up and saw soldiers who neither resembled nor wore the uniform of Azerbaijani *askaris*. It was the Russians.

During the night an armoured train, just one, had crossed the ephemeral border of the ephemeral independent Republic of Azerbaijan and deposited Red Army soldiers at Baku's sleeping station. In a matter of moments, without a shot being fired, the Azerbaijani army had melted away. The Republic was dead and victorious Russia was reclaiming its subjects.

With my own eyes I had seen the end of a world.

PART TWO

I

I saw with my own eyes the end of a world, namely, the ephemeral Republic of Azerbaijan, and with it came the end of my childhood. 'What, Madame, at the age of thirteen?' Well yes, and why not? The departure of my stepmother, two of my sisters and my brother for Paris came as a psychological shock, and opened my eyes to the cruelty of the world. Isn't that the point from which to date my break with childhood? To my mind, the definition of childhood is very simple: belief in stability and the goodness of the world. Take away that belief, and childhood comes to an end.

Am I overcome with emotion at the joy of innocence and child-like naivety? Not at all: I abhor that state of innocence precisely because it is ignorant of the real world in all its magnificence, horror and divinity. To accept the world and love it just as it is—herein lies the glory of mankind. It would be too easy to love a good world.

The departure of my two sisters induced in me a sense of injustice, which I found hard to bear; though bear it I must, as there was nothing else I could do. In theory, my father and I were supposed to join them later—in theory... In fact, I remained on my own, overcome with a sense of yearning, of having been wronged and wrenched apart from loved ones. True, my eldest sister Leyla stayed behind, but she was married, and a mother, and so capricious, so rarely there that she became quite elusive; there was no connection between us. Our governess Fräulein Anna was more highly strung and unwell than ever. Devastated by the decline of her sight, she used the little strength she had left to look after my nephew; and if she should turn to me, my reserved nature and stupid pride stopped me accepting her affection. Even more distant was my relationship with my father, as he was extremely reserved and cold. I was intimidated by his presence, afraid almost, and my only feeling for him was frosty respect.

So, I was alone with my first major sorrow. The departure played a decisive role in my psyche, inclining me towards pessimism for many years. A while later, I saw my first death (I don't include the anonymous bodies swinging from nooses in the public park). My maternal grandfather lay on his bed, his corpse swollen with dropsy and covered in a sheet, as though he were a secret, shameful object that had to be hidden from public view. No, I didn't love him and had never loved him. His death caused me no pain, and even seemed a deliverance—a deliverance from the interminable visits we paid to him once a week throughout his long illness: mortal hours that we spent at his sickbed, hours when we did not know what to say, how to kill the minutes; seconds that stretched into eternities at the spectacle of a man dying, unloved. I had come to long for his death—why hide it?—as must his wife, who had become his faithful nurse, as must all those who suffered in one way or another from the poor, dying man. What about the patient himself? He was said to be afraid of death; but his illness was so awful that it might have made him long for a final peace. All his life he had so feared this death that he forbade his closest relatives to speak of it in his presence. According to an ancient oriental belief, death does not take anyone who builds. Inspired by this, my grandfather built house after house as soon as his vast fortune, derived so suddenly from oil, permitted. By the time of his death, he had built more than sixty houses. He seemed to collect them, as other people collect snuffboxes or postage stamps. But superstition had lied: despite the last house being under construction, death had no compunction in coming to look for Grandfather Musa.

So, it was the first time I had seen the corpse of a relative—I looked at the body without love but with unbounded curiosity, coupled with fear. Grandfather had far more prestige to me dead than he had ever had in life. Where was he? In what other world, in what unimaginable void did he now think and live in the manner of the dead? I gazed in horror at the sheet covering the corpse; a large bulge indicated the location of his stomach, swollen by illness. His exposed face was not improved by death; he had a long, bony nose, hollow cheeks covered with a white beard, dotted with just a few dark hairs, evidence of an old colouring of henna. His sunken mouth turned inwards, seemingly drawn inside by a force still intact within his body. Then an obsession began to grip me, one so revolting that I find it hard to acknowledge—but I would like to get as close as possible to the truth: I wondered, with shudders of revulsion running through my body, what that mouth might smell like. It pursued me for months, poisoning my dreams with its imaginary breath. I felt like a monster and was disgusted at myself. The obsession eased very gradually until it eventually disappeared. I returned to it today, of my own choosing, following the guiding thread of memory.

After the corpse had been washed, it was placed on a litter in the middle of the large room, according to Muslim tradition, and covered in a cashmere shawl. Prayers were said over the corpse. A string of mullahs succeeded one another in the room, which did not empty for two days. Women were not admitted; veiled in black, they sat on the floor in other rooms, reciting the Koran and weeping. I wept with them, not out of grief for my deceased grandfather, but carried along by their emotion and, especially, out of bitter regret that I was there and not in Paris with my sisters.

The funeral was impressive. A dense crowd, stretching farther than the eye could see, surrounded the litter, which rocked the body, now like that of a child, small and defenceless. Only the men, heads covered with a fez or an astrakhan hat, followed the litter.

For a week chicken pilaff was given out to all comers: hundreds of poor people came to mourn the dead man and afterwards to eat their fill from the enormous copper cauldrons, used to cook the meat and rice. Then everything returned to normal, and talk began about the deceased's legacy. His immense fortune was to be shared among his four granddaughters and his wife. I wasn't terribly interested in this fortune, as it seemed unreal to me, and in this I was not wrong: I was never to take possession of it; it was never to enslave me.

The Red Army's reconquest of Azerbaijan returned us to the bosom of the Russian Empire, which in the meantime had become Soviet. Capitalism was dead; we possessed nothing now.

My father, the family, the whole city were stupefied as they struggled to grasp that everything had finished—or rather that everything was just beginning. The naive dreamers of a Pax Azerbaijani, of a great, future Muslim empire, mourned their foolhardy visions; those who loved their wealth lived in fear and trepidation. Believing they were millionaires by divine right, they called upon Divine Mercy to ensure the preservation of their fortune. But to the outrage of the believers, Divine Mercy seemed to have abandoned them and joined their enemies. There were more Red soldiers in the city by the day; then came the commissars and spring blossomed with its buds and butterflies, committees of this and soviets of that. Spring had arrived, pristine and lovely, without a care for the affairs of man, transcending them in its eternal glory.

Despite the call of the glorious weather, my father went to ground, not daring to leave the house. His ministerial, tanned-leather portfolio lay abandoned in a drawer; there was no longer a parliament or parliamentarians, only poor men ignorant of their fate. During the two years of this rickety republic on the margins of Russia, the whole of Baku had repeated complacently, 'We are independent. It was declared in Geneva. *They* would never dare to come here. And we are armed, while *they* are exhausted by the war and civil unrest.'

My father was devastated, almost prostrate. He constantly ground his teeth, and I could imagine the dialogue going through his mind, the reproaches he made to himself: he had not left Baku in time; he had not transferred money abroad; he had got caught up in his ministerial functions, which, in the light of what followed, seemed derisory. The tan portfolio was empty now and sentries no longer guarded his residence. My father paid dearly for his blindness.

Life dragged on for a time, as we waited for something decisive to happen. Then, one morning, my father was arrested; minister, rich man and president of a reactionary party, he had no hope of escaping the vigilance of the new masters.

The next day a commission came to inspect our house and the inspection concluded, not without reason, that we did not need so many rooms for so few people. The same day, a commissar, accompanied by his wife and members of staff, moved in with us.

Our first contact with the world of the revolution was cordial. The commissar's wife, a petite blonde with a snub nose, often invited us, that is to say Leyla and me, to take tea with her; it was served in our finest tea service (she denied us nothing) and accompanied by literary conversation. She was a passionate reader and though she usually discussed only books with suggestive covers promising the heights of intellectual pleasure, and tragic titles, such as *A Captive Heart* or *A Secret in the Night*, the intention was none the less good and a sign of a curious, romantic spirit.

Aunt Rena, who still lived on the top floor of the house, and Fräulein Anna were incensed that Leyla and I should accept 'that woman's' invitations. On the one hand, though, we thought it politic to do so, and on the other we were burning with curiosity to know more about this unfamiliar world. Perhaps you are surprised that a child should be invited to join adults for tea. I was neither mentally nor physically a child, despite my age. I looked like a young woman and spoke like one too, and I could certainly keep up conversation with the wife of the commissar. I already had more extensive literary baggage than she did. My evenings at Aunt Rena's devouring all the books in the library had not been in vain. So we spoke about literature and quizzed one another about our respective worlds, especially when the commissar husband joined us. A curious man, with a very agile mind, he wanted to understand this strange life that we led: half-Islamic, half-Western. He hated all religions, holding them responsible for most of humanity's misfortunes (the revolutionary slogan 'Religion is the opium of the people' is well known). He wanted to convince us of it, and sometimes succeeded, but as soon as we had left, our atavism would regain its hold on us.

These instructive tea parties did not last long. Summer was coming and my father, from whom we received regular letters during his incarceration, wanted his mother and his daughters well away from the city, in the country, which seemed to him a refuge from the social vicissitudes. We could not see him nor be any use to him staying in town, so we obeyed him.

In summer Baku is the most desperately stifling, dusty city, and we always felt the call of the countryside in spring. Moreover, too many people were being arrested; people were afraid—afraid for their worldly goods, afraid for their lives. We were in a hurry to leave the city and be reunited with the pools and trees.

2

I was overjoyed to see them again! The gardeners were as busy as ever looking after them. They would soon leave, as our fortune had abandoned us. But while waiting for things to be decided, they stayed on, unpaid; they could still live off the estate. Free from anxiety about the revolution, the sheep thrived and potatoes grew in abundance. The air remained heavy with its usual fragrance; the scent of honeysuckle and the stronger scent of climbing jasmine perfumed the terraces, carrying into our rooms. Things remained as they always had been. That summer could have been any other summer—nothing seemed to have changed. The clear sky laughed at revolutions, beneath it the sea shone blue, while the earth was gracefully fecund. This contrast between the serenity of the world and our growing anxiety filled me with melancholy; it was poignant—and poignancy is what I began to feel, contemplating the eternal resurrection of nature compared to the brevity of our life.

It was several years since the summer I had pictured my stepmother in Paris with Leyla. Now, I still pictured her in Paris but with my other sisters. They had sent us letters and photographs: they were elegant, happy and pleased with life. They lived in a large apartment on the Champs-Élysées, which they had rented from Gaby Deslys, a star of that era. Champs-Élysées! A name that overwhelms with longing those who are not there.

I was idle from morning till night: my studies, which had been irregular at the best of times, were now abandoned completely. 'At least revolution is good for something,' I thought to myself with grim humour. Only the piano found favour with me from time to time. The rest of the time I strolled in the garden and read a little, but my main occupation was daydreaming, the daily bread of the dissatisfied. That summer I found a new place where I could give myself up to daydreaming in perfect peace. It was a rock inside the vineyard, bordered by poplars. No one ever went there and in the silence of the hot afternoons I could wallow in visions and sensations. I stretched out on the rough rock, facing the glittering sea. Behind me the poplars formed a solemn guard of honour, the wind playing in their branches. Sometimes clouds would blow lazily by, while the poplar leaves rustled more than ever. Fascinated, I followed the clouds' progress with my eyes. They emerged from behind the horizon, passed over the sea, arrived above me and disappeared without trace behind the tops of the poplars. A blue sky appeared for their pleasure: a high sky, a pure sky, it spoke the solitary language of eternity. Seeing it so calm, so detached from the wandering clouds and the wandering humans with their miseries both great and small, I took it for eternity itself—a strange feeling that was sometimes so strong it made me weep.

I was soon not to be so solitary. My cousin Gulnar and her mother arrived in the country; all the rest of the family had stayed in Turkestan for lack of transport. I was overjoyed to be reunited with Gulnar, as I had rarely seen her that winter. I was bound to her by old ties of friendship, a friendship mixed with admiration for her originality. Brazen, cynical, light-hearted and deeply immoral, Gulnar transported me to a world very different from my own, one that delighted and frightened me in equal measure. She was nearly sixteen and seemed to have the measure of life; her lively mind took surprising changes of direction for someone who was basically unpolished. Sensuality seemed to ooze from all her pores and determined her whole personality. She had a violent desire for men and despised them at the same time. Still inclined to fall in love, the more in love she was, the more she found reasons to despise the object of her passion; I think that she unwittingly hated whoever could subjugate her, albeit only for a while. It's difficult to imagine quite how flirtatious she was; I think it must have been an effort for her not to flirt with her brothers and her father, the handsome Uncle Suleyman. Tall and slim, her body was very different from that of our compatriots, whose breasts and other protuberances expanded unreservedly in all directions. No sooner had her breasts begun to appear than she squashed them mercilessly in a brassiere of strong linen. Likewise, she squeezed her abdomen into punishing corsets. She could be proud of the results, and indeed she was, contemplating her reflection with satisfaction. She had velvet eyes and thick, sensual lips, which gave her a rather piquant, Negro look. As soon as she encountered a specimen of the male gender, she would turn her face towards him and fix him with a sultry gaze. Few could resist her charms and she had already had numerous affairs, which stopped, however, at what she boldly called 'the gateway to paradise'.

'You know,' she explained to me in the manner of a businesswoman, 'you have to keep your virginity for marriage, otherwise you might have problems. Afterwards, though…' And she whistled. This whistle seemed to express her future full of lovers, adventures and passion. She already knew whom she would marry: a distant relative of her father's, long since approved by the family, and who had long since been enamoured of my cousin: a good, weak man, whom the heavens seemed to have specially designed to be the ideal husband to fulfil Gulnar's brilliant destiny. She was to marry him as soon as her family could return to Baku, and she hoped it would be autumn at the latest. 'I can't wait any longer,' she would say languorously. And while waiting she used all the means available to satisfy her ardour. During the worst heat of summer, when everyone took a siesta, Gulnar sometimes took me to her shuttered room, where we would lie down on her bed, covered in a clean sheet. First, she would fall asleep like a child, surprisingly quickly, pressing the length of her brown, supple body against me, her head resting on mine. We were surrounded by the silence of a tropical afternoon, the only interruption a fly buzzing around the bed; furniture creaked; Gulnar moved slightly. As usual, sleep eluded me and I lay with my eyes wide open, waiting for my friend to wake up and the game that would follow. When Gulnar's hand began to move, I knew that her nap was over. Her fingertips ran across my body, caressing me. According to the rules of the game, I had to repeat faithfully their movement on Gulnar's body. It radiated with pleasure at my touch; her eyes closed, she rose a little and covered my face and neck with fervent kisses. She did not look at me and I was not allowed to speak; she was not looking at me, but through me at those men who would one day be hers. The game gave me no pleasure; I did it to satisfy Gulnar's demands. Her authority over me was so great that I almost always did what she wanted.

She was bored in the country, where the only men to seduce were the gardeners.

'I'm bored, I'm bored,' she repeated all day long.

She shrugged her shoulders when I suggested she read or day-dream or play music.

'You get on my nerves,' she would say impatiently. 'Don't you get it? I'm only interested in men.'

So she was delighted when one day a 'Commission for the Creation of Holiday Camps' came to see us. It was an extraordinary event. Four men presented themselves at the gates of the property. When the gardeners asked what they wanted, they showed them their papers, which the illiterate gardeners were unable to read. After much mutual incomprehension, the gardeners ran to announce the visit to Grandmother, who at that precise moment was busy with one of her five daily prayers.

'What do those Christian dogs want? To see the house? They can go to the Devil... See our house? Throw them out, the faithless infidels.'

Scarlet with indignation, despite the presence of the Holy Book on the chair in front of her, she would not listen. We tried in vain to explain to her that it wasn't a matter of giving consent, that the Russians were the masters now and could not be treated like dogs, while they, on the other hand, could treat us that way, should they so desire; she did not listen to us. While all these discussions were going on, the commission lost patience and entered the house on their own authority. Grandmother covered her face, but began to curse in our own language, which the visitors, all Russians, fortunately could not understand. There were four of them, handsome to varying degrees, but all men, and since they expressed the desire to see the house, Gulnar rushed to show it to them before anyone had time to stop her. Grandmother hurled ferocious curses in her direction, but it was too late; Gulnar was already walking from room to room, the four men on her heels, paying far more attention to her than the house.

'Little whore!' shouted Grandmother, not mincing her words. 'Just look at her—see how she's wiggling her bottom like a monkey.' Then she turned on her daughter: 'It's all your fault. You're the one who's brought her up so badly. Anyone would think you're getting her ready for a brothel. And what do these men want anyway?'

Our latest explanations did not meet with success either: she didn't understand what a holiday camp was, nor what one could have to do with our estate. But we understood all too well: our house was just right for the commission's plans and the visitors said that at least half of the rooms would be requisitioned for the holiday camp. They were very courteous, though, and the person who seemed most important told us we should be proud to take in men exhausted from their services to the revolution.

'Why keep all these enormous rooms empty?' he concluded with an oratorical flourish. 'They will now provide shelter to men who come here in search of the peace and quiet of nature. In our noble cause the sacrifices of some become the good fortune of all.'

With these words of comfort they left us, but Gulnar's sighs followed them; she had certainly liked the tall blonde one with the small snub nose, who to us was utterly exotic.

'What?' yelled Grandmother. 'Russians in my house? Men who eat pigs, get drunk and think they can do what they like? Here, in my own home? Are these the men who put my son in prison? Never. I would rather die.'

There was no question of her dying, but only of giving in, since there was no way round it.

The house was divided into two wings of equal size. We all moved into Grandmother's wing, which consisted of ten rooms, so although we were together, we weren't crammed in, especially since Leyla, whose husband had just been arrested too, left for Baku and didn't come back. We each had our own room and I couldn't help thinking that it was only fair to share such a spacious house with others. But I kept it to myself.

A week later we watched a dozen revolutionary veterans arrive, all worn out to a greater or lesser extent by their exploits. There were old ideologists, accustomed to Siberian labour camps; schoolmistresses, whose eyes shone with communist faith; a Ukrainian poet who would recite poetry, then have a coughing fit; even a commissar's wife, who had apparently come to rest from her husband's exhaustion; and others whose faces and stories I have forgotten. Gulnar and I quickly got to know all these people. A few days later, we both fell in love with one of the old ideologists. When I say 'old', I'm talking from the perspective of a fourteen-year-old girl. Gregory Tarasov was a very youthful forty. He looked like a clean-shaven Turgenev, taught history in civilian life and lyrical communism all the time. Gulnar's attractions forced him to forgive us our membership of the former oppressors' class, a class to which we belonged without conviction anyway. He magnanimously overlooked this and endeavoured to enrich us with communist ideas. We weren't hard to convince—the ground was fertile. Gulnar agreed out of flirtatiousness without really listening to Gregory; she gazed lustfully at the full, handsome lips, which parted to reveal a row of shining teeth. More aware, I enjoyed following the arguments that he passionately developed before us.

'Don't you feel the injustice of these vast fortunes that are the result of the chance discovery of oil?'

We felt it.

'Don't you believe it was a flagrant injustice that millions were lost gambling in clubs, while workers died of hunger and cold in their hovels?'

We most sincerely believed it.

'And what do you think of those idle women whose only concern was to get dressed up; of those men whose interest went no further than the races, gambling and love affairs?'

We honestly had nothing good to say of such people.

He undertook our Marxist education. He did so well that, one month after his arrival, the hot blood of the newly converted coursed through our veins. Gregory looked at us tenderly, as a painter or sculptor looks at his creation, and continued his gentle moulding of our minds.

One day he went to Baku and returned with two enamel brooches depicting Lenin, pinned them on our dresses and henceforth viewed us as his own creatures. I returned his kindness, even going so far as to take him to my corner reserved for dreaming, which he immediately adopted. Every afternoon the three of us went to lie down on the rough rock, which smelt of sun and dried grapes, and we talked of a thousand and one things. Gregory called us 'his little orientals' and talked to us about ourselves, himself and the revolution.

'Almost all our great writers talked about the Caucasus,' he said to us one day. 'I have always dreamt of coming here; I've always dreamt of getting to know Caucasian girls, girls who are different from Russian girls, girls like you. You, Gulnar'—he leant over Gulnar, who was lying on her back, her hands crossed over her chest—'are like a rather dangerous plant which produces beautiful flowers. But men are wary of it. They would like to touch it, would like to smell it because they know it has a marvellous perfume, but they are frightened, afraid of getting stung.'

'Touch me,' Gulnar said without a hint of a smile, 'and you'll see that I don't sting.'

For a long time Gregory considered her face, her eyes closed.

'I wouldn't dare,' he said at last. 'If you really don't sting, I would be in even more danger.'

He turned towards me: 'I am not so wary of you and my affection for you is greater. I would have liked to have a daughter like you, to make of her the woman I have always longed for in my heart: curious, idealistic, capable of sacrificing herself to a noble cause, artistic too. But I shall soon have to go and leave you both behind. It's so sad.'

'Oh no, don't go,' cried Gulnar, opening her eyes. 'Why don't you want to touch me?' she asked passionately. 'I don't sting.'

She took Gregory's hand and put it on her neck. Gregory started to caress her there. I closed my eyes and didn't open them until I heard Gregory say in a strangled, shaken voice, 'Let's go back. It's late.'

At other times he told us about his life, a classic revolutionary life, full of danger, trouble, drama. Twice he had been exiled to Siberia and twice he had escaped. He had taken part in assassination attempts against the state, had run an underground printing press, had lived in Geneva for two years and in Paris for one. Both his wife and son had died of typhus. 'You can see that my life is hardly a round of pleasure. And you can see that I deserve this rest the party has granted me. Do the little orientals think so?'

Yes, the little orientals did think so. They were beginning to see that revolutionaries were not all monsters and that capitalism had its drawbacks. I found incomprehensible my family's stubborn blindness to the social change under way in the world. They thought they had a monopoly on stability and affluence, and were outraged when they were to be given to others too. The worker was created to work, the family for pleasure. That was their credo and anything else seemed heresy.

Gregory was not the only one to feel affection for the little orientals. Almost everyone at the camp was well disposed towards us. To these true Russians from the north, the Caucasus represented, let's say, what Morocco must represent for the metropolitan French: an exotic, far-off, rather mysterious country. Russian poets had celebrated the Caucasus, its women, its mountains, its foreignness. It was imbued with a specific emotion that almost every sensitive Russian felt when he got there. To these visitors we were 'gazelles with languorous eyes', 'girls from the harem', scarcely liberated from servitude: the 'little savages' of exotic novels.

Everyone spoilt us too, and Gulnar and I welcomed the arrival of this holiday camp, as it brought a pleasant change to our slightly reclusive lives. My aunt, grandmother and Fräulein Anna admonished us, forbidding us to see 'those people' and threatening to punish us and tell our fathers, but in vain, as nothing could stop us. Our fathers were a long way away, and we weren't afraid of the other punishments. The portrait of Lenin continued to adorn our young chests. Now we swore only by Karl Marx and his historical materialism. Gregory's influence was augmented by the arrival of a teacher. She too had given herself body and soul to the revolution, which she spoke of in maternal tones as though she were talking about her daughter. 'She's very well,' she would say happily. 'She has grown stronger; she will develop now and become robust. We must help her to flourish.'

She gave us details of workers' lives under the old regime, and we were filled with disgust at those who had exploited them so despicably. That is what she wanted. 'You have to support us with all your heart. We must show the triumph of communist ideas even in society's most hostile classes.' 'Society's most hostile classes' were enthusiastic in their agreement.

She was the daughter of minor landowners near Kiev. From adolescence, an obscure, but irresistible force had pushed her towards the people. She became a schoolteacher, joined the Communist Party and left for a destiny where her personal well-being counted for nought. She was immersed in idealism, as though in a health-giving bath. It was of no concern to her what she ate, what was poured into her glass, what she wore—all that mattered, that gave her life meaning, was the revolution and its success. Petite, slim and vivacious, she never stopped turning over socialist ideas in her head, reading or learning in some other manner. She did not daydream and did not understand when I explained to her what daydreaming meant to me.

'Daydreaming? But what about? Life is so exciting, a hundred times more exciting than the most audacious daydream.'

'But daydreaming allows you to be something other than yourself, your only self,' I tried to explain to her.

'Why be anything other than my own self? I'm happy with my life.'

That summed it up—happy with her life. Why would she want to change it? She also said to me, 'If you take action, you won't want to daydream. Try it and see.'

That was easier said than done.

3

One day Maria Nikolayevna (the schoolmistress) came to find Gulnar and me.

'My dear girls,' she said solemnly, 'I think your minds and, better still, your hearts are open to our cause. Would you like to prove it to me now through actions rather than words?'

'Yes, we would, very much.'

'Good, we are setting up commissions to compile inventories of all the villas in the neighbourhood. It's an easy job, but rather tedious. It requires pencil, paper and patience, as you have to write down everything that you find in the houses. Would you like to help?'

This was a delicate matter. It was all very well playing at being communists behind our own four walls, but it was more serious to go out with the commission and write inventories of the villas of people who all knew us. Maria Nikolayevna talked to us at length. She understood our hesitation, our fear of offending the family and the family's friends; on the one hand, she praised our sensitivity, but on the other she encouraged us to overcome it. 'Nothing in life is easy,' she declared. 'Everything requires determination and resolve.' If we really wanted to liberate ourselves, we had to start somewhere.

Gulnar and I discussed it at length. In the event, it was me who decided we would agree. Gulnar was enthusiastic where flirtation was concerned, but more circumspect than me when it came to anything else. Fräulein Anna and my aunt tried in vain to dissuade us, pointing out how awkward it would be and how shocking it was for us to belong to a movement that 'even if by some miracle it should prove to be excellent' was nonetheless responsible for the imprisonment of my father, Leyla's husband and other members of our family. But all the arguments, all Grandmother's outrage and scathing insults were water off a duck's back: we were carried away by revolutionary enthusiasm. With Lenin's portrait pinned prominently to our dresses, we sallied forth, pen and paper in hand, to conquer our destiny, which we already saw as intimately bound up with communism.

Maria Nikolayevna, Gulnar and I, with a tall, shy young man as our leader, did not make up a very imposing Inventory Commission. I'm not even sure that we would have completed our task without Maria Nikolayevna, who spurred us on with all her zeal.

Sergey, the shy young man, took a piece of paper out of his pocket. 'Here we are,' he said. 'We're to begin with your neighbour, Mustafayev.'

'Oh no, not him!' Gulnar and I cried in unison.

'Very well'—he read the second name on his list—'then we'll go to the next one, Mukhtarov.'

'Oh no, that's even worse: he's got a very bad temper and is really unpleasant.'

'Well, what are we to do? The next one is someone called Akbarov.'

'My God, he's worse still. He's known us since we were babies and won't hesitate to throw us out.'

'That's enough,' Maria Nikolayevna said. 'We're not talking about a pleasure trip but a duty. We will begin as is right and proper with the first name on the list.'

Gulnar and I gazed at her, appalled. The first person on the list, Mustafayev, was a harmless, doddery old man, but his wife was a distant cousin of Grandmother's, a redoubtable woman who might have a nasty surprise in store for us. We tried in vain to dissuade Maria Nikolayevna, but she remained adamant.

'We must do our duty,' she repeated without listening to us, 'and not look to enjoy ourselves. One must be able to take responsibility for one's actions.'

We felt only a hint of pride when Maria Nikolayevna rang the Mustafayevs' bell with an eloquent energy. At that moment historical materialism seemed more agreeable in books than in practice. A gardener who knew Gulnar and me opened the gate and, thinking of course that we had come to pay a visit, greeted us with much bowing and scraping, full of respect and cordiality.

'Balaja Khanim will be glad to see you. She is sad. It looks as though those Russian pigs are going to take her house, a plague on the lot of them and the sooner the better! I think these must be your friends! So they only speak their pig language'—he winked at us—'and don't understand what I'm saying. *Ay Allah, ay Allah*, what hard times! What is the world coming to?'

With every step we took towards the house, the little confidence we had melted away. Balaja Khanim had a near legendary reputation: she chased her daughters with a broom, beat her husband, threw jars of jam at passers-by whom she didn't like the look of; she was said to carry a revolver in the folds of her skirt, not because she intended to use it but because she enjoyed being like a man. Wagging tongues said her husband was senile largely because she treated him so badly (which shows that even in Muslim countries wives torture their husbands). When her daughters really annoyed her, Balaja Khanim would lock them in their room, sometimes for as long as a month. And we were going to compile an inventory of this woman's house...

My overactive imagination pictured the reception Balaja Khanim would give us when she learnt the reason for our visit: she would shower us with insults, throw various objects at our heads, spit in our faces (why not?), get out her famous revolver and threaten us at the very least (but you never knew—she might even fire it, if not to kill us, then to lodge some bullets in the ceiling, something she had done before).

My legs had turned to jelly and I had forgotten all my Marxist enthusiasm by the time I saw Balaja Khanim before me, veiling her face because of our companion and fixing us with her baleful, eagle eye.

'May Allah keep you! I am glad to see the granddaughters of Musselma Khanim in my home. What brings you here? And who are these people with you?' she asked in Azeri. Like all the women of her generation, she did not speak Russian.

'These people… These people…' I stammered desperately. 'We… I mean they… I mean,' and suddenly I had a flash of inspiration: 'These people are living in our house. They are dreadful; they make us follow them everywhere to help them. They want to count all the objects that are in your house. We wanted to refuse, of course, but they threatened to throw us in prison. So please forgive us, Balaja Khanim, we have to do what they tell us.'

Maria Nikolayevna and Sergey listened to my speech without understanding a word. They realized I had to explain the situation to Balaja Khanim and waited patiently.

'May cholera eat away their bowels! May Allah punish them to the fourth generation! May he turn them into a public urinal! May he make all their teeth fall out! May he impale them on hot iron! May they be sodomized by donkeys! May their tongues dry up in their mouths! May Allah increase their misfortunes and prolong their lives!'

'Is she cross with us?' Maria Nikolayevna asked.

'Yes, a little,' I replied tactfully. 'But it will pass. It's bound to.'

'Then let's make a start anyway! I'll stay in this room with you. Gulnar and Sergey can make an inventory of the next room.'

She sat down calmly at the table and began to count the furniture and write it down, without paying the slightest attention to Balaja Khanim, who was becoming ever more virulent in her choice of insults.

'And what have you got pinned on there?' she asked me suddenly, interrupting her flow and pointing at Lenin's portrait. 'A picture of a man? Have you no shame? Not only do these hussies flaunt themselves in public without a veil, they stick men on their chests! Who is it?'

'It's their leader. They forced me to wear this portrait. What can I do?'

I sighed.

'Dogs, pigs, jackals!'

She went into the next room, where it was Sergey's turn to endure a flood of insults; had he understood half of them, he would have died of embarrassment. Then we could hear them no more; it was prayer time.

Our work was long and tedious; we had to include everything in the house in the inventory—from spoons to carpets, taking in bed linen and saucepans along the way. Maria Nikolayevna gave herself gladly to the task in hand, no doubt believing that with each scratch of her pen the revolution gained in vigour. The presence of the blonde Sergey was compensation for Gulnar, as he was starting to grow on her. As for me, I was just longing for the job to end, as it was deadly boring. On top of that, though my lie had been ingenious, I was sick with anxiety at the thought of being found out and Balaja Khanim descending on me with her unused stock of jibes and insults. I was in a hurry to see the back of my Marxist apprenticeship.

That evening we were worn out, but had to face the censure of three women: Grandmother, my aunt and Fräulein Anna, who sat in a circle around us and upbraided us severely. We were insolent in our replies, claiming total independence and taking the opportunity to spread communist propaganda.

'What?' I said. 'Here is a family of five people that has thirty-four saucepans, two dozen sets of cutlery, two hundred and thirty plates and so on, and keeps all these while some workers' families have nothing at all. No, no, a thousand times no. You're all heartless, the lot of you...'

'The fires of hell are waiting for you, ass heads, hussies,' shouted Grandmother. 'While your relatives are rotting in prison, you go off and have fun with those people...'

'We are not having fun with them, we are making our modest contribution to the emancipation of suffering humanity,' Gulnar declared sententiously.

'Stupid idiot'—this was Gulnar's mother now—'if your father were here, he would give you a good beating, then you'd lose some of your airs and graces and forget about "emancipating suffering humanity". If I'd known, I wouldn't have given myself the trouble of bringing you into this world. That's all the thanks I get.'

'I didn't ask you to,' Gulnar screeched. 'If you gave birth to me, it's because you wanted to, you and your husband.'

The dispute carried on in this vein for another hour. Afterwards, we still had the strength to go and cry in Gregory's arms. He explained that nothing could be achieved in life without opposition. 'One has to suffer to become communist,' he concluded with a smile.

We worked hard for the revolutionary cause, compiling inventories of some twenty villas to the growing outrage of our relatives and their friends. The family used our age as a weak excuse for our shameful behaviour, but in a country where a girl is a mother at fourteen this pretext wasn't very convincing. Marxism had us in its thrall; Gulnar less than me, as she only wanted to please the revolutionaries staying with us, while my faith was sincere. Only my father's imprisonment stopped me from expressing absolute enthusiasm. Aunt Rena and Leyla were going to great lengths in Baku to get him released; they haunted the anterooms of various people's commissars and used all their connections; they got in touch with the workers in our former oilfields to beg them to sign petitions for his release. So far all these efforts had been in vain and my father remained in prison, where life was at least bearable. He had work as a mechanic in a workshop, which came as a great relief to him as he had always enjoyed working with his hands. But it was dangerous to be in prison at such a time. Not that Baku had the terrorism that was rampant in Russia after the resistance of the Whites: things seemed to have passed off without tragedy; none of our relatives or friends had been shot. If the worst of my father's problems were a few months in prison, that would not be too bad. Many people were now being released, and this gave us hope that he too would soon be freed. That said, he was more important than some and might stay in prison a long time. He sometimes wrote us letters full of the oriental fatalism that helped him bear his situation, which, he said, was dependent on the will of Allah; he did not mope and complain, but let destiny take its course. When I felt the stirrings of conscience and remorse about him, I responded that I was not to blame for having been born into a family of plutocrats; I did not have to hate communism, to which I felt attracted heart and soul, because my father was in prison. Gregory fanned my flames daily.

The three of us held our conferences on the rock every day now. When the heat had eased a little towards evening, around six, we would make our separate ways there so as not to attract attention. Gulnar and Gregory would lie next to one another on the top of the rock, while I settled lower down on the sloping part, and we would talk. Gregory would often stop talking, and I knew that he was caressing Gulnar. I would close my eyes and keep quiet until he started talking again. By now we knew all about his life: we knew his joys and his sorrows and the people who were important to him. We shared his enthusiasms and his friends, too. We were impatient to meet one of them, whom the party was to send to Baku and who had promised to come and see Gregory in the country. What Gregory said to us about him was just right to excite a young imagination: he talked of his heroism, his intelligence, his rectitude.

'He's the most rounded person I know—a man of steel but poetic too at times. A precise thinker yet also a dreamer. An intellectual and a man of action. He can be tender and he can be cruel; he can be everything! He is a man of many contradictions!'

A military man, he was a member of a revolutionary committee and it was on committee business that he was to come to Baku. Gregory spoke so warmly about him that I began to dream of Andrey Massarin as though I already knew him. Since the age of ten I had been tormented by the need to love to the extent that it had become endemic. What mattered to me was not so much the object of my love: it was the love itself that I had to find an object for at any cost. Since I was accustomed to collective love affairs with my sisters, their departure had left me floundering, incapable of choosing a man for myself. Gregory's descriptions came at the right time to feed my dreams. I wanted to love Andrey Massarin and wanted to be loved by him; it did not cross my mind that it was absurd to desire a stranger in this way. I looked forward to the arrival of this foreigner, as though he were my fiancé.

That day Gulnar and I went to the rock earlier than usual. Gulnar felt bitter about Gregory's impending departure and complained to me about him for half an hour. She would have liked to love him completely; she found their caresses unsatisfying, fragmentary and irritating in the extreme. She set out the situation with her customary cynicism.

'I cannot become his mistress since I'm not married yet; Selim has the right to my virginity. Gregory should stay here until I get married; then I could be entirely his. I want him so much. Oh, it's all so stupid!'

In her annoyance she was tearing out the moss that covered parts of the rock, without really noticing. She caught her finger, making it bleed, and began to swear. Then she suddenly stopped.

'Gregory's coming, but he's not on his own.'

I got up, keen to see, and with a hunch who it was. Gregory was walking towards us, his feet scrunching as they sank into the sand; he wove his way between the vines and fig trees, followed by someone with a decisive step. 'It's Andrey Massarin. It's Andrey Massarin,' I said to myself in delight.

'I'm bringing Andrey Massarin to meet you,' Gregory called from a distance, and immediately my throat dried up and my hands began to shake.

It wasn't revolutionary committee member Andrey Massarin, but Prince Bolkonsky, hero of *War and Peace*, who was walking towards me; his death had always seemed too inconceivable for me to be truly convinced of it. There he was before me, revived, with his disdainful bearing, his pensive face, his intense, serious expression; in a word, the way I had always known him.

He sat down on the rock between Gulnar and me; slim and not very tall, he wore a snug-fitting black uniform that made him look heroic and sad at the same time.

'My black knight, have you really come for me?' my soul asked. I couldn't speak, and I couldn't take my eyes off Andrey either, who didn't seem to have noticed and was chatting easily to Gulnar and Gregory.

Then he said, 'What strange countryside you've got! It's quite a surprise to someone who's just come from Russia. I've never seen such luxuriant vines, such a blue sea, so much sand. And if I'm right, this rock is your island?'

He wasn't smiling and seemed to be elsewhere.

'Yes,' I replied abruptly, though the question had not been addressed to me. 'It's our island—it's our kingdom and we are its princesses. And you, you are Prince Andrey, Prince Andrey Bolkonsky.'

Andrey Massarin paid attention to me for the first time.

'Don't take any notice of my cousin,' Gulnar said. 'She's always talking nonsense.'

Laughing, Gregory said, 'I think that's one too many titles for someone who wants to be a communist.'

My prince still wasn't smiling. 'Do you think you're Natasha?' he asked.

'No,' I cried passionately. 'I would never have betrayed you.'

I immediately flushed scarlet. Gulnar and Gregory burst out laughing. The blush would not go and I wanted to die of shame. Then Andrey smiled—a smile that was as tender as it was unexpected. He bent towards me, took my hand and kissed it twice, gently. Then he turned back to Gregory and they started talking politics.

He stayed only a few hours in the country. The car that had brought him took him away towards evening and I was left alone with his image in my mind. 'Oh, God, make me die if I cannot see him again!' I repeated this prayer all day long; he had only just appeared miraculously—was I to lose him so soon? The chance of seeing him again was minimal. Where? How? When Gregory had gone, the only possible connection between us would disappear too. I loved him regardless; I wanted to love; I gave in to my love with all the enthusiasm of my being, without a thought for the morrow. I blessed the goodness of the heavens for leaving me in the Caucasus. My only interest in geography now was in the place where Andrey was; I would have preferred a village lost in the frozen forests of Siberia to Paris, if Andrey were there.

I became devilishly skilful at directing the conversation, so that Gregory was bound to talk to me about his friend. He was happy to do so, as what he felt for Andrey was more than friendship—it was admiration. One day I said as much and Gregory agreed.

'Yes, I do admire him. Men are like objects, made of either precious or lowly materials. I don't think there's any base metal in Andrey's make-up: he is all nobility, lofty ideals and courage. When we fought side by side to take Kronstadt, his indifference to danger was inspiring and I took courage from it too. The lack of food, the cold, the pain, nothing disturbed his composure. He keeps a grip on his mind, as though it were a malleable object. It's wonderful when you think he's only twenty-five!'

I was intoxicated by these eulogies.

We were devastated by Gregory's departure. The day before the separation we spent all afternoon on the rock and returned in the evening after dinner. When night fell, we were still there beneath the vast, star-studded sky, and I knew without seeing them in the darkness and the silence that Gulnar and Gregory were in one another's arms. It was an easy transposition to see Andrey and me in their place, his black uniform blending into the night and my white dress looking like a great white bird perched on the rock. We would embrace until we had no strength left, after which nothing would matter any more.

4

We returned to the city on 1st September, when the weather was hotter than ever. Our departure was coloured by considerable sadness: we were all more or less certain that we had lost our estate for good.

We had to find somewhere to live in the city as best we could. Our house had been permanently requisitioned, but Aunt Rena had managed to keep two rooms on the top floor, the rest of which was occupied by a military band, and took me in. We ate, got up and went to bed, all to the accompaniment of music produced by dozens of wind instruments, each playing as it saw fit. The result was a tremendous din, a circus cacophony that filled every moment and was impossible to escape. Only my blessedly deaf uncle could cope, much to the annoyance of my aunt. Highly strung at the best of times, Aunt Rena now became alarmingly so; everything was liable to irritate her, but her husband remained the scapegoat of choice. He exasperated her so much that she openly wished he had been arrested.

'It's too bad,' she cried at the top of her voice to make herself heard. 'Most wives can enjoy peace and quiet today with their husbands in prison. I'm the only one unlucky enough to have to put up with you. No,' she would sigh loudly to make sure it was noticed, 'I've never had any luck.'

As for my uncle, he would shrug disdainfully, his hand still cupped behind his ear, and shout in the manner of deaf people, 'You've never had any brains.'

On the fallacious pretext that I was an orphan in need of protection, Aunt Rena made me sleep in her husband's bed, while he was relegated to a small couch, which was too short for him, in the second room. In the morning we would find the poor man on his Procrustean bed, his feet dangling off the end, his mouth open and snoring with a near grandiose power; he could even drown out the discordant music of the musician soldiers. Faced with this graceless spectacle, Aunt Rena cried, 'My poor girl, if I can give you one piece of advice, it is never to marry. A husband will annoy you during the day, bother you at night, demand everything and give nothing. That one hasn't even managed to give me a child and God knows, he has worn me out with his demands.'

I didn't believe a word: Andrey Massarin would never annoy me; he would never snore, his mouth inelegantly open; he could only light up the life of the woman at his side. But I didn't argue.

Since her husband irritated her, Aunt Rena liked to irritate him back. She had found a simple but effective way of doing it: she would talk and not shout so that my poor uncle could not hear anything. He would strain to pick something up, desperately trying to read her lips, but all he could make out were fragments of words.

'What did you say? What did you say?' he would yell, infuriated. Then Aunt Rena would nod towards the door that separated us from the rooms where the soldiers lived and put a finger on her lips. My uncle would be left guessing, eaten away by thwarted curiosity.

I loved Aunt Rena very much, perhaps because she had always been good to me. But I also loved her generosity, her grumpy kindness, her broadmindedness, her touching desire for culture, her dissatisfaction that kept her from the mindlessness into which inferior creatures easily sink. I even loved her tics, her sharp tongue, her malicious gossip, her passion for cards. Unable to sleep, we would often talk all night, lying side by side. My uncle would be snoring in the next room, the soldiers blowing into their instruments and the eternal winds of Baku, or Ba-de-Kuba,* replying in the chimney. Without the benefit of opportune deafness and both suffering from persistent insomnia, we would chat in the darkness, sometimes until dawn.

We were filthier than pigs. There were problems with the city's water supply during the intense heat of early autumn, problems that no one seemed able to fix. We bought drinking water from water vendors who walked the streets crying hoarsely in Russian and Azeri, 'Water, water. *Su, su.*'

Water was measured by the glass in this parched land, and there was no question of having a wash while the water supply and sewerage systems were out of action. We lived in filth and grime, waiting for them to be repaired; we were spared nothing, not even lice. I still remember my shudder of disgust when I found a particularly fine specimen in my comb for the first time. I shuddered at the sight of my first louse, but was indifferent to the sight of my hundredth.

There was a stench too. The musician soldiers had put buckets in their rooms, which they rarely emptied, and even more rarely washed for lack of water. They gave off a powerful smell that pervaded the whole apartment—no, the whole house; right from the foot of the stairs you were caught up in this swirl of smells, rising, falling, permeating everything and mingling with the sound of the brass instruments. I remember this as a colourful time amid the smell, the music and the filth. Difficult though it was, I don't resent it: it taught me resignation.

Thank God, we did not suffer hunger. The Caucasus was a land of plenty where one could find practically everything. Generously

---

* Ba-de-Kuba means 'City of Winds' in Persian.

blessed with natural resources, it continued to produce abundantly, and since chaos in the transport system made exports impossible, goods stayed where they were, creating a surfeit, while in many parts of Russia people were suffering from famine. Life was, therefore, much easier in the Caucasus than in the rest of Russia. So much easier that even vodka remained on sale, something forbidden elsewhere. There was no lack of hardy souls willing to go to Moscow to sell the precious liquid at a premium; they risked prison or worse, but if the trip were a success, they would come back rich.

My sister Leyla had a servant, Catherine, who regularly made this heroic journey in trains so crowded that no one knew if, how or when they would reach their destination. The smugglers had a method of choice, which the providentially skeletal Catherine was ideally placed to make use of. Aluminium containers, mimicking the various curves of the body, were attached to the smuggler's person and filled with vodka; surrounded by these liquid fortifications, they sallied forth to conquer the world. Being extremely thin, Catherine could carry several litres of vodka, which allowed her to make an outrageous profit. She brought this back to Leyla to spend on her son, whom the good woman had always loved fiercely and passionately, and for whom she was prepared to do anything.

I had been in the city for a week, when prison visiting-day came round. The prison was a long way away, in the oil-producing district of Bibi Heybat at the gates to the city, which like all oil-producing districts was a bleak, smoke-filled place where neither trees nor grass grew. On a stiflingly hot afternoon, Leyla and I made our way there; Leyla carried a large saucepan full of a delicious mutton stew, while I was laden with packages. First we had to take the *konka*, a tram pulled by two wretched nags, the only means of transport in this city of millionaires. Sensitive souls got off the tram sick at heart; it was terribly sad to see those two undernourished horses, ribs about to break through their skin, drag the tram, which was always packed to the running boards. The driver beat them constantly, and it was only those ferocious blows that kept the poor creatures pulling their burden of scrap iron and humanity.

The prison was several kilometres from the *konka*'s terminus. The road edged the sea, without any shade to protect it from the final heat of the year, which was putting in a last hurrah before disappearing until spring.

On the other side of the road grey derricks rose awkwardly towards the sky. We had driven this road across Bibi Heybat hundreds of times by car, as we left the city and entered the countryside, barren desert like all the environs of Baku but at least lapped by the sea. As we walked that road now to go and see my father in prison, I pictured all those past excursions, and my heartache, amplified by the physical discomfort of the excessive heat, grew with every step. The only remedy I found was daydreaming. I could no longer hear Leyla complaining about her husband and the heat and the revolution; from time to time I made an indeterminate sound to give the impression I was listening, allowing me to dream in peace. Prince Andrey was in Baku; maybe at this very moment he was, like me, looking at the sea; chance might lead him along the same road as me; he was suffering from the heat, like me; it united us, just as my thoughts did.

After an hour's walk, we were at last in the prison courtyard, already full of visitors. We had to wait a long time. Accustomed to oriental resignation, we patiently baked beneath the ferocious sun, fighting a losing battle against the crowd of flies attracted by the smell of our provisions. When we had been waiting for an hour a soldier appeared, who began to call us in alphabetical order. I should remark in passing that it is unfair luck (as is all luck), and invaluable, to have a surname beginning with the first letter of the alphabet, as is mine. How much waiting time is cut short as a result! And I was first to put the stew and everything else into military hands. After this event, we were entitled to another wait in another courtyard, which was also full of visitors. This wait was a long one. Then a soldier came and led us to a third courtyard, divided in two by a grille, behind which I saw my father gripping the bars, my father dressed in prison rags, my father, his frame skeletal and his beard thick. He held out his thin brown hands through the bars. I covered them in kisses, sobbing, sick with pity for him.

'Don't cry,' he said, 'you can see I'm not so badly off.'

I couldn't reply because of my tears, but his words cut me to the quick. Thin, dirty and in prison, my father did not think he was badly off; to me this resignation held far more pathos than any complaint.

A vivid memory has stayed with me from this period of painful prison visits, which shows how a seemingly trivial gesture can bring happiness and light up the darkness.

One day I came back exhausted from a prison visit. It was freezing cold and snow, a rarity for Baku, covered the pavements where my poorly shod feet (even our personal effects had been confiscated) slipped in the slush.

Once I got home, incapable even of speech or complaint, I fell onto my bed, hoping to sleep and forget the sadness of the prison, our precarious existence, our fall. But the cold of the poorly heated room stopped me sinking into dreams. I curled up on myself, a block of ice, shivering from exhaustion. And suddenly a miracle: a quilt fell onto me, bringing me warmth and release; it was heaven and I fell asleep. I will never forget the feeling of well-being descending from above that this compassionate gesture brought me. Dear Aunt Rena had understood my distress, physical and moral.

5

Gulnar's family were back from Turkestan. My cousin was overjoyed, not so much at their reunion but because their return allowed her to get married at last.

'Virginity is weighing me down,' she declared to me one day. 'When I think that some women carry that burden all their lives! Look at Fräulein Anna.' She plunged into theological considerations: 'It's ridiculous. If Allah gave us sex organs, it wasn't to let them get dried up and covered in cobwebs—it was to use them. If I were the Creator, I'd be angry if people didn't enjoy the pleasures I'd been good enough to give them.'

Her father's house had been requisitioned, like all the former oilmen's grand, and not so grand, residences. The seven members of the family had to settle for lodgings in two small rooms in a modest house on the edge of the city. They immediately turned the tiny apartment into a chaos of clutter, a turbulent parliament. This madhouse was dominated by my uncle, whose aristocratic stature and hawkish demeanour did not reflect his nature at all.

'Me, I couldn't give a damn about breeding or refinement; what matters to me is money,' he liked to say, rubbing thumb against forefinger.

His family had always been uncouth, given to untidiness and fisticuffs, but this had been less evident when they were spread out in a large, well-appointed house full of servants. Now in a confined space, deprived of domestic staff and decorum, the family showed itself in all its primitive splendour. The father and mother quarrelled all day long; the five children quarrelled with their mother and with one another. The shouting, slapping and swearing only came to an end at night when it was replaced by the snoring of half the family. Once, I had to spend the night with them and couldn't sleep. That said, it didn't take much to give me insomnia.

Gulnar's fiancé Selim came every day. Uncommonly shy, he felt that to sit in her presence was too bold for him, and he consented to do so only after numerous invitations. He would perch on the edge of a chair in the corner and observe with gentle admiration the actions, words and gestures of his terrible in-laws, whom he considered remarkable, lovable and distinguished in every respect. For Gulnar he felt only humble adoration. He hung on her every word, devoured her with his gaze and ascribed to her qualities she did not possess.

Although he looked like my uncle, he was his opposite in character; that is to say, his appearance was off-putting, coarse, almost brutal, while his soul was the most delicate imaginable. He wept when he heard of another's misfortunes, paled at the sight of blood and rushed to everybody's aid. Should someone in his presence allude to financial difficulties, he would immediately offer assistance. The four brothers were aware of this trait and the two older ones in particular did not hesitate to empty his wallet on various pretexts. This did not last long, however; nobody's fool, despite her young age, Gulnar took control of her fiancé's finances, protecting them from the depredations of her own family. Attacks on his wallet were not the only kind Selim had to put up with: he also faced assaults of a far more unusual nature. I have already said that pederasty flourished in Islamic society in Baku; many men were 'one of them', to use the expression of Baron de Charlus, though that didn't mean they despised women. Put simply, they could be said to be bisexual. Gulnar's twin brothers Asad and Ali, who were one year younger than her and very beautiful, knew how to make use of this to sweeten their material existence. So when they saw Selim's sudden reluctance to lend them money, they did not hesitate to use all their charms to seduce him—once Gulnar's back was turned, that is. But the trick did not escape the perceptive fiancée and she went to complain to her parents, spitting venom. I had the extraordinary luck to arrive right in the middle of the drama, finding Asad and Ali both slumped on chairs, flushed and dishevelled, their collars and ties torn. Uncle Suleyman went from one to the other, slapping them, shaking them by the shoulder and heaping abuse on them. The guilty parties eventually began to cry hot tears; the mother sobbed in compassion, and the two younger brothers followed suit. Gulnar observed the scene coldly, clearly satisfied with the result.

'Everyone does wrong in their youth,' Uncle Suleyman shouted hoarsely, 'but trying to seduce Selim, your sister's fiancé…'

'Yes, *my* fiancé,' Gulnar chipped in.

'And what for?' Uncle Suleyman continued. 'To cadge money off him?'

'Yes, to cadge money off him, *my* fiancé. No one's rolling in money any more after all that's happened.'

Another slap, a barrage of sobs in reply. Gulnar persisted: 'And the two of them were seducing him! The two of them together! That's how they do everything, hand in hand. I wonder what they would have done to him, poor Selim, whom even a little child could abuse.'

This time she was the one to receive a slap.

'Shut up, you little snake! A bit more decency wouldn't hurt you,' yelled Uncle Suleyman. 'You shouldn't know about such things at your age.'

Gulnar angrily shrugged her shoulders, but kept quiet. A flash of contentment lit up Asad and Ali's mournful eyes, but it was fleeting, as a fresh round of slaps rained down on them, leaving them gasping for breath. Between sobs they cast looks of hatred that seemed to say, 'Just you wait. You'll see.' But nothing frightened Gulnar, and nothing got in her way either. She wore down her parents with her brazen insistence she get married as soon as possible, and they agreed to celebrate her wedding one month after the family's return from Turkestan. 'Celebrate' is too strong a word: the hard times ruled out any festivities and a richer pilaff than usual for the relatives was all that followed the Islamic marriage contract, instituted under *Shariat*.*

This contract is simplicity itself: in the presence of the husband, the woman's father or guardian and the witnesses, the mullah draws up a legal document under which Mr X marries Miss Y and undertakes to pay her a dower if he should disown her. And that's it: the marriage has been contracted. Gulnar acquired the right to lead Selim by the scruff of the neck to their new home, three minuscule rooms that constituted one floor of a minuscule house in old Baku.

Once there, she instituted an authoritarian regime that brooked not even the faintest opposition. Selim never questioned her decrees and agreed in advance to all her whims, without even knowing what they were. Gulnar was delighted: with her house, with Selim, with the act of love. No, she had definitely not been sold a dud.

'That's the kind you want to choose—tender, weak, in love…' She talked about husbands as though they were chickens for sale at the market, 'Oh,' she continued, rolling her eyes, 'if only you knew how good it is to make love. All that fuss is no exaggeration. But it's much more tiring than I expected. I hope you'll get to do it soon too. How's it going with Jamil?'

---

* This is the way we referred to sharia in Azeri.

Now is the time to talk about Jamil, whom I should have introduced a long time ago; I avoided doing so because I find it so unpleasant.

Jamil was one of the many suitors spurned by my older sisters. Since we got back from the country, he had been working to secure my father's release. He was making a meal of it, clearly trying to please my family, and me in particular, now that I was a marriage prospect. Two sisters had rejected him, but the third might accept him, especially out of gratitude.

I loathed Jamil and found him repulsive. Was he really? He was medium height, had a good figure and took care of his appearance, aiming for an elegant look, which he carried off to some extent. I disliked everything about him from head to toe: his red hair, which was rare in the Caucasus and viewed with suspicion; his thick eyebrows above his malicious little eyes (had I been in love with him, I would certainly have found them intelligent); his unusually long nose; his mouth and the grating voice that came out of it (a wooden wheel climbing a hard rock).

He talked a lot with a profusion of gestures; he always had a great deal to say, as he was beset by excessive intellectual pretensions. He belonged to the group of Baku's brilliant young men who were almost this or almost that; he was 'almost' an engineer. He had studied in Liège for several years but not graduated. He returned equipped with some knowledge of the French language, and a Belgian mistress with whom he cohabited for several years, gaining himself in the process a reputation for perversity.

Jamil's fortune was modest on the scale of Baku millionaires; nonetheless, it allowed him to live a life of idleness and to devote himself to the favourite pastime of all Baku men—gambling.

One of Jamil's worst traits was his constant striving to be witty. Unfortunately one cannot display wit if one has none—and Jamil had none. He persisted though, even when he saw that his efforts had no effect—nothing discouraged him and he would always keep trying. He couldn't possibly be wrong! After all, it was only his audience that suffered from his failures—he never did.

As Jamil began to court me more openly—a direct result of his impending success in securing the release of my father—my revulsion for him only grew stronger. Did Jamil notice my antipathy? I answered him only reluctantly, hardly smiled at his supposed witticisms and during his visits my glum demeanour brightened only when he was about to leave.

He came to see us regularly to keep us up to date with his initiatives; he was very optimistic, thanks to the intervention of a friend who was an important commissar. My anxiety grew alongside Jamil's happiness. Though it tormented me, I came almost to fear my father's release, as it now coincided in my mind with the marriage request that would automatically follow.

I have said that I found Jamil repulsive in the extreme, and disliked both his attitude and his physique. His red hair was a major part of the problem. We attributed evil powers to this uncommon colour and it had become the stuff of legend. I had been especially affected by one of these tales, told one night by Grandmother. She said that in the olden days, hundreds of years ago, many redheads were born in a Persian village. All the families with a redheaded child suffered misfortune, which was soon attributed to the birth of these strangely coloured children. The redheads were thought to exert a malign influence and were blamed for everything that went wrong; they faced distrust and even revulsion from their own families. No one doubted their mysterious powers, their contact with the other world and their malevolent aura.

An alchemist pondered this problem for many years until fate brought to his attention an old parchment of Egyptian origin and the scales fell from his eyes. After that, the redheads began to disappear one after the other. It wasn't until the old alchemist's death that people learnt the truth from his own manuscript. 'Take a redhead and cut off his head,' the manuscript began. 'Then make incantations over it for several days, read verses from the Koran and recite magic spells.' Then the alchemist boiled the head for a long time in a cauldron with herbs and various other ingredients. After that, he placed the head on a specially prepared board and waited... If the operation failed, the head would rot; if, on the other hand, the operation was a success, the head would begin to talk of the other world, of the past and the future. The alchemist had painstakingly noted down all that the heads of his many 'patients' had told him; and all their prophecies were proved right.

In no time at all there wasn't a single redhead left in the province, so the heads fetched fabulous prices, as everyone wanted to have this fascinating experience for themselves.

Whenever I looked at Jamil, I imagined his boiled, bloodless head, eyes closed, talking about the other world, and I would be overcome with a terrible nausea. Oblivious to his effect on me, Jamil would continue his courting and his witticisms, all the while gesticulating wildly. I shuddered to think of myself in the same bed as him; my fertile imagination coupled with my knowledge of erotica painted scenes that filled me with disgust. Only by dreaming of Andrey, of Prince Andrey, could I escape these depressing images.

6

It wasn't difficult to spread communist propaganda in Baku. Although it was one of the richest cities in the world, it had no public transport, no sewers or rubbish dump. The workers lived in filthy hovels, were paid a pittance and had no recourse against the rich. The story went that my Grandfather Musa one day received a petition from his workers, demanding soap, a wage increase and more humane treatment. 'Grant them humane treatment,' he decided. There was a flagrant imbalance between the wealth of Baku's richer inhabitants and the poverty of the majority. The communists' first act when they came to power was to build an electric tramway in record time. It was bright red, as a child born of the revolution should be, and its lights shone at night. During the first few days of this apparition's arrival the populace would come out just to admire it. Other initiatives followed.

The communists set up institutions to educate veiled women. They knew that, once touched by the graces of a new civilization, these women would themselves cast off the ancestral veil, which was so clearly out of place in a Soviet republic. One such institution they founded was the National Conservatoire for Muslim Women, where my oppressed sisters received their initiation into dancing, singing and music.

One day I received a letter from the headmistress of this nascent institution, asking me to come and see her 'on important business'. I was very surprised, but responded promptly, presenting myself at the appointed hour and day at the house of a former oil baron, which now served as the conservatoire. The headmistress was waiting for me.

Zeynab Khanim was a singular person, whom I had already heard a lot about and wanted to meet. She was an educated Muslim and very musical. Her bad behaviour had always shocked the whole of Baku Islamic society, who considered her a prostitute and her husband a pimp. Unconcerned by this gossip, they continued their bohemian lives, he phlegmatic and easy-going, she wild and full of life. Striking, with a large sensual mouth and big round eyes, she wasn't pretty, but she was something better—seductive.

She fell on me as though I were her only hope (I learnt later that most of her letters had gone unanswered) and set out the situation.

'You see, it's marvellous to set up a conservatoire for Muslim women,' she told me, 'but one still has to find female teachers who are musical and know our language to boot. The vast majority of our pupils will be girls who wear the veil and speak only Azeri—in a word, backward' (she gave a scornful shrug) 'and this creates particular conditions. We need teachers like you. Oh, I know what you're going to say...' (she raised her hand to stop the words I had no intention of saying) 'that you're too young, that you won't be able to teach, that you're not musical enough. But I know what I want and I insist that you consider my offer. If you accept, you'll not only get a rewarding job, you will also be doing good work.'

I nervously asked what reward my position might bring.

'Well, you will receive six hundred million roubles a month and every week you will get various foodstuffs: sugar, dried fruit, and so on, depending on what we are allocated.'

I decided to accept, not so much for the foodstuffs and the six hundred million, which did not have a great deal of purchasing power, as to escape the idleness that weighed heavy on me; I was happy to have something to do, and what I was being offered seemed useful and potentially enjoyable. The headmistress beamed.

'This is wonderful,' she cried. 'You're the first person to accept, which will bring you luck.'

We talked some more about the practicalities of my future employment and agreed that I would begin on the first day of the following month.

Under the leadership of Zeynab Khanim, the most unconventional woman of my acquaintance, Baku's National Conservatoire for Muslim Women became a quixotic, inefficient and pleasant institution. Organization was haphazard, improvisation was the order of the day by the grace of Allah, and it was all unexpected, charming and cheerful in the image of the headmistress herself.

Having been promoted to teacher in defiance of common sense, I wondered anxiously how I would teach these young girls the principles of music; they were all from the working classes and did not know Russian, the language in which I had learnt these principles. Incapable of translating into Azeri what I knew of the mysteries of the piano, I gave up on theory and went straight into practice. I played a scale and told my poor pupils to do the same, without explanation. The black keys served as their reference points. These poor girls were both willing and talented and to my great delight were soon playing numerous scales with enthusiasm. My teaching method, which could be described as empirical, was working. In my naivety I imagined that when my pupils knew enough scales and arpeggios, I would be able to explain to them—by what mysterious method?—the correspondence between the sounds made by the piano and the small black symbols on the music paper.

My patience did not always match my educational standards,

alas. Sometimes a lack of self-control, typical of my young age, led to outbursts of swearing, of which I possessed an infinite and varied repertoire, thanks to my grandmother. I must have seemed formidable to my pupils, who were often much older than me, as I was inundated with presents; I would pretend to be offended as I received them, making the girls plead with me before I eventually accepted the gifts with an air of martyrdom. I found this childish charade very convenient and made constant use of it to protect my pride. So a rich harvest of good things rained down on me, the chosen one: sometimes an apple, sometimes cubes of precious sugar wrapped up in newspaper for want of anything else, sometimes smoked fish or biscuits.

Occasionally I came to work in an unsettled mood, wanting to do anything but teach; I would say as much to Zeynab Khanim, who promptly told me to send the pupils away until later in the day. Then she would take me to her apartment on the top floor of the house and we would make tea, chat and play piano duets. Her husband would often join us; he was a plump, easy-going man whose calm temperament was diametrically opposed to Zeynab Khanim's fiery character. Other men came too, a lot of other men, who all courted his wife, some more intently than others. During this time the Azerbaijani National Conservatoire for Muslim Women limped along; the teachers did what they wanted, the pupils too, and all was for the worst and the best in the worst and the best of all possible worlds.

One morning when I arrived at the Conservatoire to practise my profession, I found Zeynab Khanim dishevelled, excited, enthused and flushed. Not without reason: the ANCMW was to receive a visit from the Commissar for Public Education and several other dignitaries. They wanted to hear and see at first hand the state of artistic education for Muslim women, who had until then been nourished on opium, that is to say, religion.

Zeynab Khanim was ecstatic: 'What an honour, what a great honour! We must be worthy of it. Come with me...'

She took me up to her apartment, where with the help of her husband and another teacher we drew up a battle plan: we had to win the commissar's heart.

First of all, workmen were hastily summoned to build a stage in the large rehearsal hall, so all day long the knocking of hammers merged with the pupils' not always pleasant music-making. The girls were reviewed by Zeynab Khanim, who chose the best to perform pieces calculated to charm the visitors. They rehearsed zealously all week. When the big day arrived, the desired effect had been achieved and the hall had an undeniably festive air. The bust of the grandfather of communism, Karl Marx (whom I irreverently called Marl Karx when I was feeling cheerful) reigned from a pedestal; he was flanked by the busts of Lenin, Karl Liebknecht and Rosa Luxemburg, all placed on lower tables. They were almost invisible under an avalanche of coloured paper garlands, which were looped from one bust to the next, bringing them all together into a rather touching group. Red flags decorated the walls, which were lined by a forest of wilting potted palm trees. A concert piano stood on the just-finished stage, decorated with magnificent carpets requisitioned for the occasion. When the dignitaries arrived, I was to welcome them by playing 'The Internationale' on this piano.

We waited; the pupils, most of them veiled, formed a group on one side of the hall; the headmistress and the teachers were on the lookout at the windows and my good self was at the piano. Beneath the busts of the doyens of communism, the golden chairs, upholstered in red velvet, waited with us. We held our breath the better to hear the sounds that would herald the visit. At last we heard cars stopping outside the house. Making little cries of panic, Zeynab Khanim charged down the stairs at a prodigious speed; a few moments later, the dignitaries entered the hall and I attacked the anthem of the Third International with all the vigour my feeble hands could muster. When I had finished, I got up, casting a curious, hesitant glance at the visitors sitting in the red plush chairs; my heart missed a beat and I couldn't breathe... Prince Andrey was there, sitting to the left of the commissar. Panic-stricken, I rushed towards the group of pupils and went as close to the back as possible.

The programme designed to win the commissar's heart had begun; the pupils sang, danced and played on the carpeted stage. But I had eyes only for Prince Andrey, who was sitting comfortably in his chair and watching the show, his serious expression occasionally tempered by a shadow of irony. Happy to have found him, I was already upset at the thought of losing him again so soon. Chance had brought him here, while destiny would nullify the effect! I was horrified to think that Andrey would soon see me on stage again, where I was to play the last item in the programme, a bravura piece. Would he recognize me? I had spent two hours with him on the rock in the vineyard, when he had hardly looked at me and spoken all of two words to me. What would he remember of a dull young girl, only just fourteen? I looked at my reflection in a mirror opposite and found myself ugly, but especially young, horribly, desperately young. How could I hope that a man of twenty-five, a hero, a member of the revolutionary committee, would pay me the slightest attention? I abandoned all hope, indulging myself in absolute, sorrowful admiration for the black knight. Yes, Andrey Massarin was still wearing his black uniform, which distinguished him even more from the civilians around him.

The pupils worked their way through the programme. I was aware of the passing of time, bringing closer the moment when I would climb on stage. I was horrified all over again, but at the same time ecstatic that Andrey would see me.

My turn came to go on stage. When embarrassment reaches a certain point, it feels like drunkenness; I thought I was staggering and could see double, while bells were ringing in my ears. I managed to climb onto the stage and settle myself on the stool. I was to play Liszt's arrangement of Verdi's *Rigoletto*. While the musical merit of the piece is debatable, it does have an impressive number of notes and distance to cover on the piano in a minimum of time. I played the first chord and the others followed of their own volition, emerging as if by a miracle from my damp, trembling hands. I watched them as though they were not part of me, thinking they could carry on or stop as they wished. But the gods of music guided them, and quivering jelly though they were, they continued to do their job. My fingers raced along at the speed required by Liszt, so well that at a particularly lively moment in my playing, the Commissar for Public Education inclined towards Zeynab Khanim, who was sitting next to him, and said with admiration, from the bottom of his commissar's heart, 'How well she plays! From one end of the keyboard to the other! So quickly and without stopping!'

I reached the final note without mishap, to my great relief and to the satisfaction of the entire conservatoire and of the commissar, who wanted to express it to me personally. Zeynab Khanim took me by the hand and led me to his group. Then I noticed that the commissar had only one eye. While he expressed the hope that I would become a great artiste to the glory of our country, his single eye looked kindly at me. But I couldn't properly hear what he was saying, nor see very well either; it wasn't the commissar whom my eyes were beholding but Andrey, though I wasn't looking at him. Then I heard, 'Hello, Miss Natasha.'

'What do you mean, Miss Natasha?' Zeynab Khanim asked in astonishment.

'We understand one another, don't we, Miss Natasha?'

'Yes,' I said, turning white as a sheet, then bright red, feeling foolish and happy.

I thought him more handsome than in all my dreams. His dry, vigorous face, serious when he stopped being ironic, was even better in reality because it was full of life—intelligent, active, virile life; the life of a man, of a real man, with all his responsibilities, his essential courage, his aura of heroism. I thought of Jamil and the possibility of becoming his wife, and I gave Andrey a smile of gratitude for illustrating so beautifully what I wanted from my dreams.

Since the ceremony had gone well, Zeynab Khanim's complexion had regained its natural colour and the atmosphere became calmer. She led the commissar and his entourage to the dining room where the pupils were serving tea. With her infallible instinct for matters of the heart, Zeynab Khanim unerringly sat me next to Andrey.

'So, you have left the countryside?' he asked. 'Where is Gulnar, the ravishing Gulnar? Do you know that Gregory talks about her in all his letters to me? He is in love with her, very deeply I think.'

I told him that she was married to a good man and seemed happy.

'I would be glad to see you both. Do you think your social mores as they are in their current state would let you come and see me?' He gave a mocking smile. 'It would give me pleasure, great pleasure.'

He looked steadily at me. Feeling sillier than a goose and dumber than a cow, I lowered my gaze and stammered something that had neither sense nor ending.

'I can see you're shy. You're still at the age to play with dolls really.'

Pride made me forget my shyness: 'I've never liked playing with dolls. And I'll be getting married this year.'

'And that makes you proud and happy?'

I didn't answer, and Andrey said, 'In case you decide to come and see me, on your own or with Gulnar, I live at Number 14, Pushkin Street, and my telephone number is 31-34. Can you remember that?'

'You live at 14 Pushkin Street? Definitely Number 14?'

'Yes—is it really so extraordinary to live at 14 Pushkin Street?'

'Yes, it is to me. It's my childhood home. That's where I learnt to walk, to talk, to play the piano and to read.'

'Really? That is funny,' Andrey said, 'but you know I don't believe in omens. Anyway, this coincidence should persuade you to come and see me. Would you like to?'

He smiled without any hint of irony and a different man was before me. I thought I could read interest in his eyes; but I knew the power of my imagination and did not trust my impressions. False though they may have been, they nonetheless enabled me to overcome my shyness, and I began to talk intelligibly at last. Yes, I told Andrey, I would come and see him, preferably with Gulnar.

'You're afraid to go alone to visit a man, a member of the revolutionary committee at that. Brr!' He pretended to shudder.

'I know Gulnar will agree to come with me, but we might not be able to manage it in the next few days.'

'Tell her I live with a charming friend who loves to flirt with women. If my memory serves me right, this argument will sway her decision.'

Tea flowed freely and, nonsensical though it may seem, intoxicated the guests, who became more and more voluble. Eventually the commissar rose with the clear intention of proposing a toast, gesturing as though to raise his teacup like a champagne glass. However, he stopped himself just in time, going on to deliver a speech liberally punctuated with the word hope—a sentiment the commissar seemed to cherish—and with verbs in the future tense: 'We will sow, we will build, we will create, we will harvest…'

7

A harsh winter looked set to echo the harsh political climate. The wind, which regularly swept through Baku's streets in all directions, brought such low temperatures from the north that one morning the city woke up under a rare blanket of snow. Sad, heavy clouds crawled across a lightless sky. In our unheated rooms we shivered to the discordant accompaniment of the military band.

I took food to the prison twice a week, but I saw my father only twice a month. Though he had aged and lost weight, he did not seem miserable, as he was optimistic that Jamil's efforts would soon secure his release. Jamil bustled about me more than ever, filling me with bleak despair. Every time I saw my father, he never missed the opportunity to talk about the 'good lad's' efforts and praise his devotion, intelligence and tenacity. I understood all too well what lay behind his words. Aunt Rena and her husband had plenty to say in the same vein, while Gulnar too encouraged me to see Jamil as my future husband. She had another reason for wanting the marriage, which I will talk about a little later. But first I would like to emphasize that all these desires converged to weaken my own, which already tended to buckle under general pressure. Despite my European education, despite reading so many novels, despite the proximity of Bolshevism and its marital liberalism, I was still convinced in the depths of my being that one 'does not choose one's husband'. Too many, if not all, of my female forebears had been married without their own desires playing the slightest role. All these submissions weighed me down with an immaterial, but nonetheless heavy, burden. So, despite my revulsion for Jamil, despite my admiration for Andrey, I knew I would do what my family would push me to do. I put up with all the nonsense Jamil spouted in his nasal voice. I now thought he bore a striking resemblance to an earthworm: he had the worm's rare agility—supple but graceless. As he squirmed and wriggled around me, I found him slippery, soft and revolting, just like a worm. In resignation I put up with him.

My Uncle Suleyman had long cherished the idea of a marriage between Asad and me. Gulnar would have none of it. She detested Asad and claimed to love me.

'I don't want you to marry him,' she explained to me one day. 'Asad's a nasty piece of work. He'll only make you unhappy. And between you and me, he loves boys more. I'm not saying he couldn't give you a child, but where's the interest in that? He'll make love to you once a month and will continue to beat you up as he's always done. He'll be rude and mean. Make no mistake, it would be madness to marry such an obnoxious boy. I don't want it to happen.'

So when Jamil's candidacy was presented, she seized on it with alacrity. Not because she liked Jamil very much—she thought him boring and pretentious—but he was the first suitor to appear on the scene and she thought any man would do to counter the threat of Asad. Gulnar was so afraid of this marriage and so wary of any influence that might thwart her designs that she decided I should move in with her.

When my cousin wanted something, few people could stand in her way. After several discussions that she already knew were pointless, Aunt Rena sadly let me go and I moved in with the young household, where the atmosphere suited me much better than at my uncle and aunt's.

It was a strange place, the old city—inserted within the walls of the former fortress on a hillside sloping down towards the Caspian. The castle of the former khans of Baku rose in state in the middle, with ancient flat-roofed houses crowding round it. Every so often they made way for a mosque, of which there were many within the crenellated walls, and the revolution—at least in the early days—left their life unchanged; the muezzins continued to call the faithful from atop the minarets, while the faithful continued to worship Allah and his Prophet in the mosques.

When I moved to the old citadel, I felt for the first time that I was living in an Islamic city. The narrow, winding streets where only donkeys or camels could pass, the vast majority of women wearing the veil, the scruffy urchins playing jacks and swearing in the small squares under the shade of a stunted acacia tree: all contributed to this sense of the orient that was missing in modern Baku, with its new houses in the worst possible taste, its motor cars and its cinemas. It took the revolution and ensuing expropriations to bring many of the former oil barons into this neglected city, as it was easier for them to find lodgings here than elsewhere. Before these events the old city's sole inhabitants had been the indigenous, indigent population, for whom we had felt only haughty condescension. Now the tables were turned and the once-neglected city welcomed us, plunging us into the ancestral atmosphere that fortune had helped us escape. There was irony in this return to the cradle of our forebears—though we had repudiated them, they welcomed us in these times of political upheaval.

I liked living in the old city, Islamic through and through: I found its atmosphere comforting and safe. The very air you breathed whispered at every step, 'Only Allah is eternal,' 'Only Allah is wise, trust in him,' 'Nothing happens without the will of Allah.' Those of a peaceable disposition felt calmed and soothed into submission and indifference. It was reassuring to listen to the call of the muezzins, while you felt outside time watching the veiled women walk by. You might say that this is all just the author's fancy and that the reality elsewhere was just as frightening despite the muezzins, despite the old flat-roofed houses. Yes, that's true, but the illusion created by the backdrop of days gone by offered moments of remission.

I was delighted too to be back with Gulnar. We were bound by a thousand and one childhood ties, some more respectable than others. She was so vivacious, so absolutely amoral that it was beyond discussion and therefore no longer cause for concern, and so imaginative that she was a charming companion. She was perhaps slightly too self-willed, but I gave in to her with good grace, being myself still slightly childish.

Always an early riser, I would go to wake the married couple, whose capacity for sleep was limitless and who wouldn't open their eyes before midday without my ministrations. I would sit at the foot of the bed, while Gulnar, half-asleep, would recount to me the previous night's erotic exploits. With cries of horror Selim would hide his face in the pillows and pull the blankets over his head in modesty.

'What an idiot!' Gulnar would cry. 'You weren't embarrassed yesterday to…' Descriptions would follow that left Selim gasping in mortification. He would disappear completely beneath the covers, then continue to tug and twitch them violently in eloquent expression of his shame. His embarrassment never diminished, though the same performance was repeated every day—testimony to Selim's sensibility.

It was Selim who did all the household chores: he went to the market, lit the stoves, cooked our meals. Admirably trained by Gulnar, he found his servitude quite natural and it never occurred to him to rebel against his fate. In exchange he had two attractive, flirtatious women who were always smiling at him; would he have been any better off seeing us dishevelled and dissatisfied, preoccupied with household cares?

After we had lived together for a month Gulnar started bitterly to regret the disappearance of polygamy. 'Just think how good it would be if you could marry Selim too! It would be so much fun. Thank God, he's got the drive for two, and anyway nothing would stop us making love as a threesome or taking lovers. I can tell you that I intend to be unfaithful to him soon anyway. Marriage is a monstrous institution if it's not alleviated by adultery. Is a man obliged to sleep with one woman all his life and vice versa? Gregory is right.' (Actually, I recognized Gregory's opinions on marriage. 'Fidelity is unnatural, unhealthy and depressing,' he would say. 'Whoever commits to it sadly wastes away and ages prematurely. It has the same pernicious effects as masturbation.')

'Mmm,' Gulnar resumed, 'we would have a good time as a threesome. It's a real pity that polygamy is frowned upon.'

She became very pensive.

'There's no getting away from it—I have to start thinking about being unfaithful to Selim. You said that Andrey Massarin has a charming flatmate?'

'Let's go and see them this afternoon unannounced.'

I felt weak at the knees making this suggestion and took fright at my own boldness. I hoped Gulnar would refuse, as I wanted to hide in my corner. But she agreed straightaway, clapping her hands.

'Of course, and it will be more fun just to turn up than to telephone first. If Andrey isn't there, we'll go back tomorrow. Where's the problem with that?'

It never took Gulnar long to act on her decisions. She told Selim at lunch that she was going to the conservatoire with me. 'I think I'll take up the piano again, and since we don't have one, I'll have to go there to play.' She was already preparing her alibi for our future rendezvous.

Even Gulnar hesitated outside Number 14, Pushkin Street. We stood on the pavement opposite, trying to summon the courage to cross the street and ring the bell. The two-storey house, with its covered balcony on the first floor, looked benevolently at us as though inviting us to enter. It had always known us. I had lived there until I was ten and after that I had come regularly to visit my terrible grandmother, who lived on the ground floor until the arrival of the Bolsheviks. Now she too lived in the old city, near Gulnar.

At last we rang the bell.

Andrey appeared on the first-floor landing.

He came down with a light, calm step.

'It's good of you to come. I've been expecting you for ages. Come up, and don't hold it against me that I'm receiving you in your own house.'

When we left the apartment, my father had given it to one of our engineers. I had never been back. I walked into my old bedroom as though in a dream; it had been converted into a study and retained none of the aura I had ascribed to it before. When I say I walked in as though in a dream, I mean it literally. Doesn't everyone have those dreams in which objects are both one thing and another? This room was 'my room', which I immediately saw in my mind's eye as it used to be when I lived there—it had the same furniture, the same red curtains colouring the rays of the morning sun, the same carpet worn thin in one corner, the same smell, the same warm, reassuring atmosphere, but another room was superimposed upon it now, Andrey's study. This superimposition that I imagined I saw existed in my heart too: I was equally overwhelmed to be in my old room and to be in Andrey's study. Unable to say a word, I sat down on the hard, cool leather sofa beneath a bookshelf, and looked around me; then I looked at the view through the window, a view I had seen countless times. Gulnar, meanwhile, was talking gaily to Andrey, who listened with a self-contained smile to my cousin's distracting chatter. She was explaining to him how glad she was to be married.

'You know that girls here want to make love very young. Of course, there's no question of them doing it before marriage, so they're thrilled to be married.'

'Even when they don't choose their own husbands, as I think is the case in the majority of marriages?'

'Even then. After all, it's better to make love to an old hunchback than not at all. Those girls who are resourceful get by. And the others… well, it's too bad for the others.'

'And which group are you in?'

'The first, of course.'

Gulnar laughed and threw Andrey a look full of feeling. I felt uncomfortable.

At that moment there was a knock at the door and a tall, thin, greying man came in, making a lot of noise with his gleaming boots.

'Here's Biryukov, my friend and collaborator! He's a terrible man: a magician, an engineer, a linguist—he speaks seven languages—a breaker of hearts and even furniture when he's in a bad mood, which is often. What else?'

'Yes, what else? Charmed, ladies, to make your acquaintance. I know who you are without the need for introductions. Andrey has told me a lot about the two of you. Gulnar Khanim (and he pointed towards Gulnar) and here is Natasha Khanim (and he pointed towards me). You see, I know too that I should add the title *khanim* to your houri names. When I've been in a country for more than ten days, I already know its customs and begin to speak the language. So…'

And he started to gabble in our tongue, choosing his words well but mutilating them shamelessly.

'Now, allow me to kiss your hands, although it is not an Islamic custom. It is to take my revenge on your ancestors, who liked to cover our bodies with carpets and make merry upon them. But they certainly didn't get as much pleasure out of it as I am getting today!'

He kissed our hands very gallantly. 'Strange representatives of the people,' I thought to myself. 'They are just like the society men who frequented my father's house.'

Biryukov gamely courted Gulnar, who seemed to enjoy it hugely. Andrey occasionally joined their banter, while I was silent. Stupidly, strangely, I wanted to cry. Why? Because now I felt the extreme, painful complexity of life from my own experience, not from the books of others. Andrey was Prince Charming in the most literal sense, while Jamil would become my husband. Andrey was heroic and handsome and serious, and could be a hundred times more so, and I would still marry Jamil, who looked like a worm and whom I despised and hated. Ever since I had begun to dream, I had been waiting for Andrey, and here he was, a miracle, but he would leave without me. He didn't need me, and even if he did, I couldn't accept his love because the social barriers were stronger than my desire, because everything made Andrey someone to whom I had no right: religion, race, and especially his place in the revolutionary world, enemy of mine—everything separated us.

'Why are your eyes sad?' Andrey asked abruptly.

It seemed impossible to explain to him, so I smiled without giving an answer and he did not insist. But he asked me other questions about my family and about myself. When it was time to go, I felt as though we had always known one another and were destined to be together, that we clearly had so much in common—he the Russian from the revolution, me the Muslim destined for a hateful marriage.

I clung desperately to the chimera of an eternally predestined union with Andrey, but could not deceive myself.

8

Gulnar's parents decided to leave the country with their four sons. There was no question of using the normal channels; it was practically impossible to get hold of a passport, as hardly any were being issued. Uncle Suleyman had, therefore, decided to 'escape'. This heroic verb pleased him greatly: he conjugated it with sensual delight, repeated it with satisfaction all day long, artfully using it to impress his audience. The latter, although usually made up of his close relations, was carried along by it. I say 'although', because as everyone knows close relatives can usually be relied on to bring you down a peg or two and to avoid boosting your confidence. Nothing is more difficult than to shine in your own family: by some inexplicable chemistry your witticisms become platitudes, your original insights clichés, your pertinent ideas pedantry. But this harsh law did not apply to Uncle Suleyman. Respected, feared and admired, he was considered the oracle, the philosopher, the scholar of the family. He could indulge in flights of fancy in his speech or behaviour, confident of a positive reception from his family.

Considering his future escape a fait accompli, he praised unreservedly his own decisiveness, his resolution, his courage. This departure should really have been kept secret, but most people knew about it. They were to make the journey in three stages: first by train, then by cart and finally by boat to Persia.

Asked why he wanted to leave his country, my uncle would strike his chest with pathos and cry in his coarse, enthusiastic voice: 'I want to flee the horrors of the revolution. I need air.' But he didn't explain what he needed air for other than to breathe. He kept to this vague formula and no one challenged him. Only his pugnacious wife dared do so, to the great fury of her husband, who thought it compromised the aura of respect for his person. My aunt was highly critical of the planned escape. 'I want to die in my own country!' she declared angrily.

'What's stopping you, you idiot? We'll be back as soon as the Bolsheviks have gone.'

'And that will be tomorrow morning, will it?' my aunt would ask sarcastically.

'No, but it will be soon. Mark my words, my words.' And he emphasized 'my' in tones that demanded total, unquestioning respect.

'And are you never wrong?'

'Yes, I am. I was wrong the day I was stupid enough to marry you.'

A row would ensue about their respective merits and faults. When it had run its course, they would return to the precious subject of their escape.

'I'd like to know why you can't wait quietly until the Bolsheviks have gone. We've still got money. What more do you need?'

'I need air to breathe.'

'There'll be just as much here as with those bloody fools,' my aunt retorted in her usual crude language. (The bloody fools were the inhabitants of Persia, where my relatives were planning to take refuge.)

'No, I need air, air. I need air.' This declaration would be automatically accompanied by blows of pathos against Uncle Suleyman's emotional breast.

'The Devil take you, you and your children! I want to stay here in the city of my forebears, among my brothers and sisters. I want to die in peace.'

'It's a pity you don't do it right away!' my uncle cried, his eyes bloodshot. 'Then I would be rid of you! Pest, idiot, pox!'

But these quarrels with his wife did not weaken my uncle's resolve. The escape was fixed in Uncle Suleyman's mind and no human power could divert him from it. All their relatives, their relatives' friends and the friends' friends knew the supposedly secret date of departure. This constituted a lot of people and, though officially still secret, the escape unofficially became an event in which half the city took an interest. Their chances of getting to Persia, the practicalities of the journey and the necessary precautions were all popular topics of discussion in the city.

Gulnar wept to see her family go, less from affection (somewhat lacking where her relatives were concerned) than from jealousy. Not that she really wanted to leave Baku: it's just that she was always inclined to jealousy.

Only Gulnar, Selim and I were to see the travellers off at the station. They took a minimum of luggage lest they weigh themselves down on the difficult journey ahead. They did, however, take a fortune in jewellery, hidden in the most imaginative, unexpected places; luggage could be closely searched at the stations and they had to think of everything. 'Tether your horse to a tree, then put your trust in Allah,' a wise Muslim proverb says.

We arrived at the station around eight in the evening. It was very cold. The lights flickered feebly as though exhausted, and everything seemed sad and dark. I was devastated by their departure, as I am by almost all partings, which are invariably a wrench for me. The train was late, so we sat on the suitcases to wait. Everyone wept, except Uncle Suleyman, as it was beneath his dignity, but it was written On High that we were never to see that train. A dozen fearsome militiamen burst into the waiting room where we were perched on the suitcases, sobbing. They began to search the luggage. I heard one of the militiamen ask my cousin Asad a question to which he mumbled an unintelligible reply.

'What, can't you speak clearly?' By far the scariest of the militiamen, whose tangled beard and burning eyes made him look like a fairy-tale giant, lost his temper.

Asad replied again, but in the same incomprehensible fashion.

'Goddamn it!' the militiaman shouted. 'You must have something in your mouth that's making you talk like that. Open your mouth!'

Asad did not do as ordered, so the militiaman marched up to him, opened the boy's reticent mouth and pulled out a large diamond ring. The militiamen shouted in surprise and triumph, while the unfortunate travellers sighed in sorrow and despair. Our whole group was led away to a distant room. Two female militia were brought in for the ladies and they began to search us. Expert hands ran over us in all directions. There were jewels in my aunt's hair, in the children's mouths, in the hems of their clothing. My poor relatives groaned and I pitied them with all my heart, but at the same time there was something so comical about this extraction of jewels from the most unlikely locations, hardly suitable as hiding places, that I kept having the urge to laugh.

'Would you believe it!' one of the militiamen cried. 'There are millions here!'

Through her tears, my aunt hurled triumphant abuse at Uncle Suleyman. 'You're still right, are you, you old donkey masquerading as a lion? Just you try coming on all superior with me again, poor cretin!'

The poor cretin maintained an astonishing air of dignity and solemn disdain. Even when they debated taking him to prison, and us along with him, he remained fearless and his demeanour said this whole story had nothing to do with him.

'Let them go!' another militiaman intervened. 'Now that we've stripped them of their treasure, what else can we do with them? If they're in prison, we'll have to feed them and that's all we need!'

Heed was taken of these wise words. They let us go and we escorted the poor, fleeced travellers back to their house. What a pitiful return!

'Ha ha ha,' my aunt laughed hysterically. 'Isn't this marvellous! We're much lighter now, all the better to breathe the air we were meant to escape and all because of that poor idiot's madcap scheme.'

'Shut up,' her husband replied gloomily. 'You know we've still got all the gold buried in the country. There's enough to keep us going for years to come.'

If you were wondering what we were all living on, there's your explanation. All those who used to be rich still owned large quantities of jewels and gold, which they sold on the black market as the need arose. As Uncle Suleyman had said, this treasure would last for many years; and as nobody believed the Bolsheviks would be around for very long, we lived under the impression that our future was assured. With the aid of Allah and a little patience, everything would be resolved in the most satisfactory manner. These childish platitudes brought the former oil barons great peace of mind; after all, they had always thought it natural they should be blessed by fortune. It never occurred to them that fortune might have changed sides. Certainty is the prerogative of the primitive, the weapon of the innocent.

Gulnar and I had dinner at Andrey's. We told Selim we had been invited to dinner by Zeynab Khanim, who was in the know and delighted to provide our cover. The orderly with tousled hair served dishes he had made himself, which we enjoyed, though they were rather lacking in sophistication. I was in the mood to appreciate everything—food or anything else. For two weeks I had been seeing

Andrey nearly every day. It's not enough to say that I loved him: the feeling I felt for him was one of admiration, I would even say adoration if I did not fear ridicule. I will say it—I did adore him. Was it him I loved or through him Prince Andrey Bolkonsky? His attitude towards me was the same as Prince Bolkonsky's towards Natasha Rostova: a protective, deferential tenderness, untainted by any physical desire; at least, that was my perception, and even if I'm wrong, aren't things what we believe them to be? Andrey never offended me: he was always restrained in his words and gestures, a sign of rare mastery of oneself.

'When you have overcome the fear of death, there's not much left to conquer in life,' Andrey said to me one day. 'I have touched death so often that life seems to me a happy accident, not a stable state to which you have to cling at all costs. That's why I despise so many things that most people covet. Do you understand me?'

He ended almost all his sentences with 'do you understand me?' He knew I could follow his train of thought, but never ceased to be amazed.

'You're still of an age to be playing with dolls, but I can talk to you like a woman.'

'No, you're wrong. I'm fifteen—the age when women here already have children. Don't confuse me with your sisters in Russia.'

'Yes, I'll get used to this surprising precociousness one day.'

We could see Gulnar getting drunk. Biryukov was talking nineteen to the dozen, facetious as always. He told us about his highly improbable adventures, but perhaps he wasn't lying after all. Andrey claimed that at least half of his stories were true, which would make Biryukov an extraordinary character.

He was kissing Gulnar's brown hand on the slightest pretext and these kisses were getting imperceptibly higher; Gulnar's arm was a barometer clearly revealing the upward curve of Biryukov's feelings.

'When he reaches her shoulder, he'll be lost,' Andrey murmured, 'or perhaps it's your cousin who will be.'

I was alarmed at Gulnar's behaviour; if she continued drinking vodka at the same rate—a liqueur glass every ten minutes—she wouldn't be able to go home. I told her so.

'Oh, don't worry about it,' cried Biryukov. 'You can sleep here. Tell your husband you've missed the curfew and are staying with Zeynab Khanim. We'll phone to warn her.'

We all wanted to stay together, so no one raised any objection. Fortified by a sense of impunity, Gulnar started drinking even more and Biryukov launched into a new story, even more unlikely than the others. Then he began to show us magic tricks, using a pack of cards taken from his jacket. He knew some impressive tricks and we watched him open-mouthed, uttering cries of amazement. Eventually he stopped the tricks and said, 'And now I'll show you my finest conjuring trick of all. In one second Gulnar will be sitting on my knee.'

He got up, waved his hands above Gulnar, then picked her up and placed her on his knee.

'This is the most difficult trick, but I enjoy it the most.'

Gulnar laughed; she was very happy and showing no sign of wanting to get off Biryukov's knee.

'A veritable painting: *Orgy of the People's Commissars with the Daughters of Former Aristocrats*. Come into my study,' Andrey said, getting up.

I followed, glad to be alone with him.

The room was quiet, barely illuminated by a bedside lamp. We sat on the hard, cool leather sofa, and a moment later I was in Andrey's arms.

'I can do conjuring tricks too, just like Biryukov.'

Lying against Andrey, lying against a man's chest for the first time, I had my apprenticeship in happiness. For the first time in my life, I knew total well-being, perfect harmony, with all my senses. The room where I had slept and lived as a small child saw me now, still a child, but with the happiness of a woman. My body felt completely relaxed, light as a feather, while my mind was free of questions and anxiety. I had forgotten my father, who should be released soon; I had forgotten Jamil, whom I had to marry; I had forgotten my sisters and my yearning for Paris. Lying next to the black knight who came to me one day across the sandy vineyard, bringing happiness, I knew that I should not refuse it. All the social considerations inculcated by my upbringing disappeared. They all seemed stupid and pointless to me, nothing but hot air produced by killjoys.

As I lay against the black military tunic, with its appealing smell of tobacco and leather, it seemed to draw me towards another, more beautiful existence, one closer to the truth than the confines of outdated prejudice allowed. I pressed closer to Andrey and his hand caressed my hair.

It must have been after midnight as no one walked in the deserted street, no car passed. Complete calm, perfect silence reigned in the apartment too. I wondered what Gulnar and Biryukov were doing, but just as quickly forgot about them and returned to my own happiness. How long did we stay like that, without moving or saying a word? Time was no more, just a perfect moment between the past and the future.

Finally, as though emerging from a dream, Andrey's voice asked, 'Would you like to come away with me? I have to go to Moscow first for two weeks to attend the party congress, then I'll come back here for a few days, then we'll leave together for Kiev. Would you like to?'

'Of course I would,' I replied, then stupidly began to cry tears of joy.

'Don't cry. We'll be very happy.'

'That's strange,' I thought. 'Does he really think I'm crying because I'm sad? I'm crying for joy because I'm finding happiness.'

'I'll marry you, though it makes me rather uncomfortable to marry a minor.' (I sensed rather than saw his smile.) 'I will do it, however, out of love for you. Don't cry.'

But for a long while I couldn't stop. Andrey said nothing more and just carried on tenderly stroking my hair. This went on for hours, until dawn. I slept intermittently, waking up to feel an acute, overwhelming happiness, the happiness I had always anticipated. Then I would fall asleep again. I wasn't surprised that our embracing was so chaste; I found it entirely natural. I nestled against the tunic that smelt of tobacco and leather and allowed Andrey's love to wash over me. I loved him too and repeated it a thousand times, but to myself, as I didn't dare say it out loud.

There was a terrible scene between Gulnar and Selim. The poor man was ashen from insomnia and anxiety. Frightened at his own bravery in daring to confront his wife, he asked in what he hoped was a fierce voice, 'Where were you last night?'

With regal disdain Gulnar shrugged her shoulders, took off her coat and said, 'Where was I? Everyone knows where: at Zeynab Khanim's of course, since we dined with her. But we had rather a lot to drink, forgot the curfew and there you have it.'

'Oh no, you're not getting away with that! Do you take me for that husband of Zeynab Khanim's? You're not to visit her any more. The whole city knows she's a strumpet. And I've no intention of being like her husband and turning a blind eye. Let that be a warning to you!'

Gulnar turned pale, then red, then roared and leapt at Selim, snatching a clump of his hair and pulling it with magnificent energy. Selim gave a cry of pain.

'How dare you? How dare you talk to me like that? To me… how dare you?'

She was choking with rage.

'When I'm good enough to put up with a husband like you, large as a bear, fat as a pig, and a clumsy oaf to boot. How dare you? Don't you understand that if I want I'll divorce you tomorrow, in half an hour; I'll ditch you and marry someone better-looking than you, who won't dare make a scene for one little night out. You forget, my friend, you seem to forget completely that we are no longer living in an age of obscurantism, but in one of the greatest, one of the freest ages since the creation of the world.' (I smiled to myself as I recognized Gregory's ideas.) 'Do you understand?'

No, Selim seemed to have understood nothing. He roared as well, though we didn't recognize his small, hysterical voice, which was inadequate for the circumstances and didn't suit his bulk. He cried various insults, including: 'All I understand is that I've married a whore, a tart. I'm sure there were men at Zeynab Khanim's. The whole of Baku knows she's a procuress to beat them all, and I think she even receives gifts for it. Tell me who was there and what the two of you did, tell me.'

'Well, we drank and we… Is that what you want me to tell you, you idiot? Very well, I'm telling you—are you happy now? If you like it, I'll do it again, and if you don't, I'll do it anyway.'

Selim charged towards Gulnar, clearly intending to hit her, but Gulnar was more slippery than an eel and darted behind a table.

'With all that flesh you think you can catch me and hit me?'

Selim gave his wife a wild look, then collapsed onto a chair, crying like a baby. He sobbed and mumbled and we couldn't understand a word. Tears ran down his poor, kind, ugly face, distorted by grief.

'Tell me, tell me'—at last we could make out snatches of words—'tell me it's not true. You're breaking my heart saying such foolish things. Tell me…'

Gulnar raised her eyes to the heavens, 'Oh, men!'

She was wavering between the desire to tell the truth and the desire to spare Selim.

'Oh, of course I lied.'

Selim stopped crying, wiped his eyes and even managed a miserable smile.

'On the other hand,' Gulnar continued, 'I want you to understand that I will be unfaithful to you one day. Really, it's too sad to sleep with the same man all the time. It's like having to eat the same dish every day. I'm going into a decline, I can sense it. If you would prefer a divorce...' Gulnar conceded this indulgence with a regal gesture.

'No, no, anything but that.'

'Good, then we won't discuss it any more.'

And Gulnar sailed out of the room with majestic dignity.

9

Jamil's friend the commissar finally obtained my father's release. He was freed in late December after nine months of incarceration. Since we hadn't known his release date, no one went to meet him and he left the prison on his own. He went to his mother's house, and as we lived close by, an elderly relative came to tell us of his arrival.

He sat on Grandmother's bed, tired and pathetic. The sagging flesh, trembling hands and bags under his eyes all signalled his defeat. But after just an hour he was beginning to recover; the trembling was less pronounced and his gaze was firmer.

'It doesn't take much to defeat a man, or to revive him,' Andrey told me one day.

It took only one hour of freedom to revive my father. Andrey was right as always. Looking at one and thinking of the other, I put my finger on the dilemma I had been wrestling with since the man I considered my true fiancé had left for Moscow. Andrey would be back in a week and spend just three days in Baku. Everything had to be sorted out with my father by then. I was gripped by panic at the thought of it. I knew I was timid, especially with him: I was still afraid of him, though he had never spoken to me harshly, only with an icy reserve that made cowardice of my timidity. It was madness to imagine talking to him about my fiancé in the revolutionary committee.

'So, are you happy?' my father asked me, something he rarely did. 'Are you happy with your work at the conservatoire? You're all grown up now.'

'You need to marry her off, son, and soon,' Grandmother intervened. 'She's gadding about on her own, her face uncovered, with all these men around. It'll be no surprise if they all end up loose women. Huh, much good it's doing us, all that damned European influence! And you've gone through so much! Why? Why, I ask you?'

My father shrugged. Grandmother began to cry, but they were strange tears—tears of fury interspersed with invective against Christians in general, whether Bolsheviks or not; she still considered life in religious, rather than political, terms. She's behind the times, I thought, but how could I explain it to her? And why explain it to her? To confuse her even more? What would she say if I married Andrey, a Russian? A Russian, A RUSSIAN! It was a crazy enough idea that her granddaughter might marry a non-Muslim! But if she found out that that Russian was one of the mob that took away her house, her money, her son, what would she say then? It was better not to think about it. But I had to, as Andrey would be back in a week. I broke out in a cold sweat at the thought of what I had to tell my family. I would rather die! But if I didn't tell them and did nothing, Andrey would leave without me. I was racked by indecision, which must have shown on my face.

'What's wrong with you?' my father asked. 'Are you ill? You're shaking.'

'It's the cold, and I'm not feeling very well either.'

An inner voice told me to seize the moment—to plunge into the icy abyss and say my piece, come what may. I was about to speak but lost my voice. 'You've lost your voice, so you can't speak,' my cowardice rejoiced. There was a knock at the door and friends came in. I didn't have to fight with myself any more. My voice returned immediately and so did my courage… just when I couldn't use either.

Jamil saw no reason to delay his marriage request and spoke to my father the day after his release from prison. To me at least, it looked as though he were demanding payment for services rendered. My whole family seemed to think his behaviour perfectly natural, though, as they already considered Jamil my unofficial fiancé. My father summoned me after the visit to tell me of Jamil's request. He made the following speech:

'Jamil obtained my freedom. Without him, God knows how long I would have been in prison. That's not all. I want to leave the country and you know how difficult it is to get a passport. But his friend the commissar might be able to get hold of one for me. I don't want to twist your arm, but I am asking you to think about it. I would like to add that Jamil is a fine young man. He's educated, broad-minded, resourceful and he loves you. Why not marry him? But let me repeat it, nobody is forcing you to marry him. Sleep on what I've said and give me your answer tomorrow.'

Why not marry him? Because I love someone else, I should have replied, but I looked down and said I would think it over. I hated my father as I left. By telling me that he still needed Jamil, he was blackmailing me; he was profiting from my sense of duty and gambling on my filial affection. But I didn't feel affection for him, quite the opposite, and I didn't want to sacrifice myself so that he could leave the country, while I had to stay behind with the hated, detested, execrable Jamil. I clenched my fists as I walked out, weeping tears of rage, though I realized how powerless that rage was.

I hadn't told Gulnar anything about Andrey's plans. Something kept me back from opening up to her: maybe it was fear of her cynicism or her brutality, or the impression that she wouldn't understand the intensity of our feelings. Gulnar believed in loving men, not in loving one man. She would think I should marry Jamil first, then do whatever I liked. I could hear her say, 'You marry Jamil, he gets your father's passport, then you do what you want.'

The day after the night at Andrey's she was concerned to know if I had managed to keep my virginity.

'The question never came up,' I replied.

'What? It didn't come up at all? Andrey didn't want anything from you? You didn't have to refuse him anything?'

When I again replied in the negative, she said, 'What an imbecile!'

I didn't object, but was aware of the gulf between us.

Gulnar thought about it: 'You were right not to sleep with him. Basically, it's always a bad idea to spoil the merchandise.' Gulnar never suffered from stylistic scruples. 'I like Andrey more than Biryukov. Just between us, his conjuring tricks don't go as far as the bed. It's a good job I don't give up easily, or I might have been put off by my first experience of adultery.'

'But I don't think Andrey just wants to sleep with someone,' I ventured timidly.

'You poor thing, you're so stupid! Even if he lo-o-o-oves you' (pronounced with a sarcastic tremolo), 'it won't stop him sleeping with a pretty girl.'

And Gulnar gave a self-satisfied look at her reflection in the mirror.

I was drained after the conversation with my father and lay down on the couch that served as my bed. The apartment was cold, empty and silent. My mind too was cold, empty and silent. There was nothing but a void inside me. Exhausted, incapable of rational thought or further struggle, I fell asleep.

The whole family came to celebrate my father's release, a pilaff made by Grandmother the centrepiece. Clean, freshly shaven and rejuvenated, my father was as cheerful as his withdrawn and often melancholic nature allowed. That morning he had asked for my answer to the Jamil question. Against all expectations I mumbled that I would do what he wanted and since he wanted the marriage, that was that. Jamil had been informed straightaway and now that he was officially my fiancé he squirmed around me, more like an earthworm than ever, and put all his wit into paying me compliments. With Andrey far away, I was powerless to combat my cowardice, and let destiny take its course, telling myself that it still might be changed by some unforeseen event.

In the large room that constituted my grandmother's whole apartment, and where my father had been living for the past two days as well, two dozen relatives furiously tucked into traditional pilaff. Since the table wasn't big enough to seat everyone, half the assembly sat on cushions on the floor. This didn't bother anyone—they saw furniture as a dispensable European import. Ordinary people still lived their lives on the floor without recourse to tables, chairs or beds; they sat cross-legged on the floor to eat and slept on mattresses that were rolled up during the day.

Aunt Rena was there, highly strung as usual and chain-smoking; when she looked at her deaf husband she would be sure to make some nasty comment about him, but his carapace of deafness guaranteed my uncle's peace of mind and he continued to devour enormous quantities of moist, steaming white rice.

My eldest sister, whom I didn't see very often, felt no compunction about displaying her boredom. She had good reason not to be cheerful, as her husband was still in prison, but she did not make use of it: hypocrisy was never her forte and she did not hide her indifference towards her spouse. No, she was just bored. She yawned all the time, pointedly looking at her watch.

Fräulein Anna was there too. She had been with our family for more than twenty years and was considered one of us, even by my fierce, traditionalist grandmother, who made an exception for her Christian religion. Fräulein Anna kept turning her kind, increasingly myopic eyes towards me. I didn't have to tell her about my sadness, she could see it for herself; but she did not mention it, as I had chosen not to. She looked at Jamil with disapproval. Aunt Rena had told me that Fräulein Anna tried to dissuade my father from encouraging this marriage; she thought I was too young and Jamil not right for me, but her views went unheeded. I forgot to mention that Jamil was twenty years older than me.

The redoubtable Uncle Suleyman was there with all his family, and they were soon to disrupt our gathering. I've already said that my uncle had always wanted me to marry Asad. He thought one of the richest heiresses in Baku should keep her fortune in the family, not squander it elsewhere. That I had lost this fortune did not trouble him. Didn't he have it on good authority that this eclipse was transitory? 'The Bolsheviks will soon leave' and we will recover all our wealth.

You could tell from his sulky, glowering demeanour when he arrived that a storm was brewing within, waiting for the opportunity to break out in dramatic fashion. He didn't look once at Jamil and even when he offered him his hand, he very rudely looked away. By contrast Asad and Ali did not stop staring at my fiancé, pulling ironic faces and sharing private jokes. Nobody could miss this insulting behaviour: only Jamil, made immune by his happiness, failed to notice and continued to pay me sickeningly banal compliments. He did not make jokes on this important day, reserved for more serious matters.

After the sumptuous pilaff, accompanied by chicken and grilled sturgeon, the samovar was brought in and tea was served. This was the moment my father uttered the fatal words: 'You all know the good news: my daughter is going to marry Jamil.'

Scarcely had the words been uttered than Uncle Suleyman lifted his impressive head, looked at my father with blazing eyes, then slammed his hand onto the table, making the teacups jump.

'Aren't you ashamed to talk to us of good news? You should die of embarrassment to give such a pearl' (he pointed to me) 'to such a runt.'

Jamil was given a menacing stare which made him jump like the cups.

'Be quiet,' Uncle Suleyman shouted, though Jamil seemed to be struck dumb in astonishment. 'Be quiet. I've still to settle accounts with your future father-in-law.'

He gave the table another thump, rattling the cups all over again.

'You've always robbed the lot of us!' he shouted at my father. 'You've always taken advantage of managing our poor father's firm to chip away at us penny by penny and keep our hands off the inheritance. If those poor girls' (pointing to my aunts) 'hadn't found rich, model husbands who knew how to make money other than by robbing their closest relatives, they would have died of hunger. You would have reduced them to begging on the streets.'

Pandemonium ensued. Even Uncle Suleyman's loud voice was lost in the racket. Everyone was shouting at once—begging, threatening, imploring, agreeing and disagreeing. My father got to his feet, as did my uncle, and they hurled abuse at one another, though we could make out only snatches in the general hubbub. Asad and Ali were ecstatic, as they loved nothing more than a good row, and here they were at a gala performance. It was balm for their souls, sending them into raptures of glee. Their eyes shone, as they ran from my father to theirs as though to stoke their respective fury or at least to maintain it. They behaved like devils, gesticulating and cackling with malicious joy.

With a supreme effort to shout more loudly, Uncle Suleyman made himself heard at last: 'Yes, yes, and now you're taking this poor girl and throwing her into the arms of this bloody fool just because he's promised you a passport to go abroad. She has always been Asad's fiancée! Just look at the boy' (addressing the whole assembly). 'He's handsome, strong, intelligent. He's a model son and will be a model husband. But no, this monster has decided he needs a passport and everyone else can go to hell. May Allah punish you, if there is an Allah!'

Jamil charged towards my uncle, shouting in a strangled voice, 'Shut up or I'll kill you!'

'What with, for God's sake? Your moustache?'

And Uncle Suleyman took hold of Jamil's small, fine moustache and tugged it hard.

'I'd give you a slap if you weren't my fiancée's uncle. If I had a weapon I'd kill you...'

Aunt Rena and her husband held back my father, who wanted to get at Uncle Suleyman, while my uncle was restrained by Gulnar and Selim. Grandmother yelled, entreating Allah to calm his zealots, while my sister was finally enjoying herself. A horrified Fräulein Anna held her head in her hands, groaning and repeating from time to time, '*Ach mein Gott! Ach mein Gott!*'

Suddenly my uncle broke free from Gulnar and Selim and yanked the tablecloth, sending everything crashing to the floor. In a grand apotheosis, the samovar fell with a clap of thunder, spilling boiling water everywhere, accompanied by the chime of smashing cups. Uncle Suleyman left the room, his family on his coat-tails, every inch Genghis Khan departing a ravaged battlefield. He was never to see my father again.

Four days after this memorable evening, I received a note from Biryukov: Andrey would be back the following day and asked me to come and see him in the afternoon. My heart was trembling when I rang his bell the next day. The orderly told me that Andrey had a visitor, so I went into the drawing room and sat on a sofa near the window. I looked at the view, which I had seen thousands of times before—the drawing room had been our classroom. Here I had struggled to learn the piano; here I had formed the Gothic letters of the German language, studied the Russian ABC and tried to draw the arabesques of Arabic script.

The door opened and Andrey came towards me. I threw myself into his arms, seeking in their protection comfort for my distress.

'Let's go to our couch, our universe,' he said.

This couch was a hideous piece of furniture, like all the leather couches that were widespread in the Russian empire at this time. Narrow, hard and cold to the touch, it gave off a hostile air rather than inviting relaxation. But for me and for Andrey it was, as he had said, our universe, the place where our love overwhelmed us for the first time. We sat down and Andrey took my hands in his.

'Have you done it? Have you spoken to your father? All right, there's no need to answer—I can tell from your expression that you haven't done anything. Why not? Are you afraid?'

I hung my head. Andrey let go of my hands.

'So you've changed your mind? You don't want to come away with me?'

'I do, I do!'

I had shouted so loudly that I blushed in embarrassment.

'I don't understand. You want to come away but you haven't said anything to your family. I'm leaving the day after tomorrow. I think you should have spoken to them by now.'

'I daren't.'

'Do you want me to go and see your father?'

'No, no, don't.'

The idea of a meeting between Andrey and my father made me weak at the knees.

'So what are you going to do then? Do you want to leave without saying a word? I want you to come, but I have to say I think it's rather cowardly to run off without saying a word. Don't you think so?'

'Of course I do, but I am a coward.'

'Then you will have to be a coward and leave without any warning. It might be the simplest solution after all.'

Andrey saw my dejection and tried to inspire me with courage. He told me that I needed to be braver and reject the influence of my family, who would remain stuck in the past, stagnating and growing increasingly bitter about a world to which they could no longer adapt. I should leave with him, live with him, live and not rot away with my relatives.

'Do you know what it means *to live*? It means to influence things, people, events—to pursue a clear goal in the vast complexity of a great country. It means to know one's duty and to do it; it means to feel strong; it means to transform one's smallest tasks into grand gestures. To live is to be intense, passionate. We will burn brightly together.'

Andrey smiled.

'See, you've turned me into a poet. You're so young, so touchingly young! I would like to make you into someone strong, fulfilled, useful. Do you want me to?'

Of course I wanted him to! The question wasn't that, it was whether I could do it.

'Yes, I want you to,' I replied in a strong voice and felt that I could.

Andrey looked at me and his normally impenetrable face lit up with tenderness.

'You'll see,' he said. 'You'll never regret your decision.'

He accompanied me to the front door.

'I'll send you a note tomorrow to let you know the time of departure, as I don't know it yet. Come here, as I can't pick you up, and we'll leave together for the station.'

Before opening the door, he took me in his arms, holding me tight, and said for the first time, 'I love you.'

He still held me tight. 'Trust me. I'll be waiting for you the day after tomorrow.'

Then he opened the door and I was out in the street, calm and sure of myself. I looked back. A ray of sunlight shone into Andrey's eyes; he screwed them up, smiling. I smiled back and the door closed.

I laughed at Jamil's supposed witticisms; I was even starting to like him now I had decided to leave with Andrey. Jamil was making plans too. After we were married we would go to Tiflis* for a few days, while we waited for my father to receive the famous passport that would finally allow him to go overseas. We would meet up with him in Batumi and see him off.

'Do you like the plan?' Jamil asked me.

I liked everything.

Gulnar came in and handed me a letter. 'It's from Zeynab Khanim,' she said.

I knew the letter was from Andrey, so I went into the next room and opened it with trembling fingers. Andrey had set our rendezvous for ten o'clock the next day at his apartment. I went back to Jamil.

'When I think how happy your father will be when he can join his family at last!' said the grating voice. 'The poor man has suffered so much, he deserves this happiness. Do you know of the old belief that the amount of happiness in the world is limited? The amount remains the same but changes destination. So when you are unhappy, you can console yourself with the thought that your unhappiness is allowing someone else to be happy. And the reverse, when you are happy, you are taking the same degree of

* Now known as Tbilisi.

happiness away from someone else, maybe your sister. It's a curious idea, isn't it?'

I imagined my father deprived of his passport, deprived of the hope that reconciled him to life, cruelly banished from his state of euphoria when I left with Andrey. I was gripped by anxiety again. *I couldn't leave.*

'I'm sorry, Jamil,' I said. 'Could you leave me alone? I don't feel very well all of a sudden.'

I couldn't bear the sight of him any longer, couldn't bear the sound of that hideous voice which enveloped me like an immovable shroud. It was only eight in the evening but I went to bed, wanting to die and be done with these insoluble problems once and for all.

Then I called Gulnar and told her everything I had been hiding from her. She was outraged. 'How could you hide it all from me, your confidante, your lifelong friend? You've always told me everything.'

But I was crying, so she stopped criticizing me.

'You will go and see Andrey tomorrow at ten,' I said, 'and explain everything—about the passport, Jamil, how I can't hurt my father and all the family. You will explain it to him, won't you?'

She promised and, coward that I was, I took four sleeping pills so that I could get to sleep to escape my sorrow. The next day I awoke at around ten with a terrible headache and a deathly taste in my mouth. All was still in the silent apartment. Gulnar was at Andrey's and Selim must have been out shopping. I was too tired to get up. It was raining outside and cold in the room. I was overcome by a sense of great unhappiness. 'When you're unhappy, that allows someone else to be happy.' I remembered Jamil's words, but they were no use to me: I couldn't be kind with this sense of bitterness inside. I only cared about my own fate; the rest of humanity could perish—what difference would it make to me? Something irreparable had happened, something that would change the direction of my life—for better or worse, I didn't know. What I did know was that I had lost Andrey. The black knight, the wonderful man whom I could have admired, perhaps loved, my whole life, was at this moment leaving Baku for good. I could have gone with him, but I was in that bed, so crushed by despair that I didn't have the strength to cry.

I heard the door to the apartment open and close and a few moments later Selim walked into my room.

'Where's Gulnar?' he asked.

'I've no idea. I've only just woken up—I'm not well.'

Selim had been downcast since Gulnar's revelations, his shoulders permanently hunched, but he fussed around me, too much for my liking as I wanted to be alone.

'Let me go back to sleep, but if Gulnar comes, tell her to wake me up.'

I turned to face the wall and Selim left the room.

Gulnar didn't come back at eleven, when she would normally have been home, nor at midday, nor in the evening, nor the next day. Quite simply, she did not come back at all. Selim discovered that a small suitcase was missing, as well as two dresses, some underclothes and toiletries, and I realized the truth, though I couldn't tell the poor man.

'How could she do it? How? How could she leave without saying a word? Not even to you. Do you swear?'

I could swear with a clear conscience.

Selim seemed to have gone mad: he would cry, then fall into a pit of despondency from which there was no rescuing him.

'How could she have done such a thing? Leave without a word, without a thought for the pain it would cause me? For the agonies of uncertainty I would suffer?' he kept repeating.

His grief was so constant, so violent, that I forgot my own a little, though it was deepened still further by jealousy. I had no doubt that Andrey had left with Gulnar instead of me. I imagined what must have happened: she was tired of Selim's doleful complaints (he couldn't get used to his wife's infidelity but he couldn't leave her either) and 'wanted fresh air' (she couldn't breathe living with Selim, she had kept telling me recently). She also wanted to become Andrey's mistress, as she liked him a lot, so she had decided to take a small case and go and meet him in my place. The Gulnar I knew would have told herself that she wasn't taking any risks and that she might in fact come out on top. Cold and calculating, she must have propositioned Andrey, who in his disappointment and resentment thought 'Why not?' and agreed. She hadn't worried about Selim's grief or mine, or about the scandal that her flight would cause in the family. Gulnar followed her desires without scruple and with no concern for anyone else. A happy disposition that allowed her to live as she saw fit, her conscience clear, her soul at ease.

I sat in a small, gloomy room with just one narrow window, waiting to get married.

In the next room a mullah was drawing up our marriage contract in the presence of Jamil and his witnesses. When the signatures were placed at the bottom of the paper, I would become the wife of a man I hated. I held a book, which I tried vainly to read. Those who claim that reading is a consolation for everything cannot feel very deeply—a powerful emotion leaves no spare mental capacity; it takes over, hypnotizes you, stops you thinking of anything else. I had already found out for myself that life was more eventful than fiction; books seemed flat to me, still do, in comparison to reality. So I read the words of the open book without understanding their meaning: I was constantly tormented, haunted, by the idea that I would 'belong' to Jamil. I knew what this verb meant: Jamil would have the right to get into my bed, he would have monstrous rights over my body. Not that my body felt anything yet—it was my imagination that was torturing me. I closed my eyes and saw the mouth that would have the right to put itself on mine; I saw the hands covered in red hairs touching my body; I heard the grating voice say tender things to me that I didn't want to hear from it. But more than anything I was horrified at the thought of living with Jamil, whose presence I could hardly bear for an hour; I would have to put up with him for a whole day, ten days, a year, years, a lifetime! I was tortured by regret. But I didn't cry: my pain was so closely mixed with hatred for my father and Jamil that it stopped me falling apart.

The door opened and I hid my book, because according to the rules of the game I should not be reading but be absorbed in the idea of marriage. I got up. With tears in their eyes (this was part of the ceremony) my aunts appeared en masse and announced the good news: I was married! 'What joy!' I cried ironically. Aunt Rena hugged me tightly—I didn't complain. It was useless.

I was fifteen years and three months old, while Jamil was thirty-five.

10

That evening we took the train to Tiflis, where we intended to wait for my father to leave for Batumi. We would join him there to see him off as he sailed for France. He was waiting for his passport, the famous passport that Jamil's friend the commissar had promised to obtain. A promise bordering on miraculous in those still revolutionary times, so much so that this passport was referred to as a thing of fable or legend. Bets were made—would he get it? Wouldn't he get it? The commissar had given assurances though; in accepting Jamil as his son-in-law, my father was barely settling the rather significant debt he owed him.

The station bore the signs of troubled times: the war abroad, the civil war, and general wear and tear had all made themselves felt on the railway. An unusually long train was coupled to a wretched little locomotive, which seemed exhausted before it had even started. The dilapidated carriages lined up along the astonishingly filthy platform, jam-packed with a throng of defectors lured by the Caucasus and its relative prosperity.

My father was there, calm and taciturn, as were Fräulein Anna and Aunt Rena, who were crying instead of me; Leyla was giving practical advice to the frightful Jamil, who was hovering over me. He looked awfully like a worm that had momentarily taken on human guise. I could hear his grating voice, which I hated more than ever, to the left of me, to the right of me, in front of me and behind me; it flooded me, overwhelmed me, hemmed me in on all sides.

We had the good fortune to get into a compartment for eight, where some fifteen people were already doing battle.

The journey lasted two days instead of the standard twelve hours. A carriage took us to the home of friends of Jamil, who were expecting us; they were Georgians, hospitable as all Caucasians are, but real chatterboxes. They dazed us with their questions, which we had to answer, though I was very tired. At last they took me to my room, to our room, rather—it was time I understood that my room was now Jamil's room too. I was alone with him, my husband. There was a bed, a large double bed. I sat in a chair and began to cry; I could no longer bear the enormous weight of my regrets, the constant image of what was and what might have been. I would soon have to lie down in the bed with this Jamil, who turned my stomach; I would have to bear his flesh against mine; I would have to let him caress me, do a deed that I hadn't thought about when Andrey took me in his arms, a deed that now seemed hideous to me. Jamil was wriggling around me.

'What's wrong with you?' he asked in his grating voice.

For the first time he had used the informal 'you', and this familiarity, unjustified by any affection, felt like a humiliation. I didn't answer. Even if I'd wanted to, how could I have done so? What words could have come out between the strangled sobs?

'Be good now and get undressed,' he continued.

I shook my head violently. 'Certainly not that,' I said to myself. I was vehement in my thoughts, rebuffing Jamil, covering him in violent blows; I killed him so I no longer had to see him or hear him or know that a Jamil existed somewhere with rights over me.

'What to do? What to do?' he asked out loud, at a loss.

He left the room and came back with a glass of water, but I pushed him away so strongly—him and his glass and his water—that the liquid spilt. Then Jamil sat on the bed. I was still crying, but the tears were not so profuse.

Suddenly I heard snoring; looking through my fingers, which I had pressed to my tear-streaked face, I saw Jamil half-lying on the bed, fast asleep. He seemed worn out. This gave me a sense of freedom. I got up, turned off the light, quickly got undressed in the darkness and furtively groped my way into the bed. I fell asleep straightaway. I woke up with a start when I felt a hand touch my breast. I hit out in the dark, catching Jamil in the face. He gave a cry and I jumped out of bed.

'If you touch me again, I'll get dressed and spend the night in the armchair.'

'I'm your husband,' Jamil cried angrily.

'I don't care. I hate you.'

'Why, for God's sake? What have I done?'

I didn't answer. Minutes passed during which Jamil must have been waging an internal battle.

'Very well,' he said eventually. 'Come back to bed and I won't touch you.'

I lay down at the very edge of the bed. I reassured myself by imagining the space between us as an impassable ditch. Jamil did not move any more.

The few days we were to spend in Tiflis became three months. All the commissar friend's magic was powerless to speed up the issue of the passport. I sometimes wondered if my sacrifice had been in vain. But I enjoyed living in Tiflis, which I much preferred to Baku. This beautiful city was lively and gay, and only rarely did you feel you were living in extraordinary times. Those who still had money could enjoy good restaurants, theatres, the ballet, shopping. Jamil sold a diamond ring, which made us rich for a while. We went out a lot with Jamil's many friends, went to the theatre and on trips, in short led what is generally considered a dissolute life. It was what

I needed: I hadn't changed at all in myself; I still loved Andrey and thought about him all the time, while I hated Jamil.

For two months I turned my back on him when we went to bed, picked up a book and with manifest hostility pretended to read. Jamil would cry, complain about my cruelty, try gently to caress my back but not dare go very far, oppressed by the wall of silence and hostility that I put up against all his attempts. When he became too forward, which usually happened after an alcoholic dinner, I pushed him away brutally, and succeeded in disheartening him with my harsh words. But I felt no pity for him and enjoyed hurting him. I considered him hateful: physically repulsive and morally weak.

I was exasperated by his desperate desire to be witty at all costs, a desire that was practically manic and never left him. He was spiteful and boastful, mean too, except if he was gambling, when he cheerfully lost money. There was no limit to his boasting. He boasted about everything: his intelligence, his education, his family, his clothes. Since his marriage he especially boasted about having married one of the richest heiresses in the Caucasus. That memories were all the heiress had left of her fortune did not deter him: the memories were dazzling enough, especially since he considered Bolshevism an accident of fate and our impoverishment a temporary phenomenon. So I had to hear him take shameless delight in my past riches, which, though they had ceased to exist, gave him a reassuring sense of grandeur and increased his self-esteem (not that there was any need for it at all; his self-satisfaction verged on madness). Everyone who came near was doomed to hear all about the size and precise value of my momentarily disappeared assets. Jamil was downcast when he couldn't extract cries of admiration or envy from his audience, and quivered with pleasure when his public took the bait. At those times he would be expansive and treat me with even greater consideration than usual—for Jamil always treated me with a great deal of respect, the sole pleasant consequence of his admiration for my fortune. Here perhaps was the reason he bore my revulsion for him as patiently as he did. It wasn't my own personality that inspired this respect, but the fact that I was 'the daughter of such a man'. I could have been deformed, an imbecile or a shrew and Jamil's attitude would have been the same. As the 'daughter of such a man', I was immutable, above the fray, in some way fixed in eternity; everything might change, worlds might collapse, but I would remain 'the daughter of such a man'. An attitude that was to my advantage, but reinforced my scorn for Jamil.

Everything served to stoke this hatred, as happens when one is ill-disposed towards someone. Gestures that would have appeared harmless from other people irritated me from Jamil. The way he ate, dressed, spoke, all disgusted me. But I also took a sadistic pleasure in hating my husband; sometimes I would even take a seat so I could see him better and enjoy, yes enjoy, my hatred. I stirred it up the better to savour it. Fortunately he wasn't aware of my feelings (I say fortunately out of a residue of pity) and put my 'reserve' down to the extreme modesty of a young girl—or at least pretended to.

The longer we stayed in Tiflis, the more I loved the city. Eventually we rented a small, furnished apartment in a central street, but we still ate in restaurants; my education had not included the culinary arts and I didn't know how to boil an egg. I made sure to maintain this convenient ignorance: I was disgusted at the thought of looking after Jamil, which was enough in itself to keep me from making any effort. Add to that an ineradicable tendency to idleness and daydreaming, typical of many orientals. The hours I spent in this state were among the best of my life; that was when I lived entirely with Andrey. Somewhere a long way from me, he lived his life of action, 'burning bright' as he followed his desires, alone or with Gulnar; this latter detail remained uncertain as we had never heard news of my cousin. My grief at the thought of them was perhaps fading slightly, though it remained strong enough to cloud all possible joy.

We were surrounded by an ever-growing crowd of friends, most of whom were poker players. Jamil seemed to attract them—he was considered one of the best poker players, I was going to say in the world, but I will say more modestly in the Caucasus. What happens when poker players get together but poker? And there was plenty of it. Our house became a club where poker was played from afternoon till dawn with breaks to troop off to a restaurant for sustenance. Fed, watered and rested, the poker players would resume their places at the green baize tables with renewed vigour. Jamil and his friends played with intense commitment; no social cataclysm, war or similar disaster could have stopped them. They played for high stakes; everyone still had lots of gold and jewels to sell, since in the Caucasus we were only at the start of the revolution. I often joined them. I had learnt to play poker at the age when other children learn to read; in my family young and old were passionate, fervent players. Lessons from Jamil, an incomparable teacher, added to this firm foundation and I soon became a player destined for a brilliant future. Carried along by the others, I sometimes stayed up all night smoking and playing, hooked in turn by this passion. Whether or not such a pastime was suitable for the mind and body of a young person of fifteen is a dilemma I am not competent to resolve.

The wife of one of the poker players befriended me and decided I should spend less time playing cards and more time going out with her. 'With a regimen like that,' she told me, 'you'll be old by the time you're thirty. Why, you're worn out at the card table.' So I would leave Jamil with his fellow players and go out with my new friend.

She was a strangely gentle, phlegmatic and perverted woman. She spent her time looking for lovers, whom she had no trouble finding, thanks to her deceptively soft, cat-like physique. Men were easily seduced by her large eyes, very short nose and mouth, which was almost always half-open to reveal dazzling white teeth. Short and plump, she moved gracefully and talked sweetly. This was the woman that befriended me.

'We're such physical opposites that we can't harm one another's chances. Quite the reverse: by complementing one another we'll attract more men.'

I didn't feel any need to attract men, nor to discuss it, so I didn't answer. Despite my reserve, Salome (this was the name of the young woman, who was Georgian) found her way into my heart through her persistent kindness. She extracted from me a confession of my love for Andrey.

'What? You loved a Bolshevik?' she cried in horror.

'They're still men,' I ventured.

Willing to see the man rather than the label, Salome accepted the idea.

'Well, we have to get used to the idea after all. It's true that the commissar who lives in our house is very handsome.'

She sighed.

'He never looks at me. I'm still afraid of them though.'

'To be honest, life isn't too terrible in Baku or Tiflis.'

'That's because they haven't had time to deal with us yet. Just wait.'

Whatever the reason, life in Tiflis really was pleasant and easy-going. Their sizeable wardrobes still allowed people to dress very well, while their stocks of gold and jewels, sold at regular intervals, ensured their lifestyle, as I've already said. If many of them had their houses requisitioned, nothing stopped them renting more modest, but quite adequate, apartments. When they got together, it was hard to tell we were supposedly living in a state of revolution. The well-dressed women, decked out in jewels, and men playing cards were characters that could have been found anywhere in capitalist Europe. It was hard too to imagine the dreadful social upheaval under way in Russia, which was bound to reach the Caucasus soon too.

But let's get back to Salome. My revulsion for Jamil was obvious to those who knew how to look, and my friend soon began to question me about my relationship with him. She was astounded to learn that I had not yet become his wife.

'What? Don't you sleep in the same bed?'

I admitted that we did.

'So what does Jamil do then? What do you do?'

'I turn my back to him and read.'

'What about him?'

'Oh, him!'

'What do you mean "Oh, him"? Doesn't he try to get close to you?'

'Yes, he does.'

Salome began to lose patience.

'Please explain yourself. Doesn't he do anything, say anything?'

'He does, he complains all the time. It's constant and turns my stomach. If you only knew how often I wish I could kill him like a flea. I would love to roll him between my fingers, to crush him until there's nothing left of him. But yes'—I was suddenly in the mood for confidences—'he does try to get close to me, to my back to be more exact, as I turn my back to him every night. And every night it's the same tiresome performance. First he complains, while I keep reading. Then when he sees that his complaints have no effect—every night he hopes I'll change my mind because of his complaining—he gets close to me and tries to caress me. My dear Salome, physical repulsion is torture.'

'But you might be his wife anyway, my young friend. You know it can come just as well from behind,' she laughed.

'Definitely not. I'm not a little girl and know what I'm doing.'

'So he's happy to use the service entrance?' Salome burst out laughing and I blushed.

'He would like to,' I said, deeply embarrassed.

'And all this time you keep on reading?'

'Yes, I force myself to.'

'That's priceless! And what are you reading? Something instructive?'

'Very. At the moment I'm reading Dostoevsky—*The Idiot*.'

'So you need a lover before Jamil has the chance to profit from a mistake and marry you properly. If you let him do it, you'll be put off love for the rest of your life.'

Once she had got this idea into her head, Salome couldn't let go. I was wasting my breath explaining to her that I didn't want a lover. She wouldn't listen to my explanations and pursued her idea.

'Let me get on with it. I'm ten years older than you and know what you need.'

She began to take me out more often. We got into the habit of going out every afternoon, leaving our husbands absorbed in their cards.

Summer was progressing in all its splendour: divine heat, unchanging sky, flying birds, trees in leaf, flowers and fruit. Only in summer am I truly alive—that's when I thrive in body and spirit. One of our resourceful friends had transformed his garden into an outdoor tea salon, where on most days we would spend several hours. It was the most pleasant spot imaginable in the heat. Chestnut trees around a pond, rose bushes dotted over a carpet of grass—that was all, but it was a lot. It had cool air, birds, iced chocolate, of which we drank two, three, sometimes five glasses a day, until we got indigestion or were sick of it, but that didn't stop us starting again the next day.

One evening I became Jamil's wife. Out of a need for protection? Out of a sense of the inevitable? I don't know myself. I did not turn my back to him as usual, I did not pick up my book; I got into bed and lay motionless, waiting for what I could not escape for ever. Jamil took me in his arms and I did not resist.

11

We finally got a telegram from my father in late October announcing his imminent departure. We took the train straightaway and joined him in Batumi.

We found him rejuvenated by hope—his look, his demeanour, his gait, everything about him appeared stronger. He was standing tall again, both in mind and in body. He was staying with friends, though their lodgings were less than commodious—Batumi was experiencing a severe housing shortage at this time. As for us, we ended up in a peculiar hovel, overlooking the sea, a vortex of all the winds in the world blowing in through the badly fitting doors and windows. The leaky ceiling too was open to the rains in every season. But we discovered this only later, as the sun was shining like a fanfare in a radiant sky when we arrived in Batumi. While we waited for the boat that my father was to take, we strolled down the promenade looking out over the Black Sea, which despite its name was bluer than the Caspian. Ridiculous palm trees, reminiscent of feather dusters, decorated the promenade. Children played in the sand—it all seemed so peaceful and humdrum. But the reality was anything but—there were revolutions in the world, partings and defeats, and everything seemed funereal to me.

The two men at my side were talking non-stop. Jamil was the dream son-in-law: he venerated his father-in-law only slightly less than Allah and his Prophet, and listened to and obeyed him without demur. My father's appreciation was evident and he dispensed his advice liberally, encouraging Jamil to ask his commissar friend for passports for the two of us, too.

'It was difficult to request passports for everybody all together, but once I've gone, you can start again for yourselves.'

Jamil agreed. I would have been delighted at the prospect of going to Europe, had it not seemed so distant and improbable.

The stormy sea hurled drunk, demented waves crashing over the jetty towards us. The boat pitched violently, as it slowly pulled away from the land to which I remained bound by invisible cords, harder to break than material ones. This boat would reach another shore where I could have lived, had my parents not decided otherwise; I would have known neither Andrey nor the man to whom I had supposedly been given for the rest of my life. Dripping with rain, my father smiled to us above the ship's rail and grew smaller and smaller. He was soon the size of my thumbnail, then merged with the grey mass of the boat.

I wanted to go back; I thought grief had given me a fever and wanted to curl up in my bed, my refuge against all the ills of the world. On the promenade the ridiculous palm trees bent gracelessly in the violent gusts of wind. It was almost as wet and windy in our house, or rather in our room, as it was outside. Bowls placed on the floor revealed the weak spots in the roof, of which there were many.

I went to bed feeling mortally tired. My fever wasn't imaginary: it rose along with my grief, mirroring its climb to the heights of utter loathing for life.

Jamil fetched a doctor who diagnosed appendicitis. I readily slipped into illness with no desire to get well. I wanted to be ill, free from responsibility, disgusted with everything and everyone.

Long days passed in this room, which grew colder and colder. The autumn rains had begun; I heard the drops fall into the bowls on the floor. Draughts of air raced round my bed unhindered. When I braved them and sat up for a moment, I saw the grey sea, the grey street, the grey sky; the rain merged everything into a desperate uniformity; I had the sensation of eternal rain. My imaginings were bleak and bitterness poisoned every moment. I saw my father reaching Constantinople, Paris, the Champs-Élysées, my sisters. I wondered if they ever thought of me. I wondered what the course of my life would have been had I left with them, but above all I was tortured by my uncertainty about Andrey. I imagined myself with him in distant cities—mysterious and beautiful; our life together could only be beautiful! The fever turned my reverie into delirium; we lived in a palace of crystal, inset with gold and diamonds; we savoured strange dishes served by invisible jinns, for we were alone in this palace, wonderfully alone, without masters or slaves, without children or parents. The world existed only for us, full of trees, flowers, scents—and silence. I craved absolute silence, the better to hear Andrey's voice, the better to love him—nothing should distract me. I would wake up to reality from these ramblings, my loathing intensified.

The doctor decided I should be taken to Baku and arranged to have me repatriated in a hospital carriage, due to leave in a few days.

So I was wrapped in a blanket and carried onto a grey carriage, marked with a red cross. A nurse settled me on a couchette against a wooden partition, behind which constant groaning could be heard—from a typhoid patient, the nurse explained… I was well aware of the danger of infection from a louse bite, and lice were plentiful in our post-revolutionary world, but far from frightening me, the prospect gave me hope of ending the nightmare in which I was trapped.

After two days of pain and fever I was back at Baku station, semi-conscious, and then in my mother-in-law's house. Little by little I emerged from the nightmare and let myself live again—because I was young and because somehow I had some hope of a future.

Fräulein Anna came to see me almost every day. She was still living at Leyla's, sharing a room with my nephew, but was thinking of going to join her sister in England, who had long wanted her to come over. It would be easier for her as a foreigner to obtain a passport than for us, citizens of Russia. She had nothing to show for the long, difficult years spent with us; we were ruined and could do no more for her, but our spiritual destitution was greater still, as we even refused to show her gratitude.

She sat at my bedside. I could see her head, now white, bending over her knitting—the only work her failing eyesight permitted her. She fixed her blue gaze on me with affectionate concern, filling me with gratitude. But my long-established habit of keeping my feelings from her (when they were good) meant that I looked indifferent. I never said much to the poor woman anyway and now replied in monosyllables. But Fräulein Anna talked—she talked about everything, especially about her forthcoming journey, which she was dreading. But since she could no longer be of service to us and was even becoming a burden, she felt obliged to leave for good. Fräulein Anna always wept at the thought of this separation, which seemed cruel to her, while I wondered with astonishment why she loved us. Even if you acknowledge that you love 'despite' and not 'because of', should there not still be a limit to the 'despite'? She must have loved us despite a thousand and one reasons, and I am still amazed at this saintly woman's capacity for self-denial and love.

She left us not long afterwards, frail and nearly blind. First, she had to travel the length of Russia, still in total chaos, to reach her native city, Riga, and her journey was long and arduous. Nonetheless, she made it to Riga, and from there, after many adventures, to England, where this gentle soul found her sister and the affectionate atmosphere she needed but had so cruelly lacked with us.

Though their former home had been expropriated, my in-laws all still lived together in one house. I had three brothers-in-law, each noisier than the last, who liked to eat, talk and quarrel. Their mother was a constant martyr to their lively disputes, never wanting to declare any of them right or wrong, as she thought she owed them all equal protection. Since the death of their father, Jamil as the eldest son had made himself referee of their internecine quarrels, which tore the brothers apart and him with them.

My mother-in-law spent her time cooking to satisfy her sons' insatiable appetites and bemoaning their inability to get on with one another. She very much hoped that I would make things better: 'My daughter, who will henceforth be the light of my old age and the consoler of all my ills' (she spoke in flowery language reminiscent of the *Arabian Nights*), 'you must bring all your brothers into harmony. Why do they argue? For no reason, for no reason at all. I listen to them sometimes and say to myself: you brought idiots into the world because you are an idiot—that's Allah's just punishment for your sins; he always knows what he is doing. May he bless you, let me say in passing, you and your belly!'

And she would give what she thought was a furtive look at my flat stomach, which she hoped to see swell as a result of her son's ministrations. But she had to wait for this transformation, which must have caused her great sorrow, for in Islamic countries a household without a child is considered cursed. Crying or sighing, she would get back to her baking, roasting and simmering. '*Ay Allah*,' she would say, and the chicken would jump in the frying pan, '*ay Allah*,' and the sauce would bubble vigorously.

I had to deploy all my diplomatic talent, all my now meagre energy, to stop myself being force-fed like a goose.

'You don't eat anything,' my mother-in-law would sigh when I had consumed two plates of soup, half a chicken, several plates of rice and a dessert. 'She will become thin as a rake and the whole of Baku will say they don't feed her properly at her husband's house.'

12

Time passed. The commissar friend promised us a passport in the not too distant future. Pessimistic by nature and by superstition, I didn't set too much store by this and feigned indifference. I threw myself back into piano playing after long months of neglect. I read a lot in French and English and even started to learn Persian; I went out for walks; I played poker with my aunts, taking delight in calling their bluff and infuriating them; but I never forgot to daydream, my great consolation.

One day the door to my room opened without anyone bothering to knock and in walked Gulnar. I gave a cry of shock, as she threw herself into my arms. I didn't know how to behave—for all her faults I still loved Gulnar, but what I considered a betrayal had come between us. I did not return her kisses and, aware of my reluctance, she plunged into the heart of the drama with her customary resolve.

'Listen, don't be such an idiot! Why shouldn't I have made the most of Andrey since you were giving him his freedom? It's absurd to hold it against me! Perhaps you think I've taken something from you? You're wrong! Andrey slept with me but it was you he continued to love. You should understand once and for all that they are two different things. While we're on the subject, you're a woman now. Do you like it, making love?'

She was trying to distract me from the scarcely closed wound to my heart. I didn't go along with the trick and disengaged myself from her embrace.

'I can't get over your betrayal.'

'God, you're infuriating! What betrayal are you talking about? You didn't want Andrey any more so I took him. Your jealousy's extraordinary.'

I was starting to think that she might be right, so I took another line of attack: 'And do you think it's forgivable to run off without a word to anyone, without consideration for your parents, without pity for poor Selim? Well, it isn't! Whatever you may say, it was disgusting to go off with the man I loved.'

'You're all backward, riddled with bourgeois prejudice, dim-witted and only fit to be thrown to the dogs!'

Gulnar sat on my bed, settled back on the cushions and started talking as though in a dream: 'If only you knew how wonderful it is to live without traditions and habits. How every morning seems fresh, ripe with new experiences, how everyone you meet might change your life!'

I realized that Gulnar was repeating the words of some recent acquaintance. She was gifted and adaptable, able to model herself on whomever she happened to meet. But beneath each temporary persona her underlying self remained intact, only growing stronger under all these, often contradictory, influences.

'I didn't stay long with Andrey. We went to Kiev first and stayed there a month. Then he was sent to Moscow to some kind of congress—don't ask me what about. You know I couldn't give a damn about politics! Well, I had a really good time there, which didn't go down too well with Andrey. I think he didn't really like me at all. He was so obsessed with you that he didn't even let me talk about you. Whenever I tried, he changed the subject and if I persisted, he got angry. Everything would have been different if he had loved me like he loved you! We did make love a few times at first, very few let me repeat. One day in Moscow he brought a male friend round and that was the end of our liaison.'

'Even so, aren't you mad to behave so badly?' I couldn't get over Gulnar's casual attitude.

'Behave badly? You mean "sleep with him"? What's bad about that? It does two people good, yet people have the nerve to call it bad! Humanity is so stupid! You too, you fall into the same trap! I didn't think you were quite such a fool. Anyway, how did poor Selim take my escape? I hope he got over it.'

'You mean you haven't been to see him? When did you get back? Where are your bags?'

'I got back an hour ago. I left the suitcases at the flat, but Selim wasn't there. I came to see you before going to see my parents.'

'That's nice of you.'

I was softening.

'And I want to ask you something. I would rather go with you to see them. It's a bore to go on my own. Do you want to come?'

I lost my temper.

'You've got some nerve. You take Andrey away from me—'

'I took Andrey away from you? It's you who let him go. I just seized the moment so we wouldn't all lose out. I didn't take your Andrey away.'

'You took Andrey from me—'

'I didn't take him from you—'

'You took him from me—'

'No, I didn't.'

'Yes, you did.'

'Damn it. All right, I took him from you (though that's not true at all). So what?'

'Well, that's it.'

'Well, now we've agreed I took Andrey away from you, what's stopping you coming with me to see my parents? Go on, you know that deep down you're my sister, that we've always lived like two sisters... You won't refuse me this small favour?'

I was sitting on the edge of the bed, frowning in indecision. Since Andrey had never loved her, the question had changed: Gulnar hadn't really taken anything from me. She might even have increased his desire for me, if her presence had been a constant reminder.

'Well?' Gulnar asked.

'I don't know,' I muttered.

Then she had her arms round me again. 'My dear little cousin! Don't push me away—it hurts!'

She had tears in her voice and, more convincingly, in her eyes.

'Really I only love you and Mama! So forgive me if I have anything to be forgiven for. Lets go back to how we used to be—doing everything together! Say yes, please say yes!'

I had tears in my eyes too; I was still jealous, but I wasn't so sure of myself any more, and I genuinely loved Gulnar, though I loathed some aspects of her character.

'Where is Andrey?' I asked.

This question must have shown Gulnar that I was considering forgiving her—I wouldn't have asked if I'd still been really angry.

'He left two months ago now for Ankara. I haven't heard any more of him since. But all his friends said he would go far. And I'm not talking about geography,' she added, smiling, 'but about his career. They trust him with diplomatic missions.'

There was a pause, while Gulnar seemed to be thinking.

'He's attractive, Andrey, very attractive, but he's hard. He never showed me the slightest tenderness.'

'He is tender and he's kind too!' I cried.

And I started to cry. Gulnar hugged me and caressed me. When I was a little calmer, she asked, 'Is he really tender?'

'He was with me. Extremely.'

Gulnar shrugged her shoulders.

'Perhaps. I'm not disagreeing with you. He never stopped being cold towards me. One day he waved his revolver in front of me—he was playing with it and pretending to aim at me. "Would you kill me?" I asked him.

'"Of course. I wouldn't hesitate if it meant doing my duty!"

'He spoke so seriously it sent a shiver down my spine. This may be what drove me to leave him. But we're getting off the point. Do you want to come with me?'

I wiped my eyes. I really didn't have to be jealous.

'All right, I'll come with you.'

She covered me with kisses and we left the house, reconciled.

'What are you going to say to them?'

'I don't know. That I was abducted?'

'You take a suitcase and other things and want to say you were abducted?'

Gulnar chewed her lips.

'I'll see.'

'Why did you come back anyway?'

'Because the man I was living with began to get on my nerves. Since I didn't have my eye on anyone else, I decided to come and see what's going on here. But don't worry, I won't be staying long in this miserable dump.'

Gulnar pushed me in front of her and I opened the door. All the family were drinking tea around the samovar.

'I've brought someone to see you,' I said casually.

The whole family gave a cry of astonishment. My aunt blanched, her lips trembled and she threw herself on Gulnar, covering her with kisses.

'Before you embrace her, ask this slut where she's been!' Uncle Suleyman roared in his gruff voice. 'And who with? Who-o-o with?'

'No one, Papa. I left because Selim was tormenting me with his jealousy. I wanted a change of scene.'

'Ha, ha, ha!' Her father gave a devilish laugh. 'Selim was tormenting her! Selim who couldn't torment a flea! Whore!'

Gulnar drew herself up and said proudly, 'Not everybody can be a whore!' The peerless dignity with which she uttered those words had to be seen to be believed.

'Be quiet! Don't be so insolent!' raged Uncle Suleyman, then immediately contradicted himself. 'Tell me what you've done and who with?'

'All right, I left with Maria Nikolayevna, the woman I met at the country house. You know, the teacher! She took me with her to Moscow, where I worked in a nursery school.'

I had always greatly admired Gulnar's wit and presence of mind, but I became truly convinced of her superiority to me when I heard how glibly she could lie. She lied so effortlessly that more intelligent men than Uncle Suleyman would have been taken in. But her brothers Asad and Ali were on the lookout. Lying was their daily bread; they were just as good at it as Gulnar and not easily fooled. 'Huh,' they said in unison, reigniting their father's doubts. He looked at his sons and his daughter in turn, trying to divine the truth.

'Why didn't you let us know you were leaving? And why didn't you write to us after you'd gone?'

'But I did, Papa. I was surprised and hurt when I didn't receive any reply. You know what a mess the mail is in—the letters must have all got lost. Is that my fault?'

'Pull the other one!' said Asad.

'You must be joking!' Ali echoed.

'And you can be quiet too,' Gulnar shouted at them, infuriated by their malicious comments. 'I've no hope of behaving as well as you. If you think I don't know what you did with little Aslan, or with other children, girls as well as boys, then you're wrong. Worse still, you're thieves, liars and traitors!'

As usual in that family, everyone started shouting at once—father, mother, the other little brothers. In the midst of the fracas the door opened to reveal Selim, white as a sheet.

'I knew from her luggage that Gulnar was back...' And unable to continue he rushed over to her and clasped her in a desperate embrace. 'I knew you'd come back! I knew it! I've been waiting for you all this time!'

And he cried for joy. All the family, even Asad and Ali, were moved.

Gulnar quietly went back to living with Selim and life resumed its old pattern, except perhaps that Selim seemed more inclined towards melancholy. Gulnar was voluble on the subject of her supposed stay in Moscow and the nursery school (here she adopted a virtuous tone that suited her script perfectly), dredging up Maria Nikolayevna for the good of the cause. She became genuinely emotional talking about the little children she had looked after, their kindness and gratitude. She made up the things they said and did with a real flair for invention.

'You should be writing novels,' I said admiringly one day.

'Maybe later when I lose interest in men. It can't be as much fun to write a novel as to live one!'

And she clicked her tongue several times to show her enthusiasm.

After a month in Baku she was already bored and planning her getaway. She didn't know yet to where or how or with whom. I envied Gulnar her adventurous nature, so different from my own timorous, hesitant character, which might have cost me my happiness. I didn't know then how much I would change; so much so that as I now describe my former self, I feel neither compassion nor sympathy for her. Such is the miraculous effect of time, the magician that both creates and destroys.

13

Spring was painfully beautiful, promising happiness that would never come. The weather warmed up, the buds swelled on the trees. Worst of all were the days when the sun played on everything, animate and inanimate alike; when the sparrows sang their hearts out, heedless of being in the Caucasus or France; when the whole of nature gleamed and glittered in one great celebration from which I felt excluded. The deep blue of the sky seemed to hold the secret of happiness, as far out of reach as the sky itself, but always sought after, waited for. For me, as for many others, waiting had become my dominant state, the essence of life, and remains so to this day.

We were waiting for the passport that would allow us to go abroad; the commissar friend's promise had become a realistic prospect. I got out the suitcases, or rather a suitcase, as I wasn't expecting to take many things with me, and put it in a prominent position on a chair. It symbolized the anticipation of freedom and happiness. When I felt sad and downhearted, just one look at the symbolic suitcase would revive my hopes.

When she came to see me, Gulnar gave the suitcase an envious look: 'You've got all the luck,' she said harshly. 'You're going to France, you'll be able to sleep with Frenchmen. They're supposed to be very good lovers, better than any other nationality. Oh,' she sighed, 'I would like to have lots of lovers, masses of lovers. Whenever I see a likely man, I want to become his mistress, to play a part in his life. Don't you feel that desire too?'

No, I definitely did not feel that desire.

'You're a man's wife. If you had gone off with Andrey, he might have been the only man you knew. It's a good thing it didn't happen! There's a glimmer of hope left. Does he still disgust you, Jamil?'

I was categorical on the subject: poor Jamil still disgusted me.

'If we see each other in a few years' time, who knows what I might hear about you!'

To be honest, I didn't expect very much. My difficult character made life so hard and seemed to me to be incompatible with Gulnar's hopes.

The birds went on singing, Gulnar went on looking for lovers and I went on playing the piano, until the day Jamil came home, beside himself. Our hopes, which until then had remained vague promises, were becoming reality, tangible reality—he had seen the legendary passport, harbinger of another world, another life. A few minor formalities later and this world, this other life, would be ours. My reaction was unexpected and stupid—I collapsed onto a chair in tears. 'Stop crying, you poor fool, you utter fool!' an inner voice whispered, but I couldn't help it.

My mother-in-law came out of the kitchen, skewer of meat in hand, to see what was going on. When she heard the news and saw me crying, she joined in. One hand grasped the skewer, the other wiped away the tears streaming down her hollow cheeks.

'*Ay Allah!*' she groaned. 'You're both going to leave me! Me so old and yet to see the joy of a grandson emerging from your belly. I'll be all alone with those three devils, who will tear each other apart before my eyes!'

Next to appear was the maid. Having listened to her mistress's woes, she sat on the floor and began to cry too, out of solidarity.

There we were, the three of us, weeping and sighing, while Jamil walked anxiously from one to the next, close to tears himself.

I enjoyed drawing up my list of farewell visits. Jamil and I watched with alarm as it grew longer and longer: his family, mine, our relations, his friends, my friends, our friends. How much free time would we need to go and see them all, to hear them sighing, crying and doling out advice? I started crossing out more and more names; whole families disappeared at the stroke of a pencil, dubious families were struck off; distant kinship justified ruthless rejection until the list appeared manageable. But before I left the Caucasus, perhaps for good, there was one visit I did not cross off, though it would be my longest—to the countryside that I had loved so much. I wanted to take my leave of all that had been dear to me during my childhood: all my silent friends—inanimate to others, but always alive to me.

At the railway terminus I got a place in a carriage, where other travellers were already sitting. There was no special greeting for me from the coachman, as he did not recognize me, nor did the horses' bridles sport any of those colourful woollen pompoms I had liked so much that I wanted them on my own hats. But there was the usual long journey across the desert, full of holes and stones—though a tarmacked road was already under construction by the revolutionary government: another justifiable topic of propaganda against the former oil barons!

The carriage did not enter through the gate as it used to do, but stopped by the side of the road. I took my leave of my travelling companions, the carriage continued on its way and I was alone. The estate was quiet during this season, inhabited only by a few gardeners—I couldn't see a living soul.

I went up to the iron gate and gave the knocker a clang which must have shattered the peace for miles around. I had a long wait, but eventually the gate opened and Firdusi, our former head gardener, appeared. Unkempt and at first looking wary, his expression changed as soon as he saw me.

'My good *khanim*, may you enjoy heavenly blessings!' he cried in delight. 'I'm so glad to see you here. We only see those foreign pigs now! What brings you here?'

I explained that I was leaving Baku to join my father in France.

'Ah, your father, your father! He was good to us, your father! May Allah protect him! So you are all leaving, one after the other? You are abandoning us! What will become of us? How long are you staying here?'

I told him I would be glad to spend the night if he could offer me hospitality.

'To whom would I offer hospitality if not to you, my master's daughter? Khadija, Sofia and Sevar will be very glad to see you!'

These were Firdusi's three wives, of whom the oldest was thirty and the youngest fifteen. When they saw me walk in with their husband, they cried out in welcome and surprise and rushed over to embrace me warmly. Their six children and three cats ran around us, and a mangy dog bounded in. They were triumphant when they heard I was to spend the night with them, but plunged into mourning when they heard I was to leave Baku. They snapped out of it only when their husband told them to make me as lavish a dinner as possible. I left them where I had found them—busy in the kitchen. I wanted to make the most of the fine afternoon that God had put at my disposal.

The gardener's house, big enough to accommodate all his family and two other gardeners as well, stood at the entrance to the estate. The masters' house was in the middle of the garden and could not be seen from there. I asked Firdusi to leave me on my own and walked towards the house, down the long avenue of poplars. Here was where I felt truly at home, among *my* poplars—as straight as ever, unbowed by the revolution. Hundreds of rose bushes were already starting to stretch out tiny leaves in the warm sunshine. The only sound I could hear was the scrunch of sand beneath my feet. Everything looked the same as in the past—a deceptive impression that did not last. On the contrary, everything had mysteriously changed, because I had changed. I had been part of this world, as a grain of sand or poplar branch was part of it; no boundaries had separated me from its inhabitants, and at times our lives had merged. But that world had gone: in its place was another world, outwardly similar to the old one, but lacking its vital essence... Its soul escaped me. Was it taking revenge as I was about to leave it behind? It was avoiding me, ignoring me, excluding me from its embrace.

I climbed the steps of the large pool and sat at the edge of the water, which was as green and opaque as ever. Never again would I see this water, which my childhood had filled with monsters and sirens, or its reflection of walnut trees and clouds, my walnut trees and clouds. It was a concept I couldn't fully comprehend. I dipped my fingers into the cold water as I had done a thousand times before. The setting remained the same, but the times changed; I was seven, ten, thirteen; I dipped my fingers in the water while Asad and Ali chased each other round the pool's rim, the width of a jetty; I dipped my fingers in the water and Fräulein Anna scolded me; I dipped my fingers in the water and Aunt Rena called me to come and fasten her dress.

When I had exhausted my memories of the pool, I headed to the house, to which Firdusi had given me the key. First of all, I visited my grandmother's kitchen; I could see her sitting on the floor, sweating profusely, swearing, doling out smacks to the children, insults to everyone and blessings to some. Now the cold, sad kitchen seemed abandoned by the world; I shivered to see it this way, dead. The whole house seemed like a corpse, its soul stolen away. I sat at the piano and played a few chords, deliberately choosing some cheerful tunes, but they sounded flat, funereal to me. I quickly closed the lid. I walked through the house from room to room, the impression of death growing at every step. I stopped on the terrace and sat on the bench. The sun was setting in a clear sky where birds soared effortlessly. The rays gilded the sallow stones of the house, while the still bare branches hung down to my feet, bringing them a touch of warmth. The house, abandoned by everyone, seemed to be looking at me in gentle reproach: 'You too?' it asked. Yes, me too. I left the house with its heartbreaking melancholy and went to the vineyard. I lay down on the rock where I had met Andrey. Then I sat up as I had done when Gulnar told me that Gregory was bringing another man to see us. I watched Andrey approach in his black uniform: Andrey, Prince Andrey, Prince Andrey Bolkonsky! He had been all I dreamt he would be, but I let him leave without me. 'That's what you chose,' I said to myself, 'so stop complaining!' Then I drifted into a long reverie that touched every subject.

All would be dead to me—the poplars, with their rustling by turn soft and brutal, the vast house that saw me return every summer a little taller, the blue depths of the sea, everything I loved at the time when I thought life would be just a succession of rosy mornings and death would have no meaning for me. Never again would I see or hear or smell this world that had been my sole, gentle universe for so many long years. Now I understood that things, people, feelings were destined to disappear one after the other; that instead of happiness life was separation and regret; that at every moment something escaped from us, fell away irrevocably, and this is how it would be my whole life long. These were the truths that the sea, the sky and the poplars taught me in farewell.

The passport lay open on the table, where all our visitors looked at it with a mixture of respect, envy and superstition. There it was, the neatly bound, brand-new passport, so long coveted and so miraculously obtained, a symbol of freedom and adventure, both paper and wizardry at the same time. Gulnar did not leave my house at all: three-quarters of the time she behaved quite arrogantly, saying nasty things to me and succeeding in being thoroughly objectionable.

'It's only cretins who have all the luck! You could have left with Andrey but you didn't! You missed a wonderful opportunity to change your life for the better. So it would only be fair if you had to pay for your stupidity with a miserable life! But instead you're going abroad! No, no, it's insanely unfair! I hate you.'

With that, she threw herself on my shoulder. God knows how long she would have sobbed there if I had let her! But I didn't have the time to comfort her. We were leaving that night and I still had visits to make. I invited her to join me.

'All right,' she said, wiping her eyes, 'that would be better than nothing.'

We began with her family, whom we found at each other's throats. That morning Uncle Suleyman had inadvertently left his wallet out and Asad, thinking he was alone, had extracted three hundred million roubles to buy a few packets of tobacco...* But one of the little brothers had been hidden under the table playing with his lead soldiers and had witnessed the scene. He had wasted no time telling his father.

'I didn't bring you up to steal from my wallet!' he raged.

'Only from other people's!' Asad growled.

He received a slap for that—not a rational argument but one that always had an effect on Asad, who admired force. Defeated, he said no more. My aunt shed a few tears, then everything returned to normal.

---

* Inflation was at record levels.

'So you're going?' Uncle Suleyman gave a shrug. 'With your midget husband instead of…?'

He made a solemn gesture towards Asad, who was behind him. My cousin used his strategic position to make an obscene gesture in my direction.

'You'll be sorry one day that you didn't marry him!'

My aunt intervened. 'Oh Suleyman, stop getting at her. As if you didn't know the child was just doing what her father wanted.'

Her husband turned pale.

'Don't mention him to me—that murderer, that thief, that bastard—'

'Be quiet! He is my brother and this child's father, after all.'

'No, I will not be quiet. You should have chosen another brother and she should have chosen another father. He's robbed us all of your father's inheritance—'

'That money's mine. Why are you sticking your nose in?'

'That money's yours? Do you think I'd have married you without the prospect of an inheritance? With your looks? With your breasts like tobacco pouches? With—'

He didn't get the chance to finish. My aunt grabbed a cushion and brought it down on her husband's head; the two little brothers clapped their hands—the two older ones must have been delighted but kept it to themselves. Gulnar gave a tactless giggle. Uncle Suleyman's reaction was the least expected, as befitted such an essentially original man.

'All right, let's talk about something else,' he said gruffly, putting the cushion on a chair.

And a peaceable conversation ensued. My aunt served a farewell tea, by the end of which we were all emotional. We reminisced about the good old days when we were rich, respected ('Though not respectable,' Gulnar added), envied and even—joy of joys—hated by some.

'I remember a charity evening at the governor's residence. That pretentious Taghi Ruslanov entered fifty thousand roubles on the donations list. I had to sign straight after him so I wrote seventy thousand. You should have seen him turn green with envy! The thug wanted to kill me! I was laughing in my beard!' He recalled other memories in the same vein, all about crushing others with his wealth. 'Money is beautiful!' he concluded with poetic fervour, and all the family sighed with him, except Gulnar, who waited a moment before saying in honeyed tones:

'Well, it's a good thing it's all over—the reign of the plutocrats, the exploitation of the workers, the whole shebang!'

'Idiot,' shouted her father. 'Did you learn this nonsense at the school?'

'More like in the beds of the gentlemen of the Third International,' Asad hissed.

His mother exploded: 'Spawn of Satan, you'd eat your sister alive if you could!'

And they were off again, quarrelling. I got up and said firmly, 'I have to go. I've still got to see Grandmother and Aunt Rena.'

This put a halt to the discord and ushered in a touching farewell scene. Even Uncle Suleyman became almost sweet, which wasn't like him at all. Just as he used to do when I was a child, he touched my breasts, saying, 'Titties, titties,' and wiped a minuscule tear from the corner of his eye. My aunt cried openly. Asad and Ali pinched my bottom, but gently to show their goodwill, and the two little brothers clung to my skirt. At last I managed to leave and Gulnar and I walked the short distance to my grandmother's house.

She was not sweet. She was highly suspicious of any country outside a circumference of fifty kilometres. Once past the fifty-kilometre mark they were all equally far away—France, Crimea, America or Batumi.

'Well,' she muttered, 'tell your father he should come back soon. As for you, you'd do better to bring children into the world here, rather than running about all over the place where people will have no respect for you. Well, Allah's will be done!'

She said the Fatiha in my honour, then dismissed me with a parting shot—don't become a whore. She must have thought all her granddaughters had the requisite qualities for the profession, as she never missed a chance to caution us against this temptation.

My poor grandmother was no longer the woman overflowing with vitality, authority and virulence she had once been. Age was taking its toll, of course, but so were the social changes: she saw their effects, without appreciating their causes; she understood none of it and suffered as a result; she resigned herself to it, strong character that she was, but this resignation left her diminished in body and soul. She was no longer so ready with her insults, gave orders more gently, got angry less and less. Poor Grandmother—she would have felt at ease only in the era of Islamic stagnation, but was condemned to live through unprecedented upheavals… She died not long after my departure, Allah's name on her lips.

Aunt Rena cried a lot. I was her favourite niece and she thought we would never see each other again. She felt old, miserable and alone. That's what she told me, without heed for the feelings of her, fortunately deaf, husband. His deafness was getting worse, making communication with him extremely annoying. We had to shout words into his ear several times, straining our voices so he could hear. He often resorted to pencil and paper now to spare everyone the wearisome effort.

'It would be better if he died,' declared Aunt Rena with quiet cruelty. 'He's neither use nor ornament. He bores himself and everyone else.'

'Come, Aunt, if those were the criteria, there would be hardly anyone left on earth! Useful people are rare.'

Aunt Rena made a dismissive gesture, then was convulsed with sobs.

'You will see other countries, other nations, other people. I've never been anywhere but Russia, because of him'—nodding scornfully towards her husband—'who always promised me a trip to Nice, but didn't keep his word. You're young, you've got your whole life ahead of you. Whereas I…'

The poor woman broke my heart, but at the same time her pain made me obliquely happy at the thought of a limitless future stretching before me like a field, a field that was empty now but could at any moment be covered in thousands of plants, fruit and crops of every kind. I didn't think it could remain barren or be covered in thorns. Those are not ideas that occur on the threshold of life.

The more she cried, the more I rejoiced: 'You're young, you're not staying here, you're not trapped for ever in your marriage, everything, every experience can still be yours!'

Disconsolate, tears streaming down her face, Aunt Rena clasped me to her heart for a long time. Of course, I was sorry for her, but I couldn't stop a growing sense of elation at the contrast between our fates.

Only my three brothers-in-law, my sister and Gulnar accompanied us to the station. The station did not seem so filthy now; there were not so many refugees from Russia; the trains were not so packed. Things seemed to have changed slightly in the past few months. Our compartment had a standard complement of passengers and seemed almost clean, but maybe I was looking at the world through rose-coloured spectacles.

The last kisses exchanged, I got on the train. The bell gave the three regulation rings. The carriage was shaken by a great groan, echoed by Gulnar and Leyla, then the train slowly began to move. The platform went backwards, the station too. Tears of joy clouded my vision; just a touch of sorrow at leaving those with whom I had lived for so long lay beneath a great sense of happiness. The lights of Baku soon disappeared and the train plunged into the night, accompanied by the regular jolts that give every railway journey a strange rhythm and melody. But in the midst of my happiness a pain rippled through me that I had been less aware of recently: the thought of Andrey. In leaving Russia I was leaving him too, with little hope of meeting him again. Where would I be now if I had gone with him? In what town, what climate, what circumstances? Today I no longer ask myself such tortuous questions. All life that *is*, by definition cannot be different. An act is never down to chance but to the mysterious logic of all existence. If I do something, it's because I cannot do otherwise. So why be tormented by supposed mistakes? Whoever professes this philosophy does what he has to do with a calm spirit. When things go badly, it's because they are bound to go badly. A simplistic philosophy? Perhaps. Fatalism? Most definitely.

14

I was seasick the whole six days it took the wretched boat to cross the Black Sea.

I set foot on Turkish soil a total wreck, but I revived in just a quarter of an hour and began to study the new country with interest.

In the new climate of this young Turkey, women already wore shorter veils, even revealing their faces. Many wore just a small veil, similar in style to a nurse's veil, but in different fabric and all the colours of the rainbow.

As a Muslim woman, I had to follow the custom of the country. I adopted this headgear with enthusiasm as I thought it flattering, and sported it in gauze, in tulle, in crêpe de Chine. Before long, though, I had had enough of Constantinople and began to wait for the passport that would allow me to leave for France. In a letter my father urged Jamil to stay behind in Constantinople and wait for him, as he had to return on business and would need his help. Ever the perfect son-in-law, Jamil acquiesced and dealt only with my passport. We had to obtain visas from the innumerable countries crossed by the Orient Express on its way to France—a task so arduous that it took two months. I spent my time walking around Constantinople. Thanks to the paucity of my own culture, thoughts of lost Byzantium did not trouble me, as they might have done another visitor. I saw Constantinople only as a city of sultans and Muslims. So, peace of mind intact, I went for my walks, admiring the unique location of this city washed by the sea. Every day I made a pilgrimage to a mosque, until I had visited them all; then I started again.

Another attraction of Constantinople at that time was the Russian nightclubs, which gradually made their push westwards, eventually reaching Paris. The city teemed with Russian émigrés. The men argued, sold jewellery or accepted whatever job they could find; the women often tried their hand as courtesans—with success, on the whole. They claimed a good rate and had no shortage of admirers.

My husband took me to the most elegant nightclub, the Black Rose. I think we went in particular because of a *consommatrice*. (This was the name given in Russian to the ladies who encouraged miserly clients to consume the services on offer.) It didn't bother me, and I made the most of these visits. I had never frequented such places, which seemed to me the quintessence of the dissolute, elegant life, the kind of which one dreams when one is not a serious young person.

Russian songs flowed thick and fast, as did the champagne. Strange to say, the patrons did not enjoy themselves at all in this 'place of pleasure', at least they did not enjoy themselves in the commonly accepted sense of the term. They were overwhelmed by a special nostalgia, largely the fruit of music and melancholy songs, and would have felt robbed had they been served gaiety instead of this noble sadness. 'One comes here to weep, not to laugh,' a regular told me, unsmiling, after I had shared my impressions. 'Don't forget that we have lost everything: our country, our fortune, our tsar...' He gave me a harsh look. 'Of course,' he must have thought, 'she's a barbarian, a Muslim, not a real Russian; she doesn't have a drop of Slav blood in her veins, nor a drop of blue blood either' (he was a prince). 'What does it matter to her that our Holy Russia no longer exists?' That, or worse, is what he must have been thinking, but raising his glass, he said aloud, 'Long live our Holy Russia!'

I raised my glass too, out of politeness. My interest in Holy Russia was mild at best, but all that money had not been spent on my education in vain. So I raised my glass and sipped some champagne to show my goodwill. I knew that these poor people were to be pitied, as they had in effect lost everything. As had we all, in fact.

With all these visits to mosques and nightclubs time passed rapidly, though not rapidly enough for me, as I was in a hurry to leave Constantinople, especially since Jamil would be staying behind. My sisters hardly mentioned him in their letters; they would casually send regards, barely observing the proprieties. Jamil felt resentful, and hurt, too. He thought he was excluded from the family, and he was not wrong: my whole family, with the exception of my father, was outraged at this marriage, which only exceptional circumstances could have produced. My sisters had already rejected Jamil's advances, considering him ridiculous. They gave him no quarter, as they thought him too old for me and inferior in every respect.

So he was worried, with good reason, to see me leave alone for Paris. One evening, he wept. 'Yes, now that you're going to join your family, now that none of you need me any more, no one will care if I disappear… quite the contrary! Your sisters and your stepmother despise me and will stop at nothing to turn you against me.'

So feeble were his powers of perception that he did not know how much I hated him already; a little less perhaps than at the start of our marriage, but I still hated him consistently and with no prospect of improvement. No one needed to turn me against someone I had never favoured in the first place.

I made some cowardly protestations, reassuring him that he would join me in Paris and that his fears were unfounded, but in my heart of hearts I hoped for the reverse. I desperately wanted to be rid of his voice and his wriggling, bothersome presence. I also wanted to be free of this obsessive gambler.

His passion had become all-consuming. On arrival in Constantinople, his first concern had been to find other Baku émigrés who, like every resident of our city, played poker to their dying breath. On evenings when we didn't go to the Black Rose, Jamil would get carried away gambling, while I would wait for him like a good girl in the furnished apartment we had rented in order to economize. Our stay at the Tokatlıyan, one of the two most expensive hotels in Constantinople, had cost us dearly, but it had not entered our heads at that time to live in a more modest establishment.

So, while I waited for him in our apartment, Jamil slowly but surely lost all the money made from selling the last of our jewellery, until the day he told me we didn't have a penny left. When a man accustomed to having money no longer has any, his first reaction is to go and borrow some. So Jamil borrowed a tidy sum but it lasted only a week, funding three trips to the Black Rose and four to the poker club. Meanwhile, he wrote to my father to explain our situation and ask for his help. In Jamil's defence I should say that he had suffered a crazy run of bad luck ever since we docked in Constantinople. Accustomed to winning by and large, he could not conceive of a change in his fortunes, and kept on playing, certain that luck would return. But it did not. After every poker evening he would return home crushed. I would be waiting, sometimes until dawn, unable to fall asleep.

'You see,' he explained, sure of finding a sympathetic ear (not for nothing was I granddaughter, daughter and niece in a long line of gamblers), 'you see, I draw a full house and my partner puts down a flush. I draw a flush and he shows me four of a kind. And it went on like that all evening! What a streak of bad luck!'

He started tearing out his red hair.

'You should stop playing.'

My advice was half-hearted, as I was sure it would be ignored.

'Yes, you're right. I won't play any more,' Jamil said humbly, certain in turn that he would play, if not the next day (we could go to the Black Rose for a change), then the one after.

From one loss to the next, from one expense to the next, our debts grew at disconcerting speed. Jamil did the rounds of the moneylenders who were still prepared to take us on. But increasingly, as events took their familiar course, said lenders turned us down. Several times lack of money meant we had to forgo food in our sumptuously furnished apartment. We would empty our pockets and, if fortune smiled on us, we would find a few coppers to buy bread and a tin of sardines. Jamil would have readily watered this repast with his tears, as his hearty appetite was indignant at such a frugal dinner. He was also frightened by our poverty, the result of his fatal obsession, fearing it would give another trump card to his 'enemies'. (He meant my sisters and stepmother.) I did not take it as seriously as him: I found our poverty amusing, believing as I did that it was temporary and I would soon escape it. And I was delighted to dine on sardines: as a child I had loved tinned sardines in oil and dreamt of being old enough to buy as many of them as I liked and gobble them down on my own—or, if need be, with other people. I had finally reached those years of relative independence when I could buy what I wanted and I seized every opportunity to fulfil my innocent dream. I would devour my dish of choice, Jamil's complaints ringing in my ears.

He would take up his refrain: 'So you will leave, of course, but what will become of me? When will your father come? And will he send me any money? We need it for your journey, never mind anything else.'

These remarks would annoy me, especially made in the grating voice I had heard too often.

'You're getting on my nerves!' I would reply callously.

Then he would begin to cry. He would be too upset to eat his sardines and I would polish them off, bones, skin and all.

A week before my departure we received some money from my father. It wasn't a large sum but enough to pay our most pressing debts, buy my ticket for France and leave some for Jamil's poker. For two evenings the gods of the card tables smiled on him and he won. So we went back to the best restaurants and resumed our evenings at the Black Rose.

Encouraged by our temporary wealth and a stunning sky, I decided to make some final excursions to Prinkipo, Therapia and other classic pilgrimage sites.

But what moved me most were the cemeteries around Constantinople, with their tall, straight cypresses and their tall, straight gravestones. That was where I felt most Muslim: in a place dedicated to peace I do not like crosses, rich, overblown mausoleums and flowers. I like simplicity in death—I like the ascetic appearance of a Muslim cemetery. The last one that I visited in an Islamic land was located on a hill overlooking the Bosphorus. The beauty of the sky, the place, the sea merged to create a vast, perfect loveliness—a source of suffering more than pleasure, but a strange kind of suffering with joy welling up beneath it. An initial sense of the transience of beauty gives way to an awareness of perfection as an eternal quality, an unchanging constant.

Beneath the cypresses the air vibrated in the early heat. This familiar cemetery gave off no air of melancholy, just the impression of peaceful sleep. It slept with its pointed stelae, sometimes crowned with a stone turban; only the cypresses kept watch. Here death seemed merciful, the gentle mother of the living. On the other side of the Bosphorus, I could see Asian Turkey; farther to the east I imagined Ankara, where Andrey should be. The happiness I felt changed to nostalgia. I was aware that we possess only snatches of happiness—I am now convinced of it—and these snatches fall but rarely into our ever-outstretched hands.

Forgotten, the mosques and the streets and the people; Constantinople, you remain to me that enchanted hillside, covered in pointed stelae; you are the blue sky above the water and the cypresses; you are this carefree profusion of beauty, this calm reflection of paradise. Moments lived on this hillside, you will never leave me; you will die with me, suspended somewhere in my memory. And if, as I hope, all the beauty we reflect returns to eternity upon our death, you will even become immortal.

At last I held in my hands the passport covered in visas in a host of European languages. Two days later I went to the station, accompanied by Jamil. The Orient Express, all sleeping carriages, looked like a rich relative of the train I had taken from Baku. With all its lamps lit, it shone like a grand celebration amid the grey of the station.

I took my place in my compartment, helped by a very pale Jamil. Disconsolate and distraught, he asked me every two minutes if I would write to him.

'Yes, of course,' I replied in good faith.

'And you won't forget me?'

'Of course I won't, of course I won't,' I reassured him, also in good faith.

But he must have had a premonition of a permanent separation; he embraced me, his expression at once fearful, respectful and imploring.

'I feel that I'm about to lose you,' he said, sitting down on the couchette and bursting into tears.

What could I do? What should I do? I reassured him that that was not the case; I talked to him about the future as though we would share it, consoling him as best I could. Jamil calmed down a little then. One minute before departure he left the carriage. As I looked at him above the door curtain, that minute was longer than eternity. I too wanted to cry, but for joy at leaving this man with whom I had been united against my will by the malice of fate, both of us victims of dramatic circumstance. The train moved off. Jamil walked next to my window for several metres; then, when the train gathered speed, he wanted to run, but the platform was too crowded and he had to stop.

The last words I heard in his grating voice were: 'You will write to me, won't you? You won't forget me?'

The train gathered speed and the crowd became a shapeless mass in which I could no longer make out Jamil. I sat on the couchette and cried too. I held in my hands a great piece of happiness; I clasped it against my heart, offering my fervent gratitude to God, who had given it to me without my deserving it. I spent the whole night sitting at the open window. I could not bring myself to go to bed, let alone go to sleep. The night was dark and balmy. We crossed mysterious lands that did not appear on ordinary maps; there lived knights and dragons, mermaids and goblins. But whatever they were, they all sang and the train plunged into their song, breaking it up and scattering it far and wide, where it reformed and returned to us. So we advanced from melody to melody, from fabled land to fabled land, until morning. When the sky grew pink in the east, I lay down for a moment, fully dressed, and fell asleep.

I soon woke up and found the same joy intact, solid, almost too heavy to bear. I straightened my veil (yes, even in the train I continued to wear the Turkish veil) and went to the restaurant car for breakfast. The moment I walked in, my joy vanished. I realized that I was alone and surrounded by strangers, men travelling on their own to boot, and I was terrorized by the thought. I must have been a comical sight, with my veil and my expression of a frightened savage let loose in a hostile universe. I thought everyone was looking at me, and they might well have been: my attitude must have seemed strange to all these civilized people. My consternation grew; I kept my eyes lowered as I drank my coffee in an agony of fear and confusion. Now I realized the danger to which I was exposed; if a man or men took it into their heads to rape me, they had only to come into my compartment, where I would be defenceless before their lust, at their mercy, there for the taking. Then I started to miss Jamil's male presence, my protection against these hazards. I gulped down my scalding coffee and hurried back to my compartment, where I double-locked the door.

Mealtimes were torture for me. When I heard the bell, my heart would start pounding and I would delay leaving for the dining car until the very last minute. My compartment was my harem—I opened the door only to go and eat or to let the couchette be prepared for the night. That was when I was happy again. During the day we travelled through familiar countries, but at night we would wander in an unknown world, crossing nameless empires and mysterious kingdoms.

But utter exaltation, equal to anything I'd ever dreamt of, or experienced with Andrey, came at dawn on the fourth day on the approach to Paris. The warm air carried the fragrance of the fields. The meadows divided by lines of trees, the wooded hills, the lakes and rivers all awoke to daylight, suffused with pink from the rising sun. In the sky motionless clouds appeared to be awaiting sunrise before starting their journey. 'Your life seems to be spent in the clouds,' Andrey told me one day. Yes, that had been the best part of my life. Now, as I approached the wonderful city where endless possibilities awaited me, I sloughed off my earthly past like an uncomfortable garment. I came to my new life receptive, open to everything, bringing with me from that past only its finest part—that spent in the clouds.

Brief Summary of the History of Azerbaijan at the Start of the Twentieth Century

I was born at the very end of 1905, the year of the first (abortive) Russian revolution that followed the disastrous Russo-Japanese war. I was eight when war was declared in 1914, eleven in 1917, year of the oh-so-victorious October Revolution.

Still a child, I could hardly comprehend the course of events or piece together history. I thought I remembered that the Turks had occupied Baku at a time when they were not yet defeated, and that the English had succeeded them after the defeat of 1918. Now, having consulted historians, I have drawn up the following timetable:

In May 1917, Azerbaijan, along with other neighbouring peoples, profited from the civil war in Russia to break away from the empire and declare itself independent. But Armenian revolutionaries—the Dashnaks—led by Stepan Shaumyan and supported by the Bolsheviks, seized the country for a short time.

It is during this short time that we fled to Persia to escape severe reprisals and potential massacres.

This is how a Soviet text presents the events of that period: 'However, in the early summer of 1918, the situation of Soviet power in Baku worsened... The interventionist Germans and Turks longed to seize this oil-rich region. Russia, which at this time was itself waging a bitter struggle against the forces of intervention and internal counter-revolution, was unable to support the inhabitants of Baku. On 31st July 1918 communist power was temporarily overthrown. The city was first occupied by British troops, then Turkish ones.'

During this period of anti-communist reaction, twenty-six people's commissars were shot. When the communists returned to power, they erected a monument to commemorate them. The bust of Stepan Shaumyan, 'one of the leaders of the legendary Baku Commune', stands atop a tall pillar in a Baku park.*

When the communists were defeated, we were able to return from exile to Baku, where the elections of 7th December 1918 handed victory to the social democrats, the Musavat Party, which was my father's party. He was named minister of commerce.

On 5th January 1920, the government of Azerbaijan was recognized *de facto*, though not *de jure*, by the Allies. This recognition was short-lived, as the country was reconquered by the Red Army on 27th April the same year. I have written that I witnessed the end of a world, our capitalist world, when at night I saw lorries full of Red soldiers from the window of our house.

My father was imprisoned for around ten months. His only thought on release was to join his family in Paris—without me. In spring 1921, I entered a sort of prison—marriage with a man I hated. It was two months after my fifteenth birthday.

I in turn was able to emigrate in spring 1924, leaving for good my country, to which I no longer had any connection. It joined the Soviet republics. Since my family has remained famous in the annals of Azerbaijan, and since I am its last representative—or almost—the Soviets invited me to come to Baku. But I did not accept their invitation. I would be lying if I said that I do not regret it now.

Banine

Paris 1985

---

* Stepan Shaumyan's monument in Baku was dismantled in 1990. [Translator's note.]

Photographs of Banine and Her Family

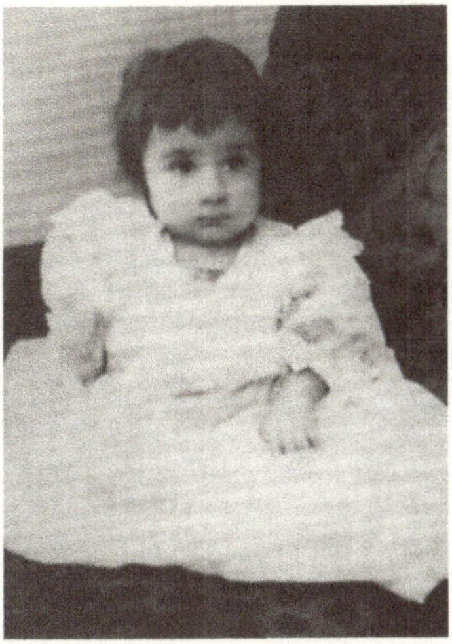

Banine, probably before her first birthday

Banine's mother (right) with two of her aunts

Banine's father

Banine's grandmother

Fräulein Anna

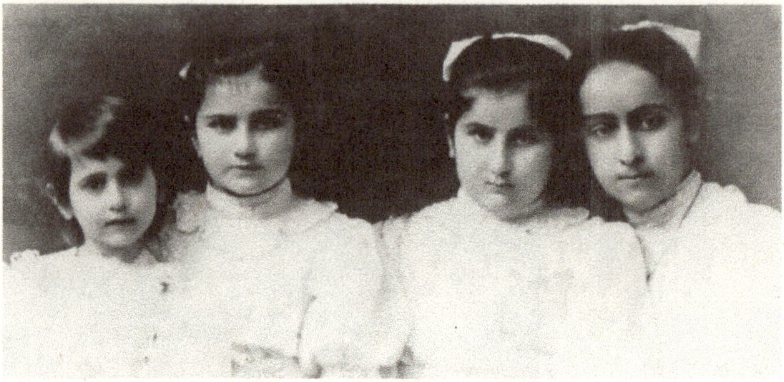

Banine (left) and her sisters

Poker at the country house

In the garden of the country house. Left to right: Banine's father, Uncle Ibrahim, Amina and one of Banine's sisters. The uniformed man in the background is unidentified.

Banine's father (left), with his brother and nephew

Banine at 16

Banine's husband, Jamil

Banine in Paris, 1931

ALSO AVAILABLE
FROM PUSHKIN PRESS

AVAILABLE AND COMING SOON FROM PUSHKIN PRESS CLASSICS

The Pushkin Press Classics list brings you timeless storytelling by icons of literature. These titles represent the best of fiction and non-fiction, hand-picked from around the globe – from Russia to Japan, France to the Americas – boasting fresh selections, new translations and stylishly designed covers. Featuring some of the most widely acclaimed authors from across the ages, as well as compelling contemporary writers, these are the world's best stories – to be read and read again.

MURDER IN THE AGE OF ENLIGHTENMENT
RYŪNOSUKE AKUTAGAWA

THE BEAUTIES
ANTON CHEKHOV

LAND OF SMOKE
SARA GALLARDO

THE SPECTRE OF ALEXANDER WOLF
GAITO GAZDANOV

CLOUDS OVER PARIS
FELIX HARTLAUB

THE UNHAPPINESS OF BEING A SINGLE MAN
FRANZ KAFKA

THE BOOK OF PARADISE
ITZIK MANGER

THE ALLURE OF CHANEL
PAUL MORAND

SWANN IN LOVE
MARCEL PROUST

THE EVENINGS
GERARD REVE